FORUM GRONINGEN

Edited by
Erik Dorsman, Toon Koehorst, NL Architects,
Jannetje in 't Veld and Niek Verdonk

nai010 publishers

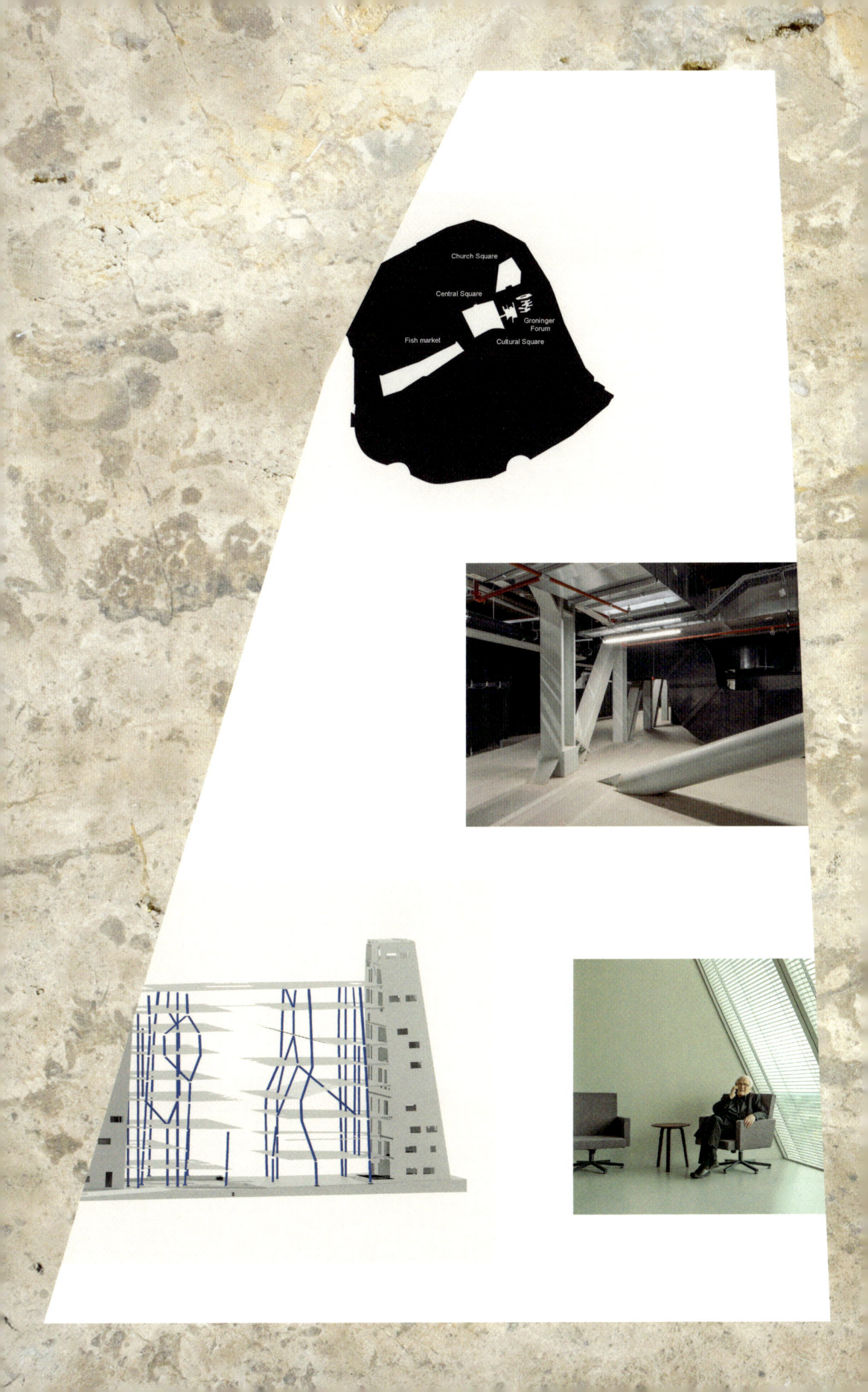

Church Square

Central Square

Groninger Forum

Fish market

Cultural Square

3

5

Sectie

C

Contents

14

CITY

Chris Zwart

The Turbulent First Years of a Building that Seems to Have Always Been There

It is four o'clock in the afternoon on Friday, 29 November 2019. Richt Pander, head of public services at Forum Groningen, walks nervously through the entrance hall of the brand-new building. It is due to open in an hour, after years of preparations. The buzzing sound of the escalators warming up fills the space. Her colleagues put the last things in their places. Richt peers outside with a concerned look on her face. There is hardly anyone on the Nieuwe Markt, Groningen's newest urban plaza. Were the critics right after all? Would the locals not be interested in the Forum at all?

Between around 2006 and 2014, the local media had devoted few positive words to the Forum. Some claimed the building would be a financial disaster, a 'Trojan house'. For others, the concept was nothing but hot air, merely a marketing ploy: a bottomless pit based on a worthless plan. This jazzed-up library was nothing less than an assault on the city. There was great scepticism not only among journalists, but also among some politicians and the city's inhabitants. What did they want with a big, expensive building that would house nothing new?

Despite the doubts, the Forum is a reality. And how! It has now been open for three years, albeit with closures due to the coronavirus pandemic. How has the building fared in that time? What happened during the first months? And how does the final building compare to the original designs?

From Castle in the Air to Packed Building

When the Forum opened its doors for the first time on that Friday in November 2019, no one involved in the building had any idea how it would be received. The majority of people questioned for an RTV Noord survey shortly before the opening were still against the Forum. Would anyone turn up?

The fears were unfounded. By five o'clock, the Nieuwe Markt was completely full. In the first few days, there was a queue from Popkenstraat to Saint Martin's Church and around the corner past the Vindicat building. "Everyone here was pleasantly surprised," says Gerda Vrugteman, programmer and project leader at the Forum. "I get goosebumps again just thinking about it. It's difficult having a concept you believe will work but which can't be demonstrated until the building actually exists. Until then, it's a castle in the air. We needed the building to show how we wanted to weave the various programmes together."

There was no time to sit back and enjoy the enormous turnout. The Forum was completely overrun from the very first minute. "At one point we had a member of staff at each escalator to stop people and let them through in groups when there was some space upstairs," says Richt Pander. "Over time, we realised how many people the building could handle and stopped them at the front door." The twenty-five flexible employees that Forum hired shortly before had their first working day during the opening. "There was no time to train them," Pander recalls with a laugh. " 'Here's your shirt,' we said, 'you're standing by this escalator, put it on! Just smile. And if you have a question, here's a walkie-talkie.' We really threw them to the lions, because we didn't know what had hit us either. But it went well."

Total
Surprise

After the crazy opening, the Forum had an equally bizarre first year. It was incredibly busy until Christmas. In January, a month when fewer people usually venture outdoors, the building still received hundreds of thousands of visitors. And the influx didn't stop in February either. Exhibitions opened, all sorts of large and small events were organised in the building, and curious visitors discovered every part of the building. Every new building has teething problems, and the Forum was no exception, but there was hardly time to solve them. No sooner had one knot been untangled than the next problem arose, while all the internal systems still had to be fine-tuned: from cleaning and catering to security.

In the meantime, there was no stopping the stream of visitors, who went through every door they saw open, even entering spaces they were not allowed into. And because people were mostly looking up in amazement, they didn't pay attention to where they were walking, which resulted in accidents. At the top of each escalator, people stopped to gaze at yet another beautiful floor, causing congestion everywhere. The virtual-reality headsets were used so intensively that the wires had to be replaced within no time at all. And the predicted catering turnover for a whole year was achieved in three months. "We could barely cope," says director Dirk Nijdam. "Some days the tenth-floor restaurant sold more than two thousand cappuccinos. It was almost impossible to keep up; the baristas were driven nuts."

Despite the hectic pace, there was also joy and relief. Before the opening there had been fears that the public would only complain and criticise, but the people of Groningen embraced the Forum. The low expectations due to negative advance press may have helped to make the finished building an even greater positive surprise. The way the architects had moulded the varied programmatic components into a single form was an immediate hit.

"In those first months, I really felt how proud I am of this building," says Gerda Vrugteman. "Thank God it works, I thought, and people understand why we're doing this." The storm that raged through the building subsided only with the emergence of the global pandemic. Just as the Forum was starting to find its rhythm, the coronavirus sent the Netherlands into lockdown. When the building was forced to close in March 2020, it had already clocked up more than a million visitors, with more than twenty thousand on the busiest days.

Although the lockdown killed the Forum's momentum, it had its plus side. "For some of us, the lockdown was almost a salvation," says programme coordinator Daphne de Bruijn. "We had worked so hard. People were at the end of their tether. But for an organisation that had reached such a high, it lasted far too long." The closure allowed for some technical finishing touches to be made, but for a few months the Forum was unavailable to the people of Groningen even though it had immediately proven its worth within the short time it had been open.

A large part of the Forum is intended as a covered public space, with city squares where you can spend an hour just sitting and watching the world go by, just like you would outside. And while it wouldn't have been the first time an architect's intentions didn't match how a building is actually used, here it worked out exactly as hoped for. The Forum is light and spacious on the inside and opens up to visitors, making them feel comfortable. Despite its enormous scale, the building retains a human dimension. You don't feel lost in it. It's a place to hang out in, not just for a quick photo opportunity. The term 'urban living room' has been used so often it has become a cliché, but it is an accurate description. "We made very few compromises in the interior," says Dirk Nijdam. "We went all the way." Smart solutions made it possible to spend money on extra quality. "For example, we had the backs of cabinets made with cheaper wood. That saved us a hundred thousand euros, which we could invest in the architectural design of the cinemas."

Above all, the Forum was intended to be a building for everyone. And that principle has become a reality. Since it opened, the building has welcomed visitors of every age group, from small children to the elderly. The building is not intimidating. If you've got half an hour to kill, you can take a seat in the public gallery on the ground floor. You can take shelter in bad weather without any further obligations. Interestingly, the building received large numbers of visitors over the Christmas and New Year period in 2019/20. Those who didn't have family or friends to spend the holidays with, or who didn't feel the need to, found a place in the Forum with like-minded people.

One group that was attracted to the Forum from day one is students. Whether from the University of Groningen and the Hanze University of Applied Sciences or vocational trainees or secondary school pupils. Foreign students have been especially quick to make the building their home, spending hours here every day and bringing visiting friends and family with them. Some of them are probably new to Groningen and did not know the city without the Forum. They've never even heard of the Naberpassage. The Forum also attracts the proverbial loitering teenagers. Not yet old enough to get into bars and clubs, they meet here in the evenings. Daphne de Bruijn has noticed that they mainly hang around on square 4 and on the roof: "I never thought beforehand that the building would work for young people in this way. We're trying to attract them with our programmes, but they're coming anyway."

The strength of the Forum is that everything is possible and nothing is compulsory. You can spend money there, but you don't have to. It is there for the city – not only on paper, but also in practice. Its accessibility makes the building special. "If you made people pay to access the roof, for example, you'd have a completely different dynamic in the building," says Richt Pander. "The atmosphere is determined by the liveliness and openness we have now."

Before moving to the Forum, film programmer Ruben Allersma wasn't sure the building was what Groningen needed, but is now fully convinced by the concept. "Yesterday I was having lunch and looked down. I had a view of the whole building. It was buzzing. It's really alive here. Two men in suits were having lunch in the public gallery. A few metres away, an elderly lady was reading a newspaper under a lamp. A few teenagers were watching films in the media seats on the film square. I thought: yes, this really works."

Dirk Nijdam explains with a grin that when he walks through the building, he straightens up every chair that is out of place. He knows exactly which piece of furniture belongs where and why. But in a large, public building such as this it's only natural that people move the furniture around – it shows that they feel at home. "Perhaps the most wonderful thing for me is that people were using their laptops in every part of the building from day one," says Richt Pander, "as if the Forum had always existed."

The Forum was intended to be a cultural building, with the specific identity that that entails. The only problem was: a building exactly like this one did not yet exist. So, what was that identity supposed to look like? It was up to the architects to give the Forum its own character, to fuse the various elements into a whole that is greater than the sum of its parts. It had to be an open building, but with intimate spaces. The different elements, some accessible to all and others requiring a ticket, had to merge on the squares in between: an interesting puzzle for the architects.

Shortly after his appointment as director in 2013, Dirk Nijdam redefined the concept that had been used until then. The Forum would no longer be a House of Information and History as initially intended but a place focused on the present and the future. During inspirational visits to modern libraries in cities abroad, including Aarhus in Denmark and Chester and Manchester in England, confidence in the concept grew within the organisation. "I had the feeling that all the successful elements I saw in those buildings would come together in ours," says Richt Pander.

Wonderland was initially conceived at the centre of the Forum but because that would have meant you could hear screaming children all over the building, it was moved to a corner of the building. Late in the process of defining the interiors, the floor originally intended as offices made way for the comic-book museum, Storyworld. The office space was reduced in size and moved several floors higher up, where the workstations now connect directly to the public parts of the building. "You won't find better office spaces anywhere," says Daphne de Bruijn,

"the natural light, the clouds and the sun contribute a great deal. I never realised the view would be so amazing, and how that makes you feel."

An excellent – and by no means accidental – characteristic of the Forum is that you come into contact not only with other people but also with a variety of subjects and activities. You learn all kinds of things in a playful way, even if you hadn't planned to. As the Forum's representative, Gerda Vrugteman sat down with the architects and interior architects to translate the public programme into a brief for the building. One space that stands out for her is the Smart Lab on the sixth floor. Designed by architects deMunnik-deJong-Steinhauser, it is a completely new kind of space for which there was no existing reference point. Because the digital workspace has glass walls, it invites curious visitors and introduces them to modern technology. With 3D printers operating in front of the windows, it has the effect of a shop window, where passing visitors regularly stop for a while. "It has become a very accessible space," says Gerda. "That's exactly how we envisaged it together with the designers."

What they could not have envisaged beforehand are the spontaneous initiatives that quickly took place in and around the building. It has witnessed celebrations for Chinese New Year, salsa dancing on the Nieuwe Markt, and every three months an orchestra plays a Haydn symphony in front of the public gallery. And the parking garage also turned out to be more than just a carpark. Coordinator Frits Haverkamp has seen just about everything down there: "Many couples have their wedding photos taken up on the roof.

Then they come down and see that it's also very beautiful here. They get permission from the council and have some more photos shot down here." The parking garage has served as the location for a video by a local rapper and has also hosted photo shoots with expensive cars, usually with the raw concrete inner wall or the artwork *Turmoil* by Nicky Assmann as a backdrop. Frits also regularly sees all kinds of people in the garage who haven't come there to park their cars: homeless people looking for a quiet corner to sleep in, students who think they can sneak in unseen, skateboarders who have discovered that the garage is a paradise. He emphasises that everything is continuously monitored, so unwanted visitors are spotted straight away. The artwork is a different story; it attracts a large audience. "People used to come down the ramp in droves to see it, resulting in dangerous situations." Nowadays art lovers are allowed to ring the bell and Haverkamp lets them into the garage in a safe manner.

Despite the great variety of beautiful spaces inside the building, the *pièce de résistance* is the roof. It is accessible to everyone, doesn't require a ticket and you have the best view imaginable over the city. For the first time in history, it provides a view of the tower of Saint Martin's Church from above. A selfie with the tower is probably the most popular photo taken in Groningen in the past two years. Daphne de Bruijn recently visited the roof with her seventeen-year-old son. "He looked out over the city and began to reorganise it, as it were, removing a building here, adding another there. It made him think about what he considers beautiful and ugly. It inspired him to look at his own city from above."

Over the years, programme components and functions have shifted considerably. It is therefore all the more fascinating to see how closely the realised building corresponds to the very first design. The Forum makes perfect sense, and functions just as it was conceived.

Redefining the Cinema and the Library

There was never any doubt that the Forum would house a library and a cinema, but precisely what form they would take was uncertain. In the building, the cinema has become a contemporary cultural venue of the highest standard. Like the library, it could never have undergone that development at the old location. "Looking back now, I think: we were really just mucking about on the Hereplein," says Ruben Allersma. "We have the best auditoriums imaginable, with the best picture, the best seats and the best sound. Everything is perfect." There is still a place in the Forum for lovers of art-house films, but the programming has been consciously expanded. With the occasional quality blockbuster, the cinema attracts a wider audience than before. "We got two extra screens as a gift, which has allowed us to go wild with special film programmes and premieres that you might not expect in an average cinema. It's fantastic to see that we're attracting so many more young people as a result."

To come up with the ideal cinema, the team visited movie theatres throughout the Netherlands. Interior architects &Prast&Hooft were given a list of keywords and quickly conceived a design that was close to what the organisation had in mind. "In terms of atmosphere, it had to be a combination of chic and kitsch," says Richt Pander. "The shade of pink they chose is wonderful. It also gets dirty very easily, by the way." She smiles. "And those lights are perfect too, it gives the feeling that we really wanted. It took us a while to attune everything exactly, but it worked out very well." The film square is now the most popular seating area in the building. Most of the people you see there don't even come to see the films.

In the Forum, the library has also undergone a transformation in line with the development that libraries have witnessed over the past ten years. Of course, lending books is one of its functions, but the library is increasingly becoming a place for debate, cultural manifestations, and digitisation. "Yet in many Dutch cities, in the most beautiful locations, there are still libraries with rows of bookcases. They're like cemeteries," says Dirk Nijdam. The library in the Forum had to be completely different, more like a bookshop, a lively place where books are displayed in a way that makes you want to grab them. There are just as many books as in the old library, about 97,000, spread over various locations. Mini-living rooms with armchairs invite you to read a book on the spot, and that is exactly what happens. The library has gained almost two thousand borrowers, including many young people and small children.

"Libraries have had a social dimension ever since they came into being," says Daphne de Bruijn. In addition to lending books, they derive their right to exist from a wide spectrum of activities. In the Forum, the library is a place where people come into contact with each other and can work on their own development. They learn to read and write, learn to speak Dutch or receive help with online communications with government agencies. In this way, the building opens the door to the digital world, and thus to the future.

Showered with
Compliments and Prizes

"Urban society needs a place, emotionally and historically determined, where the most important events of urban life can be shared, where it can experience togetherness and solidarity. The inhabitants of the city and the surrounding areas also need this centre to attend to important matters in an appropriate atmosphere and to experience remarkable things. The centre allows every city dweller to experience something exceptional. For him it is the 'source of warmth' [...]."

This passage comes from the *Doelstellingennota* (Objectives Memorandum) for Groningen's city centre, commissioned by the city council in 1971-72. Max van den Berg, a councillor at that time, played a crucial role in this study, planting the seed decades ago from which the Forum has emerged. And although the policy document related to the city centre, it can be applied just as well to the building: a centre within that centre. The Forum is precisely the kind of place where people meet, where things can be seen and experienced, and where you can go to develop yourself, be inspired or enrich your life.

The Forum had to be voted on by various municipal executives, who raised questions time and again. "Looking back at the entire process, it's a miracle it ever got built," says Dirk Nijdam. "It was all down to chance, luck and good timing." Sometimes it was due to the perseverance of a single councillor, at others to two votes in the city council. Amid all the tumult, the design stood firm.

All in all, the Forum, including the parking facilities for cars and bikes, cost about 150 million euros. That's a lot of money. But compared with similar developments, it seems like a bargain. Museum Boijmans van Beuningen in Rotterdam is being renovated at a cost of more than €250 million, and the Museum of Modern Art in New York for $450. With the Forum, Groningen has acquired a new building that brings people from far and wide: people who spend time in the city and spend money here. Together with the Nieuwe Markt, it forms a new attraction that enriches the city.

Sticking your neck out can result in beautiful things, a wait-and-see attitude usually doesn't. "Everyone involved deserves a big compliment for what has been achieved and the courage with which it has been done," says Nijdam. "It's very rare for a city to dare to construct a building of this kind in a location such as this. A building that will either last forever or become the mistake of a lifetime." Although it's still early days, it is probably safe to say that the former is more likely than the latter.

As negative as the local press was in the years prior to the Forum's opening, after actually having visited the building the *Dagblad van het Noorden* gave it five stars. The major national dailies were also enthusiastic, as was the architectural press. The Forum was the big winner during the Groningen Architecture Prize and was voted Best Building of the Year by the BNA in 2020. That same year the building won the award for Best Library of the Netherlands, and in August 2021 it was one of the five nominees for the international prize, Public Library of the Year. The building's interior design also won several awards. The pandemic meant that the parties for these awards had to be cancelled but even without the euphoria there was a real sense of pride among all those involved.

Even Groningen's most sceptical residents have now come around. Richt Pander tells a story about a visitor to the cinema on Hereplein who repeatedly voiced his aversion to the Forum over the years: "He was outraged that it was to be paid for with his taxes." A few days after the Forum opened, she suddenly found herself on the escalator behind the same man. "We can certainly be proud to have this in Groningen," she heard him say to someone next to him, without his realising it. "He said how special it was that you could get in for free and that you could go up to the roof. He would probably never have come up to me himself to admit that he had been wrong all that time. But that kind of experience is what you do it for."

Although Groningers are sober and not given to bragging, sometimes pride is the only logical feeling. Anyone who came across a building of this calibre abroad would rave about it, but when it's just around the corner we feel that we shouldn't get too excited about it. Now that the Forum is open and the locals can see that people are coming from far and wide to visit it, are walking around with their mouths open and telling their friends that they really need to go to Groningen, perhaps even the biggest sceptics now have a feeling of satisfaction. And the realisation is growing that their city has become a little more beautiful and a little better because of this new building that has taken its place in the city centre with a kind of nonchalant self-evidence, as if it had always been there.

deep.black

porschecentrumgroningen

wrongfriends.rides

wrongfriends.rides

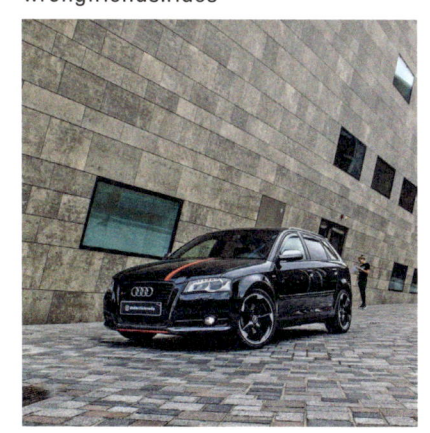

blacked.a3

gustafitgym

miladisme

ninaoosting_

m6nasaa

jakelothbruk

binnichtpatrick

miena.tara

willie_vinky

aalilatif

salam_alsasah

ilsereginastone

zarifburhani

xbowiine

ilsekwant

chevaunkepekepe

ceren_kesen

pavel_vasilev_ppv

lamonabardisa

mariannezuidema

sofiesteenhoudt

thijskoetsier

ludiekwandelen

sannemulder_official

mirtesjouke__

marcelhulshof8

justawheelchairguy

justawheelchairguy

justawheelchairguy

justawheelchairguy

shazalaura

22l791

gustafitgym

_j_anneman

merel

the_otaman

yeodimri

binnichtpatrick

ella_stol

hku.mia

johannasagner

luciennevdp

silberrr

esthervoost

lifeofmutebwa

thewoweffect.nl

Marijke Martin & Cor Wagenaar

The Forum and the City

It is impossible to understand the transformation of the east side of the Grote Markt (Large Marketplace), which finally became visible with the construction of the Forum, without relating it to ideas about and changes to this urban square as a whole. Its partial destruction in April 1945 provided the context for an unprecedented enlargement of the square, in which public bodies, with the city council at the forefront, manifested themselves much more emphatically than ever before. This story is about the reversal of the post-war reconstruction, a development that started by filling in the western half of the square and culminated in the reconstruction of its east wall and the construction of the Forum on Nieuwe Markt (New Marketplace). This process can be summarised with a term coined by the architecture historian and theorist Anthony Vidler. In an article from 1977 he wrote of a 'third typology', i.e., the traditional city, which follows the first typology, nature, and the second, the machine.[1] The reconstruction forced a radical break with the roots of the historical city. The essence of Vidler's third typology was to rectify this break, implying a return to traditional urban planning. This was propelled not by abstract theories, often embedded in ambitious social ideals, but by the historical fortunes of the city itself: the traditional city refers primarily to itself and its history. The reversal of the urban-planning consequences of the reconstruction of the Grote Markt is a rare, eloquent example of this third typology, and for this reason alone justifies an extensive elucidation.

1   Anthony Vidler, *Rational Architecture: The Reconstruction of the European City*, Editions Archives d'Architecture Moderne, Brussels, 1978, quoted in: Nan Ellin, *Postmodern Urbanism*, revised edition, Princeton Architectural Press, New York, 1999 (1996), pp. 27-28; Anthony Vidler, 'The Third Typology' (1978), in: Charles Jencks and Karl Kropf (eds.), *Theories and Manifestos of Contemporary Architecture*, second edition, Wiley Academy, London, 2006, pp. 77-79.

Vidler's ideas did not come out of the blue. They summarise trends that would come to typify the 1980s, a decade that has since been re-evaluated as a rare and fertile period of reflection on the (historical) city. Vidler fits within a design tradition whose spiritual father was Camillo Sitte, active in Vienna at the end of the nineteenth century. Among Dutch architects, it was Marinus Jan Granpré Molière who was foremost in adopting Sitte's ideas as the guiding principle for his urban-development work, including in the reconstruction plans he drew up between 1945 and 1949 for Groningen's Grote Markt. Vidler's attempt to give a theoretical-historical framework to the appeal to the traditional city related to the then-emerging school of Neo-Rationalism.

With their plea for continuity, permanence in the structure of the city and a solid foundation in the analysis of the existing urban fabric, architects such as Aldo Rossi, Maurice Culot, Léon Krier, Georgio Grassi, Rob Krier and Josef Paul Kleihues prepared the ground for the broader acceptance of the traditional city that Vidler took as the starting point for his third typology. It is noteworthy that, with the exception of the first three, all these designers have left their mark on the Grote Markt. The Berlin-based architect Kleihues is considered the originator of 'critical reconstruction', the concept that underpinned the Internationale Bauausstellung (IBA) 1984-87 in Berlin and, after 1989, the reconstruction of Berlin as the German capital. The IBA developed into a catalyst for radical innovation and a definitive break with the modernist project.[2]

Critical reconstruction understands the city as a mediator between tradition and modernity. It proposes a dialogue, rather than a break, between the two in the sense of a recognisable, legible spatial-typological development over time. Where continuity has been disrupted, the damage must be repaired. This form of reconstruction became known by the German term *Stadtreparatur*, literally 'urban repair'. The third typology, like critical reconstruction and urban repair, is an attempt to give systematic direction to the transformative processes of the historical city, which were brought to an end by the devastation of the Second World War and post-war reconstruction. The theoretical reflection that this presupposes coincides with the processing and re-interpretation of the city's architectural and urban-planning history. Because a full account of this

long and exceptionally rich history is impossible in the space allotted here, we have limited ourselves to what appears at first sight to be a motley collection of elements: plans implemented or not (not only on the Grote Markt, but also elsewhere in the city), theoretical reflections (many of which revolved around the appreciation of modernism) and concrete interventions.

The first part of this story collects the elements that have largely defined critical reconstruction and urban repair. Urban reconstruction involves much more than copying historical plans and plot structures. More recent developments also play a role in the urban planning laboratory, and we have included some of these in our collection. The role they played in the run-up to the Forum is the subject of the second part. Through this story, we attempt to make clear that it concerns a unique process that resisted the uniformity of existing administrative and professional protocols, and has the potential to be a textbook case in the contemporary handling of the city. The Forum is the culmination of this process.

2   Thomas Köhler, Ursula Müller, *Anything Goes? Berlin Architecture in the 1980s*, Berlin, 2021, pp. 30-40; Josef P. Kleihues, Heinrich Klotz, Annegret Burg, *Internationale Bauausstellung Berlin 1987: Beispiele einer neuen Architektur*, Deutsches Architekturmuseum (Frankfurt), Klett-Cotta, Stuttgart, 1986.

The Historical Square

The 'battle' of Groningen at the end of the Second World War marks a rupture in the development of the Grote Markt: after 1945 a new chapter begins. That story is tied up with the phenomenon of urban-design plans: a series of reconstruction plans followed by structural plans, zoning plans, cultural-historical explorations, visual quality plans and an armful of policy documents. However, for a better understanding of the process, we must first analyse the original square. That can be done briefly and concisely. With its collection of notable, even iconic buildings, the Grote Markt is the social and political 'heart' of Groningen, even if it is not geographically at its centre.

The Grote Markt is located in the northeast of the medieval city. Herestraat, which developed into the main shopping street after 1900, leads to it without any sense of ostentation: the square is hidden behind a small square building. Before the devastation of 1945, Waagstraat, an extension of Herestraat, was the shortest route to the square along the north wall. Only then did the Grote Markt reveal itself as a public plaza in all its glory.

Together with Oosterstraat, Herestraat forms the most important connection to the south. Before the construction of a bridge over the turning basin of the Verbindingskanaal in the 1990s as part of the new Groninger Museum, Herestraat was the main route between the station and the marketplace. Before 1945, Oosterstraat did not lead directly to the Grote Markt but ended at Poelestraat a few dozen metres away. Those approaching the square from the south would catch their first glimpse of Saint Martin's Tower above the buildings on Poelestraat and the east side of the Grote Markt. Thereafter, the tower was gradually hidden from view, only to reveal itself 'full length' once the visitor reached the square.

The relatively narrow Poelestraat runs to the east, and was for many years little more than a secondary connection to the districts built from the 1920s behind the current University Medical Centre (UMC). Sint Jansstraat runs, also in an eastwardly direction, from the northeast corner of the Grote Markt past Saint Martin's Church. Until the last quarter of the nineteenth century it was an insignificant passage, leading to a bridge over the Turfsingel. There was little to see or do there until the munitions depot, the Kruithuis, was scrapped as part of the dismantling of the city's fortifications and made way for the municipal theatre. The construction of a grammar school strengthened the regeneration of this area and led to the widening of Sint Jansstraat. The guardhouse at the foot of Saint Martin's Tower visually closed off the street. That Sint Jansstraat never functioned as a main artery to the new residential areas in the east is due to the construction, in 1903, of the UMC's predecessor, the General Provincial and Academic Hospital: one of two major national construction projects completed that year. Like Hendrik Berlage's Stock Exchange Building (now the Beurs van Berlage) in Amsterdam, it was opened by the then prime minister, Abraham Kuyper. Since then, the complex, reinforced by subsequent expansions, has formed an almost impregnable barrier. This had the effect that Groningen's city centre practically ended at the east wall of the Grote Markt.

The north wall of the marketplace is pierced by two passages. Saint Martin's Tower was attached to this wall until well into the twentieth century. Two premises away from the Tower was the Kreupelstraatje – little more than an alleyway – and a narrow passage leading to Oude Ebbingestraat was located near the City Hall. Oude Boteringestraat runs north from the market's northwest corner. Lined mainly with stately buildings, it is the city's only main artery without a retail function. The Grote Markt and the Vismarkt (Fish Market) are linked by a relatively narrow passage with the descriptive name Tussen Beide Markten (Between Both Markets). The plot structure in the vicinity of the Grote Markt was particularly intricate. The north wall originally consisted of twenty-five individual lots, while the east wall, after the construction of the pompous Scholtenhuis between 1878 and 1881, comprised eight. The majority of the buildings were shops, cafes and restaurants; exceptions were the Grand Theatre from 1929, the aforementioned Scholtenhuis and, of course, the City Hall.

The neoclassical City Hall, completed in 1810, replaced its medieval predecessor. Until 1945, its construction was the only shocking change in the square's thousand-year history. The new City Hall was the result of thorough research into the products of classical antiquity. The architect, Jacob Otten Husly, wanted to distinguish himself from earlier, to his mind dilettantish attempts to return to the pure origins of European civilisation. The building, the fruit of the nation's first architectural competition and the first in the Netherlands with a protruding portico, completely transformed the square. Where the medieval City Hall had faced north, Otten Husly's building is oriented to the east. Before 1810, the Grote Markt consisted of two more or less equal spaces that together formed a square: an elongated section along the north wall with the weigh

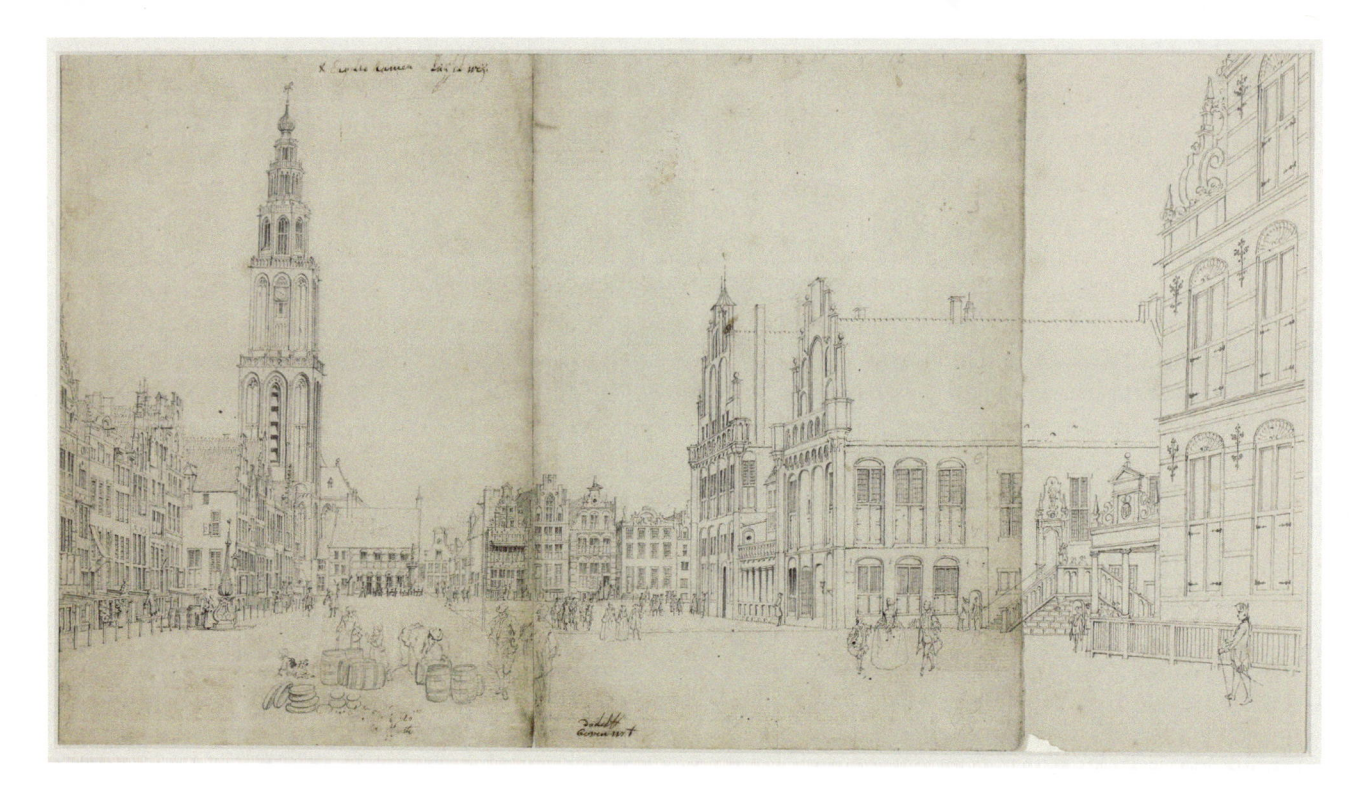

Drawing of the Grote Markt, with the tax office (Gold Office) on the far right and the Council and Wine House next to it, oriented to the north side of the Grote Markt (far left). The aerial photo from around 1920 clearly shows that Otten Husly's City Hall has been turned by ninety degrees, thereby shifting the urban development accent of the square to the east.

City

house and a more equilateral space between the old City Hall and the east wall. Otten Husly upgraded the latter to the forecourt of the new City Hall. As a result, the new building was not only architecturally revolutionary but also forced a breach in the urban composition. In Vidler's series of three typologies, Otten Husly's City Hall represents the first, that of nature. In the mid-eighteenth century, the typology of the primitive hut was seen as the metaphorical origin of architecture: with its characteristic structure of tree trunks and branches, it anticipated the classical design system of column and architrave.

The Destruction as the End of the Traditional City

The history of the Grote Markt as we know it today begins in 1945. In the last year of the war, Canadian troops entered the city to rid it of what remained of the German occupying forces. Because they had no intention of surrendering, the battle of Groningen ensued. Local historians later seized upon the war to paint a grotesque, exaggerated picture of this drama. Guided walks were established and the TV programme *Andere Tijden* (Different Times) devoted an episode to it, even making a comparison with the Battle of Stalingrad. Precisely what good the Battle of Groningen had done is a question that was never asked, but it certainly had no effect on the outcome of the Second World War. No battles were fought to liberate Amsterdam or Utrecht. In any case, the number of casualties cannot be compared with those suffered in Stalingrad, where more than a million Russian soldiers and forty thousand civilians lost their lives. Nonetheless, the fighting in the historic city centre marked a radical break in Groningen's biography. Nothing would ever be as it had been. The traditional city ceased to exist.

Selective Demolition

When the smoke from the fighting around the Grote Markt had cleared, most of the city appeared to have emerged unscathed, with the exception of the main square, which lay partly in ruins. Three of the four walls of the square had been destroyed and hardly anything had survived of the buildings on either side of Waagstraat, the two islands on the square. All the historic monuments had been spared: Saint Martin's Church with its famous tower in the northeast corner, Otten Husly's City Hall and the seventeenth-century Goudkantoor (Gold Office), a tax office that was part of the structures on Waagstraat. At the foot of the tower, the damaged guardhouse was left standing while the weigh house was

The destroyed east wall in 1945 (top) and aerial view of the area around the Grote Markt in 1947 when the rubble of the war damage had been cleared away.

demolished. Coincidence? Probably not. In all likelihood, the damage, while serious enough, was less dramatic than the authorities would have us believe. Many of the damaged buildings might have been salvageable. The maps on which the damage was recorded indicate a huge area as totally destroyed. When the rubble had been cleared away, virtually nothing remained of the north and east walls, there was a large hole in the middle of the west wall, and the Gold Office and City Hall were left alone on an otherwise empty plain.

The reconstruction of the Grote Markt began almost immediately. In fact, the director of the urban planning department, H.P.J. Schut, had contacted Granpré Molière, internationally renowned in the early 1920s for his progressive urban plans, even before the Groningen frontline approached. Granpré Molière had been a professor at Delft Technical College since 1924, where he was the first to teach urban planning. From the 1930s he was increasingly associated with anti-modernist views. This did not alter the fact that, certainly in the period before the Second World War, he had much in common with his modernist opponents: like them, he resisted historicising architecture, he sought a new formal idiom and was convinced of the need for a return to the collective. To his mind, there was no place for individualism, not in architecture and certainly not in urban planning.

Granpré Molière saw the nineteenth century as a period of decline, mainly because that century saw urban communities wiped out and culture becoming the privilege of a small bourgeois elite. Many of his modernist counterparts felt the same way. A new vision of society was needed, coupled with an architectural language that set this vision in stone. Discussions about architecture were now concerned not only with technical, economic and financial issues, the solution of practical problems, or detailing the programme behind the renewal plans, but above all with society and politics. Granpré Molière was inspired by Catholicism and saw the Middle Ages as an unsurpassed cultural heyday. Many modernists thought the same way. Ideological considerations also played a prominent role in the reconstruction of the Grote Markt well into the 1950s. And that is less remarkable than it seems. The need to rebuild the square arose directly from the consequences of the Second World War, the greatest ideology-driven catastrophe humanity had hitherto unleashed upon itself. The reconstruction was not just about a square, but about the qualities of the society that the plan had to represent. That approach has never disappeared from urban planning.

After the remains of the damaged buildings around the Grote Markt – some of them sizeable – had been removed, the square underwent a second destruction: the clearing of the network of largely private properties that neatly coincided with the plot structure. Traditionally, although the plot structure barely changes, owners are constantly adapting or replacing their buildings. This is a slow but steady process of renewal: some historians believe that the buildings are replaced every fifty to one hundred years by new or radically renovated buildings. In other words: the overall structure and urban-planning image remain intact, even if the usage shifts. In Groningen, this motor of continuous urban regeneration, anchored in the ownership of the lots, disappeared when the damaged area around the Grote Markt was completely expropriated. The traditional city was no more. Gradual transformation gave way to planning – a form of intervention that is, by definition, fairly heavy-handed and driven by interests and insights that function only at the level of the plan, never at the level of a fragmented patchwork of property titles. In the reconstruction planning, the interplay between permanent and transient parts played no role at all. It was replaced by visions of the future, often charged with outspoken social views.[3]

No Clearly Defined Programme

As far as can be ascertained, no clearly defined programme for the Grote Markt was ever formulated. Instead there was a cocktail of (sometimes contradictory) wishes. The client – the state, not the city – insisted on practical improvements, especially with regards to traffic flow. After all, the meteoric rise in private car ownership that had become apparent two decades earlier in the United States was now also expected in Europe. Through its mayor, Pieter Cort van der Linden, Groningen made it known that it was strongly in favour of defining the Grote Markt even more clearly as the city's political administrative heart. Otten Husly's City Hall spoke for itself, but if it could be generously extended with a large office building to house the expanding civil service, Cort van der Linden believed that the Grote Markt would become the beating heart of the city's government. The consequence was a drastic shift in the function of the premises around the market at the expense

3   For the reconstruction see: Cor Wagenaar, *Tussen Grandezza en Schavot. De ontwerpen van Granpré Molière voor de wederopbouw van Groningen*, Wolters-Noordhof / Egbert Forsten, Groningen, 1991.

Bird's-eye view of the first reconstruction plan (March 1946), in which the square's area would have almost doubled, its axis would have been rotated ninety degrees and St Martin's Tower would have come to stand in the middle of the east wall.

of retail and catering. This shift became even more dramatic when culture also claimed a place on the square. The initiative for this came from the citizenry itself and was taken up by the city council. Herein lie the roots of the idea to install a cultural destination on the east side of the Grote Markt. The result of the absence of a clearly defined programme was a spatial power grab by the public sector. The shift was grist to the mill of Granpré Molière's supporters, by now often referred to as the Delft School, but also played into the hands of the representatives of modernism. The new age would be collectivistic: individualism (which could easily be associated with private entrepreneurial interests) would be a thing of the past. There was no mention of the desired design of the new Grote Markt.

Farewell to the Nineteenth Century

Granpré Molière fully appreciated the Grote Markt's qualities. He considered it among the most successful medieval squares in the Netherlands and included it in his urban-planning lectures in Delft. Illustrating his fervent desire to force a radical break with the past – in this respect he was even more radical than the modernists – is a sketch in which he suggested rotating the axis of the square by ninety degrees. Saint Martin's Tower would be placed at the centre of the east wall and the City Hall incorporated in the west wall, but the National Office for the Preservation of Monuments brushed the plan aside. Granpré Molière then began to work on a plan that, from his perspective, was the pinnacle of his work for the reconstruction of Groningen. It would go down in history as the 1947 Basic Plan.

Granpré Molières 1947 Basic Plan was a manifesto of his views on the city and society. It was also a textbook example of what a daring urban plan can do – and of what would be impossible in a normal, steady transformation process. This is most evident from the interventions he proposed outside the actual plan area. Granpré Molière saw the reconstruction as a suitable opportunity to put an end to what he saw as a period of cultural decline – a view that also had currency among supporters of modernism. If the nineteenth century was the pinnacle of decay, the buildings that represented it must be demolished. The Harmonie complex, home to one of the oldest symphony orchestras in the Netherlands, was emblematic of nineteenth-century elite bourgeois culture. The same applied to the Municipal Theatre. Both could disappear, as Granpré Molière did not see the demolition of these monumental complexes as problematic. The removal of the Corn Exchange from the Vismarkt was also desirable,

perhaps even essential. This oversized building was designed in 1865 with the support of the city council to demonstrate that Groningen had become the third largest trading city in the country, after Amsterdam and Rotterdam. Presumably the building therefore ushered in a tradition in Groningen of using architecture for what much later came to be called branding. For Granpré Molière, the Corn Exchange represented the nineteenth century as a period in which economics and technology were glorified and culture was forgotten. In this case, the building's position added another dimension: it terminated the Vismarkt on the west side and partly obscured the view of the medieval Aa Church, which incidentally rises high above it. For Granpré Molière, once the city centre had been cleaned of all nineteenth-century stains, the Grote Markt could become the cultural, social and political heart of the rebuilt Groningen. All cultural facilities would be housed in a culture temple on the east side, which would be located partially behind a row of shops and cafés. This building would be emphatically dominated by popular culture, which the government was working on plans to subsidise.

Islands in a Sea

The cultural building established the programme for the east side of the Grote Markt and with it the basic principles of the design. The first problem that required a solution was determining the shape of the square. For Granpré Molière, there were only two options: either the square ran from the east wall to the west side of Guldenstraat with all the buildings standing like islands in a large plain, or from the east wall to the City Hall. In the latter case, the Grote Markt was merely a forecourt for the City Hall. Granpré Molière decided to start with the most spacious solution, which he even expanded by moving the east wall's building line backwards. This enabled Oosterstraat to lead directly onto the square and meant that Saint Martin's Tower was fully visible from that street for the first time. Here Granpré Molière apparently broke with his beloved Sitte's views and he certainly waved goodbye to the historical street plan of the Grote Markt. That was most evident on the west side of the enlarged plaza. The City Hall, a large office complex that was to serve as its extension, and the Gold Office lay like islands in a sea of open space. Because the classical architecture of the City Hall did not permit an extension, Granpré Molière decided to move the new building in the direction of Guldenstraat, which in fact ceased to exist and became part of the Grote Markt. A bridge in the form of a covered gallery connected

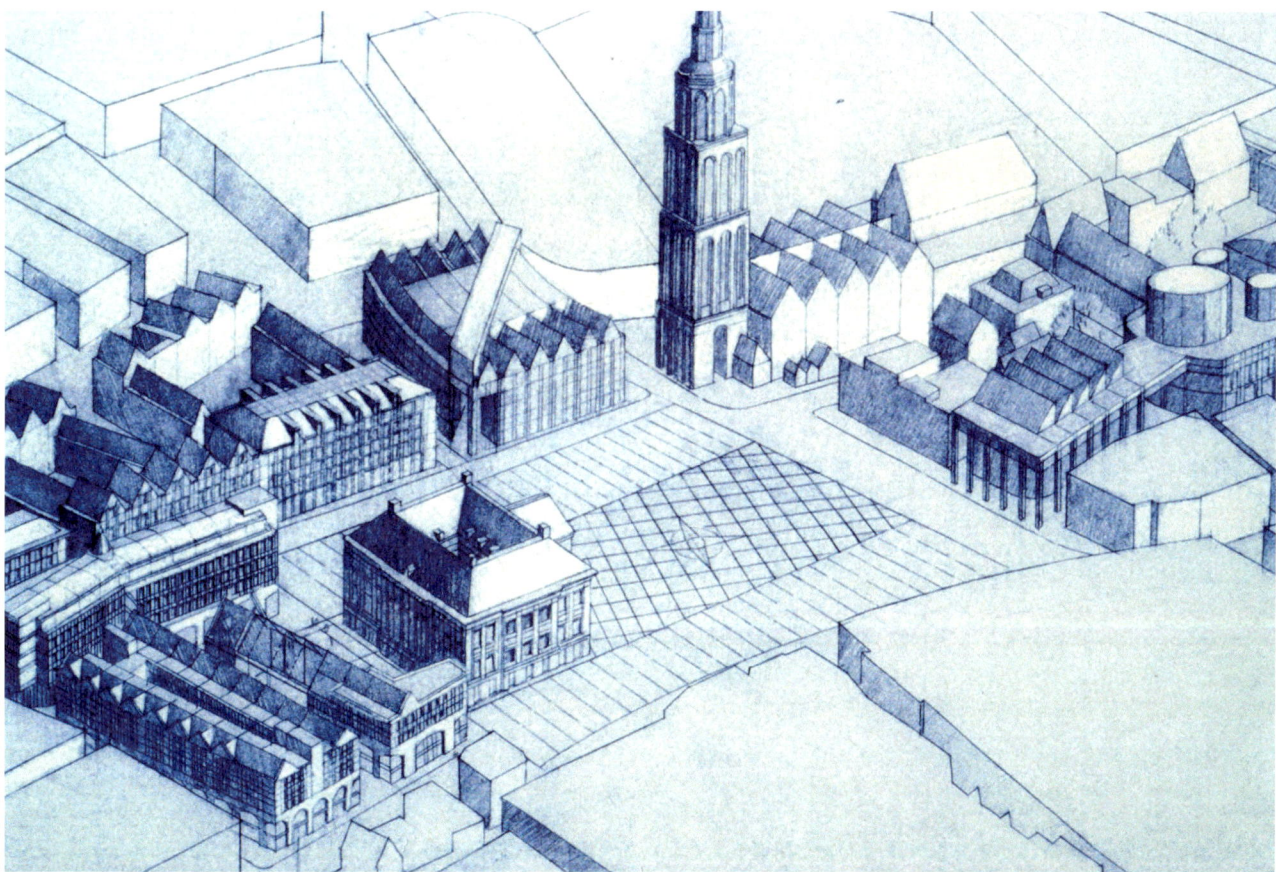

Model of the basic plan from 1947, in which Granpré Molière already envisioned a cultural centre on the east side of the Grote Markt. A cultural function on the east side was also a feature of the artist's impressions that Adolfo Natalini made of the Grote Markt in the late 1990s (designed in the context of the Nieuwe Noordzijde (New North Side) urban plan, 1997-2000).

The Forum and the City

the City Hall, the Gold Office and the new building. The latter was designed by Granpré Molière's
most gifted student, Jo Vegter, who made a series
of plans, including that for a square building with a
tower that was included in the Basic Plan 1947.

In line with Sitte's ideas, Granpré Molière's
plan clearly defined the sea of space in the heart of
the city. The traffic-control interventions did not de-
tract from this, although these were also remarkable.
At the foot of the tower, traditionally attached to the
buildings on the north side (it was not until the 1930s
that the building adjacent to it was demolished, apparently to facilitate a planned restoration), Granpré
Molière designed a wide passageway. This led to
a new square, the Kwinkenplein, which gave traffic
the choice of going north via Oude Ebbingestraat
or taking the route via Kreupelstraat, thus solving
one of the bottlenecks: the connection to the north.
An additional advantage – from the designer's perspective – was that he did not have to widen Oude
Ebbingestraat where it issues onto the Grote Markt
and did not have to compromise the closed nature
of the square. Perhaps more important was that the
tower was now detached. Although the small guardhouse would be preserved (Granpré Molière thus
prevented the mouth of Sint Jansstraat from becoming too wide), the city's most iconic structure
was now visible from top to bottom from the square
for the first time. A second remarkable intervention
was the diversion of traffic to and from the south via
Oosterstraat and the Vismarkt. This made it possible to keep cars out of Herestraat, creating a pedestrian zone, a proposal that was ahead of its time.
Too far, as it turned out: the street was not pedestri-
anised until 1968.

The 1947 Basic Plan was not implemented,
at least not as Granpré Molière envisaged it. But the
plan has left its mark on the rebuilt Grote Markt: virtually all the major urban development interventions in the plan – the enormous enlargement of the
square, the breakthrough at the foot of the tower, the
construction of a separate office building for the City
Hall connected to the old building by a bridge – were
implemented, with the exception of the pedestrian-
friendly Herestraat and the construction of a cultural
centre behind the east wall.

Urban Design as Spatial Management

Seven years of tinkering came to an end with the
approval of the 1952 Basic Plan. In the meantime,
Granpré Molière had retired so the new proposal
was designed by Van Tijen, Van der Steur and Van
Boven. While apparently a logical, pragmatic alternative to the work of their predecessor, it is in fact the
most ideological in the long succession of plans. It
celebrates the rewards of absolute rationalism, interpreted as reducing spatial planning to a technical
problem, a reduction legitimised by the pursuit of
abstraction so typical of modernism. The practical
changes are minor: the programme (including the
cultural centre), the position and layout of the City
Hall extension and the size and shape of the square
correspond to the 1947 Basic Plan. The only changes
are a slightly reduced passageway at the tower and
the widening of the mouth of Oude Ebbingestraat,
which has been optically narrowed by the use of colonnades. The practical consequences of Granpré
Molière's social manifesto, including the demolition
of many grand nineteenth-century buildings, had
disappeared.

How modern was the 1952 Basic Plan? If its
modernity does not reside in its urban design, it is
obvious to look for it in the architecture. Until the
mid-1950s, however, hardly any modern architecture was realised in the Netherlands, not even in
Rotterdam. The new plan's modernity is to be found
not in the urban design (which is no more pragmatic
or functional than previous proposals), nor in the architecture, but solely in the ideology: the plan initiates what has elsewhere been referred to as a mana-
gerial revolution. This revolution illustrates the
transition from Vidler's first typology to his second:
that of the machine. Central to this is the production process in which building types are reduced
to reproducible units that coincide with their function (family home, office building, suburban housing estate, city), and the cohesion between building and urban fabric disappears: individual premises
are no longer the building blocks determined by the
plot and shaped by public space but are stand-alone
objects. The second typology conceives architecture and urbanism as forms of spatial management
based on singular objectives and the elimination
of all aspects that cannot be traced back to them.[4]
These aspects include architectural and urban
design insofar as they have no rational justification
– at least within this line of thinking. This view is in

4   Cor Wagenaar, *Town Planning in the
     Netherlands Since 1800: Responses to
     Enlightenment Ideas and Geopolitical Realities*
     (2011), Rotterdam, 2015, pp. 357-361.

line with that of modernism but does not arise from it. The 1952 Basic Plan illustrates that the modernisation of Dutch architecture and urban design came from outside, from the worlds of planning and policy. This ideological connotation charge was later expanded with the identification of modernism with the welfare state. The latter was interpreted as social and democratic, and therefore 'open': pre-eminent qualities of modernism. This interpretation explains why the debate that was unleashed when modernism lost its dominant position in the 1990s was not about design but about ideology.

It was not until the mid-1950s that the reconstruction of the Grote Markt actually got underway. Many of the owners of destroyed buildings could not wait that long and withdrew. This was one of the reasons for the decline in the number of lots on the square – another was that modern retail was better accommodated in wider buildings. Most of the buildings were built in a style that was modern in proportions, layout and functionality, but less abstract than classic pre-war modernism due to the use of brick and decorative elements. This is characteristic of the reconstruction architecture of those years, and the result looked pretty good (and still does as long as lack of maintenance and the advance of cheap plastic window frames hasn't caused too much damage). Most notable was the architecture of the City Hall extension. Vegter renounced the 'traditionalism' of his teacher and produced a modern-looking design of white marble and extensive use of glass. He raised the building up on columns and connected it with a glazed bridge to the old City Hall and the Gold Office. At the point where Herestraat meets the Gold Office, he devised a grand staircase. In the 1960s, it eventually proved too difficult to fit the cultural centre into the limited space behind the east wall. For this reason and because it was feared that a cultural venue on the square would be at the expense of the business community, it was transferred to the Oosterpoort district just outside the historic centre. The remains of the damaged guardhouse were removed: the building blocked the entrance to Sint Jansstraat and had to go because nothing could stand in the way of the advance of the motorcar.

The Grote Markt in the late 1980s, when subservience to road traffic had effectively reduced the square to a three/four-lane roundabout with parking spaces on the edges and a bus station on the north side.

The Historical City Outlawed

If there are three concepts that typify the transformation of the Dutch city in this period they are 'the motorcar', 'modernism' and 'expansion'. All three left their mark on the Grote Markt. The square became a hub for motor traffic, which was given free rein, partly at the insistence of the shopkeepers: shops that could not be reached by car would be doomed.

In the course of the 1950s, modernism supplanted all other movements, developing a multitude of approaches and styles that met the need for buildings with an optimistic, cheerful appearance. As economic growth went hand in hand with a rapid increase in population, Groningen was not left behind. The three key concepts mentioned above help to explain why the historical city – with the exception of its monuments – was declared an outlaw. The decision to exploit the devastation left behind by the battle of Groningen to clear the entire planning area anticipated this. And both so-called 'traditionalist' architect-planners, such as Granpré Molière, and modern architects shared the conviction that the historical urban fabric must be given short shrift. In this singular way of thinking, service to traffic was the most important function of public space, even if this was at the expense of its use for leisure and of all the other qualities that would much later be grouped under the heading 'placemaking'.

Hospitable City Centre

The reversal that occurred in the 1970s can be seen as an attempt, related to the philosophy of placemaking, to reclaim public space from the car and make it suitable for other forms of use. Behind this sea change was an image of man and community that was at odds with the society that was constructed after the liberation. It was not difficult to relate the results of Groningen's reconstruction, firstly on the Grote Markt, with what was now portrayed as a technocratic approach to urban planning imposed from above. Although the most rigorous demolition and breakthrough plans were not executed after that, the machine they produced was very much alive. To change that, and also to do justice to the growing dissatisfaction with the way the city was being treated, the city council, led by councillor Max van den Berg, appealed to a number of critics. One of them was Herman Hertzberger, one of the most influential 'newcomers' who had gathered around *Forum* magazine as early as 1959. They reclaimed the artistic dimension: the architect-planner was above all an artist. The artistic side was rooted in the design and served a social purpose. This transcended the level of the material. Streets and squares served other and more important purposes than traffic. They were there for play and encounters; they were spaces where the visitor was simultaneously an actor and a spectator.

The *Doelstellingennota* (Objectives Memorandum) presented by the group of critics in 1972 contained no plan at all, but did offer numerous recommendations. The memorandum described Groningen's city centre as a site of memory, of public gathering, to experience "togetherness and solidarity" and to discover a shared history.

The authors considered it important to maintain and possibly restore the interior quality that characterises the inner city and city centre, for example in the distance between street walls in order to create "necessary seclusion and intimacy."[5] On the one hand, these intentions were linked to the importance of preserving the historically developed building structure, on the other hand, the intended sense of hospitality resulted in new construction projects.[6] On the east side of the Grote Markt arose the Naberpassage and garage, a large new building that narrowed the originally generous access to the planned cultural centre to little more than a broad alleyway leading to nowhere.

One of the recommendations of the Objectives Memorandum was to bring motor traffic under control. Groningen's city centre was divided into four parts, separated from each other by borders that were impenetrable for motorists. That put an end to the city centre as a hub and racetrack for cars that in most cases had no business there. The motorcar was also gradually pushed back from the Grote Markt.

Beyond Modernism?

As early as the 1980s, the municipal urban-planning department toyed with the idea of radically breaking with the legacy of reconstruction and thus putting an end to the hegemony of modernism. The forty years in which this movement was decisive were no more than a brief intermezzo in the more than a thousand years of the Grote Markt's existence. And if the desire to force a break with the past was the most important motivation, the Grote Markt was a perfect example (even if the urban-design breaches could be traced back to Granpré Molière).

Evidently inspired by the Internationale Bauausstellung from 1984 to 1987 in Berlin, which saw the first large-scale experiments with the concept of critical reconstruction, the municipality asked the event's curator, Josef Paul Kleihues, and later Rob Krier, one of the participants, to present their visions of the north side. In the late 1990s, Krier made a design that never gained much attention, but which nevertheless represents one of the most radical visions in the square's long planning history. He threaded the square's north and east walls together

5   *Doeleindennota* (deel 1) (Aims Memorandum, part 1), Municipality of Groningen, 1971, p. 3; 'Groningen: nota doelstelling binnenstad' (Objectives for Groningen's City Centre), in: *de Architect*, no. 9, 1972, pp. 701-705, p. 705.

6   *Grote Markt Oostzijde – Concept-Programma van Eisen Stedenbouw, Openbare Ruimte en Verkeer*, Municipality of Groningen, 27 June 2006, p. 5.

Artist's impressions of the north and east sides of the Grote Markt, designed by Rob Krier (designed in the context of the Nieuwe Noordzijde (New North Side) urban plan, 1997-2000), in which the walls of the square are joined together with the help of gatehouses, dome accents and galleries.

The Forum and the City

into a forum-like space with the help of gatehouses, dome accents and colonnades. Immediately in front of the existing east façade, he projected a continuous gallery, separated by a narrow street from a building that curves with the corner of Poelestraat.[7]

It is undoubtedly a pastiche, but it also signals a revaluation of the historic city. This revaluation was an international phenomenon that in the Netherlands can be linked to *Forum* magazine, which from 1959 was steered by a new editorial team. Herman Hertzberger, Aldo van Eyck, John Habraken and their colleagues went on to play a prominent role in the development of Structuralism: an approach that distinguishes between parts of the city that do not change or change only very slowly and others that have a higher turnover rate. Focused on the production of new buildings and districts, they always also referenced the historic city and the slow, steady transformation process that characterised cities before large-scale urban plans set the tone. The historic city made a comeback, also with the general public.

PART 2. DESIGNING FOR THE CITY

The Forum is the culmination of the reconstruction of the Grote Markt, which has been underway since the mid-1980s and in which the components described in the first part of this story played a constant role. They became woven into the mentality that gave the Grote Markt a completely new look within a period of twenty-five years, as if the city were reinventing itself, but did so by referring almost exclusively to itself: to the long series of interventions, to the thought complexes behind unrealised plans, to the *cité imaginaire*, a chest of theoretical reflections that sometimes pushed the city and urban design in a new direction. This form of self-reflection is the essence of Vidler's third typology, the traditional city, and inspired Kleihues's concept of critical reconstruction. An (urban) architecture that appeals to the traditional city refers not to external factors such as nature and the machine but to itself. Unlike, for example, Classicism (the doctrine of order) or Functionalism (form follows function), this does not have an objective set of design rules. Partly for this reason, it offers, in Vidler's words, "no panacea, no ultimate apotheosis of man in architecture, no positivistic eschatology" and heralds the end of the supposedly progressive ideological role of architecture.[8] Against this background, and in contrast to the postmodernist tendency to apply the historical image repertoire arbitrarily, the delineation of a third architectural typology should be understood above all as an appeal to the ability of architecture and urban planning to engage with the traditional city and to base an original design strategy on it. Such an appeal presupposes working with what we have called elements, but also a good dose of policy continuity. That this was possible in Groningen can only be explained by the presence of a political and administrative apparatus that consisted of a handful of local key figures and a selection of experts flown in from outside – who made their voices heard in all manner of configurations, committees, think tanks and forums. What was new was the direct involvement of the population: the owners and principal users of the public domain. Until then, they had been excluded from the decision-making process, apart from the role of the city council, which represents them. Perhaps one of the most remarkable phenomena in the passage to the new Grote Markt is that its realisation was largely determined by the outcome

---

7   Rob Krier, artist's impression of the north side of the Grote Markt (produced by John Stoel), as part of the Nieuwe Noordzijde (New North Side) urban plan, 1997-2000 (Groningen Archives NL-GnGRA_2138_3275 and 3277); Rob Krier, artist's impression of the east side of the Grote Markt (produced by John Stoel), as part of the Nieuwe Noordzijde (New North Side) urban plan, 1997-2000 (Groningen Archives NL-GnGRA_2138_3276); Rob Krier, plan of the Grote Markt (produced by John Stoel), as part of the Nieuwe Noordzijde (New North Side) urban plan, 1997-2000 (Groningen Archives NL-GnGRA_2138_3278).

8   Anthony Vidler, 'The Third Typology' (1977), in: K. Michael Hays (ed.), *Architecture Theory Since 1968*, MIT Press, Cambridge, Mass / London, England, 2002, pp. 288-294, p. 288.

of referendums, including one concerning the location of a new cultural centre on the east side of the square. We can reasonably assume that the population had little enthusiasm for the Grote Markt after the reconstruction, including the new City Hall extension. In this respect, the people of Groningen were ahead of the experts who were apparently trapped in a mental framework that had long since lost its relevance.

Reduction of the Grote Markt: the Waagstraat project

The reconstruction of the Grote Markt began in the area west of the old City Hall where the distaste for the results of the reconstruction was most pronounced. The exercise started in 1984. In addition to Jan Heeling, Abe Bonnema, Ashok Balothra and various municipal designers, Josef Paul Kleihues was also involved in this process. Kleihues, one of the founders of Neo-Traditionalism, worked in Groningen as the supervisor of the Verbindingskanaal zone and later the inner-city zone, two of the intensification zones from the 1986 structure plan.[9] In that capacity he contributed to the Plan for Tackling the City Centre (1989), in which the potential demolition of Vegter's town hall was announced, and with it the definitive break with modernist ideas.[10] The historic square, one of the elements in part 1, has been elevated to a frame of reference. Vidler's third typology, the traditional city, thus made its spectacular entrance into urban planning.

A proposal in the form of a drawing by municipal designers Maarten Schmitt and Anco Schut marks the beginning of the process of urban repair and critical reconstruction. Their sketch leaves no room for misunderstanding about the desired spatial usage of the area that was to be freed up. Along the building lines of the restored Waagstraat and Guldenstraat, Schmitt and Schut envisaged a building block strung together at ground level by a classicist gallery and divided into separate volumes above it. The façade recedes opposite the Gold Office, creating a small square that merges with the adjacent spaces. An informal openness remains in the direction of the Grote Markt with Otten Husly's City Hall

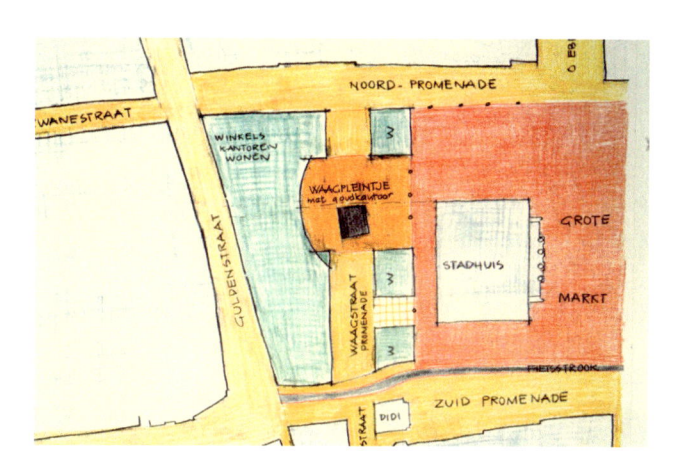

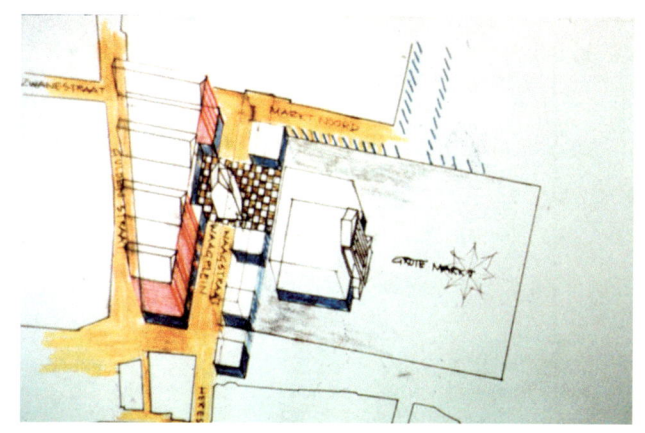

Maarten Schmitt and Anco Schut, plan and axonometric view of the urban-design concept for the Waagstraat (1989), restoring the street's building lines and those of the adjacent Guldenstraat.

9   Contact with Kleihues arose through the involvement of officials from the Department of Spatial Planning & Economic Affairs (Maarten Schmitt, Anco Schut, Niek Verdonk) at the Berlin IBA (from 1978).

10   'Richtinggevende Uitgangspunten Waagstraat locatie,' as part of the *Plan van Aanpak Binnenstad*, Department of Spatial Planning & Economic Affairs, Municipality of Groningen, 1989.

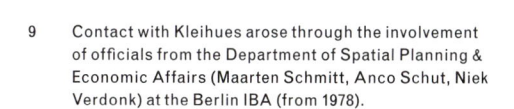

The Forum and the City

Monumento Continuo, Primary Structure,
Adolfo Natalini (Superstudio, 1969).

Nevertheless, his design was carried out and Groningen thus acquired one of the first so-called 'Neo-Traditionalist' building ensembles in the Netherlands. Neo-Traditionalism became the subject of a fierce debate between modernists and those who held freer views. The jury fulminated against what they saw as "Anton Pieck-esque kitsch" and a lazy exercise in nostalgia. But for Natalini himself, his architecture was the crystalised outcome of an era in which the modernist project had stalled, and the role of the intellectual had been redefined. In his eyes there was no appreciable difference between the hallucinatory drawings he had made with Superstudio in the early 1970s and the traditionalist façades he had now designed for the new Waagstraat: in both he was taking a stand against the – in his eyes – moralising, pretentious and, above all, deceitful 'modern project'. According to Natalini, the jury clung to the modern project's moral superiority, as if building in a different style would cast common sense, democracy and the open society into the trash. The debate took on a dimension that transcended urban planning and was fed with ideas about the city and society – one of the elements we addressed in the first part of this essay.

On 23 September 1994, barely thirty years after its completion, the 'Requiem for a City Hall' heralded the demolition of Vegter's extension. By 1996 the new Waagstraat had been completed. With its towering gallery, pronounced cornices, the combination of natural stone and brick and its saddle-back roofs, the Waagstraat, in Natalini's words, represented the historic Hanseatic city.

as a free-standing symbolic eye-catcher.[11] This municipal plan – expressly intended as part of the open plan process – gave direction to a process that led to the building up of the west side of Granpré Molière's expansive square.

The concrete shaping of the west side of the Grote Markt is the result of a closed competition for which Jo Coenen, Gunnar Daan, Koen van Velsen and Adolfo Natalini were invited. In a public vote in 1990 the people of Groningen overwhelmingly opted for Natalini's submission, no doubt encouraged by the seductive drawings.[12] That suited the city council, not only because the Italian architect's proposal fitted seamlessly with the municipality's sketch design, but also because it was attractive for financial, economic and urban planning reasons.

In the early 1970s, Natalini had been one of the founders of the famous Italian avant-garde collective Superstudio. His plan, however, was not in the least bit avant-garde: he took his inspiration from the historic city with its building blocks and compact structure. It is hard to imagine a less modern proposal. The jury was shocked. Having grown up in the tradition of modernism, they were looking for a design that represented their own time, and Natalini's plan emphatically did not do that.

11   Maarten Schmitt, Anco Schut, Dienst RO/EZ
      (Department of Spatial Planning & Economic Affairs),
      Municipality of Groningen, Waagstraat June 1989,
      and the model studies based on it, in: 'De stad, een
      plein,' thematic issue *Forum*, Quarterly Magazine for
      Architecture, no. 34, July 1990, pp. 28-31.

12   It is not clear why the restoration of the Waagstraat
      was not included in the competition conditions (which
      were, incidentally, rather loosely formulated). A certain
      jalousie de métier played a part in the fierce criticism of the
      professional jury, but also a 'submission' to the world of
      real estate. Natalini's proposal was apparently especially
      attractive for the development-investment combination
      because it was worked out in detail – technically and
      financially. See, for example, Vibeke Gieskes' extremely
      thorough thesis *Besluitvorming bij het Waagstraatproject
      in Groningen. Complicaties van inspraak en smaak bij
      architectonische kwesties*, Erasmus University, Rotterdam,
      July 1996 (unpublished), and Marijke Martin's interview
      with Maarten Schmitt, September 2011. See also: Bregit
      Jansen and Marijke Martin, *Stad vol gedachten*, Stichting
      Noorderbreedte, Groningen, 1998, pp. 31, 56.

Model of Josef Paul Kleihues's vision of the Grote Markt in his role as supervisor for the Municipality of Groningen (1988).

The North Wall: An Unappealing Urban Townscape?

Supervising the design process around Waagstraat, Kleihues expanded his vision to include the Grote Markt as a whole, placing the square in a broader urban perspective. In 1988 he proposed to reinforce the longitudinal effect of the succession of squares – the Vismarkt, Grote Markt and Martinikerkhof – with a new north wall comprising façade placed on arcades.[13] He also felt that the original quality of the square as a "public space and location of cultural and political institutions" should be respected. This required an interaction between content and form based on the traditional city – a game in which the architecture and urban planning of the reconstruction would, however, not play a role. The north side was given priority with the intention of transforming the dilapidated area behind it – as a direct extension of the new Waagstraat – into a residential space and thoroughly renewing the wall of the square. According to the councillor responsible, a new north wall would correct the mistakes of the past and give the Grote Markt a "European allure."[14] Except with a reference to narrow streets and a possible return of the tram, the envisaged 'pre-war appearance' was not made explicit. It was clear that the municipality could not ignore the chain stores and their property developers. Negotiations were also held with these parties about a joint redevelopment of the block between Oude Boteringestraat and Oude Ebbingestraat: this could be divided into smaller building volumes, with narrow streets (typical of Groningen's street plan) in between, in order to create connections with the Grote Markt. This would be enabled by the extension of the new Waagstraat.

13 For development possibilities and design models for Waagstraat since 1984 by Jan Heeling (1984), Grote Markt Working Group (1987), Josef Paul Kleihues (1988), the Municipality of Groningen (1989) and others, see: 'De stad, een plein,' *Forum*, no.34, July 1990; Okko Kloosterman, 'Groningen Grote Markt (2), Afbraak als inzet voor nieuwe kwaliteit,' *Contour*, 5/1, 1988, pp. 14-21; V. Bakker, 'Gratis stadhuis voor Groningen in ruil voor grond,' *Bouw*, 48/11, 1993, pp. 8-11.

14 'De Feiten tellen,' interview with Willem Smink, in: *Groninger Internet Courant voor Stad en Ommeland*, 25 October 2000 (via: https://www.gic.nl/nieuws/smink-nieuwe-noordwand-moet-grote-markt-europese-allure-teruggeven).

With the Waagstraat barely completed, a closed competition was organised with the participation of Jo Coenen, Rob Krier and Adolfo Natalini, three architects who represented the broad scope of Neo-Traditionalism.[15] Krier outlined the forum-like space referred to earlier while Natalini continued the Hanseatic vocabulary of his Waagstraat design. A winner was not announced, but it was Coenen who was allowed to continue with the planning, supported by the councillor and the Department of Spatial Planning & Economic Affairs.[16] That his masterplan was defeated in the 2001 referendum was due (in addition to administrative failures) to concerns among residents and local interest groups that Saint Martin's Tower would suffer subsidence and fears of a permanent excavation for the construction of a parking garage under the heart of the city – a firm demand from the chain stores. It was precisely this dependence on commercial parties that meant that, although the plan rigorously broke with the typological and stylistic qualities of reconstruction architecture, it also failed completely in its intention to match the size, scale and image of the historic city. For the time being, nothing came of the reconstruction of the north wall.

In the process, one element from our historical collection returned: the contradiction between the private interests of investors and commercial parties on the one hand and those of the local community on the other. During the reconstruction, the interests of the latter group were materialised in public facilities: a City Hall extension and a cultural centre. Now, decades later, they combined with fears that large-scale construction projects would threaten the monuments that had survived the war and reconstruction.

The Third Typology and Historical Heritage

The background to everything that took place on the Grote Markt after 1945 was the damage inflicted in the war: physically, spatially and mentally. In that sense, the destruction is a key element in our collection. But another element also plays a remarkable role: that of selective demolition. In 1945 it was decided to remove everything that stood in the way of a radical renewal of the square, except for the most important historical monuments. Less than half a century later, it was decided to protect what was historically valuable and outlaw the rest. The rest meant the reconstruction architecture on the north and east sides. There was apparently no objection to its removal, and this recalls another element: the identification of the products of a certain period as incompatible with the ideal image of the future. For Granpré Molière those were the grand buildings of the nineteenth century. For Groningen's urban planners in the early 1990s, those were all the architectural products of the reconstruction period: the buildings constructed between 1950 and 1970.

One component of the planning process described here in terms of Vidler's third typology – the traditional city – was the designation of large parts of the Grote Markt as a conservation area in 1991, including the original eastern building line.[17] The intention was to use the "existing spatial quality – an interplay of street patterns, plot divisions and buildings" as the starting point for the development of a new quality, while "respecting historical values as much as possible."[18] Linking respect for cultural-historical values with spatial and economic development policy reflects the so-called modernisation of the preservation of historic monuments. Distinguishing between those parts that need to be preserved and others where adaptation is not a problem makes it possible to use heritage values as a booster for urban renewal and reconstruction. Apparently, the administrators feared that these new freedoms did not go far enough for some parts of the Grote Markt, in particular for the north and east walls, whose unmistakable architectural and cultural-historical heritage values were deliberately neglected. The Inner City Zoning Plan of 1997 labelled both sides as reconstruction areas.

15 Adolfo Natalini, artist's impression of Waagstraat and aerial perspective including the north and east side of the Grote Markt, as part of the Nieuwe Noordzijde (New North Side) urban plan, 1997-2000 (Groningen Archives NL-GnGRA_2731_7415); Maarten Schmidt, Grote Markt / north proposal, in: *Naar een ontwikkelingsvisie voor de Grote Markt*, Municipality of Groningen, 1996, with post-war building line; Rob Krier, diverse artist's impressions (1997-2000).

16 Frits Poelman, 'Referendum Grote Markt Groningen 2001: Ferme oplawaai en euforie in geheugen gegrift,' *Dagblad van het Noorden*, 21 February 2021.

17 The procedure for designating a conservation area was begun in 1988 and finalised three years later. The protected zone roughly encompassed the area within the Diepenring and the Hortusbuurt.

18 *Cultuurhistorische Verkenning Binnenstad Groningen*, Municipality of Groningen, 2014, p. 49.

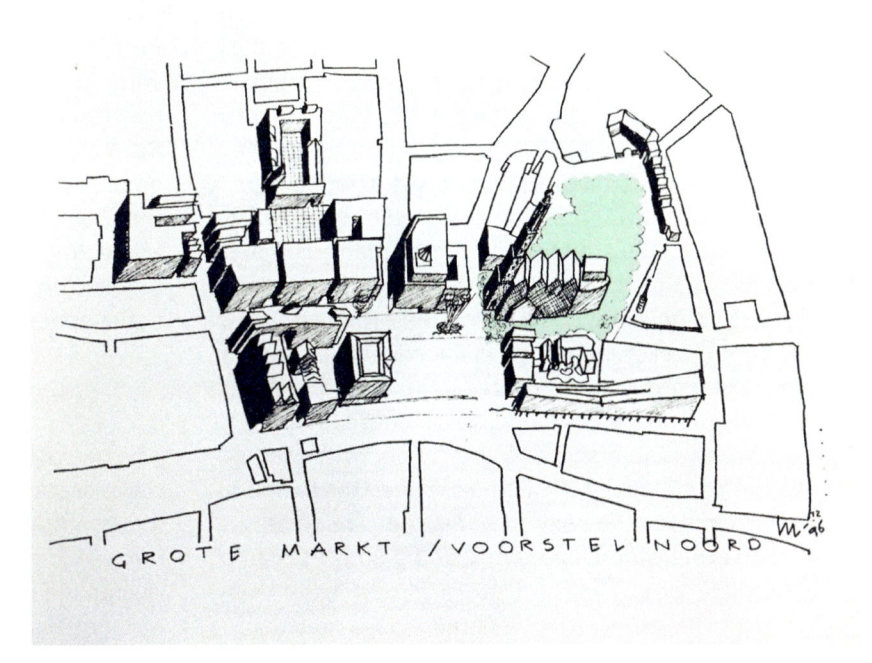

Model of Jo Coenen's plan for the north side of the Grote Markt (top right), artist's impressions of the north and east sides of the Grote Markt (left), after a design by Adolfo Natalini (both plans designed in the context of the Nieuwe Noordzijde (New North Side) urban plan, 1997-2000) and sketch by Maarten Schmitt from *Naar een ontwikkelingsvisie voor de Grote Markt* (1996).

The Forum and the City

Reduction of the Grote Markt:
The East Wall Advances

Since at least 1987 there had been talk of restoring the building line of the east side of the Grote Markt to its original position, bringing it forward by some twenty metres, which would lead to a further reduction of the City Hall's forecourt. Four years later, the historic eastern building line formally became part of the conservation area, and the 1997 zoning plan presented its restoration as a serious option. This opened up the perspective of a complete reversal of Granpré Molière's urban-design vision of a greatly enlarged square enclosed with closed walls with islands on it like chocolates on a tray. The space around the new Waagstraat was no longer part of the market square and it was now suggested to further reduce the forecourt of the City Hall. Such an operation would add valuable land for construction, which both served commercial interests and also provided the opportunity to put one of Granpré Molière's programmatic innovations back on the agenda: the construction of a cultural centre on the east side of the square. In 1959, the city council had approved a plan for such a centre, designed by Marius Duintjer, but in 1963 it was shifted elsewhere for logistical reasons. Less than ten years later, the Oosterpoort Cultural Centre opened to the public on the site of the former cattle market. This resulted in 1971 in the demolition of the legendary Harmonie concert hall: a dramatic action. It was also the first time that citizens and politicians protested en masse against the city's urban development plans. But in vain.[19] That the construction of a theatre or cultural centre was now being reconsidered is also apparent from the sketches made in the mid-1990s as part of a design study of the Grote Markt. Adolfo Natalini drew a temple-like building in the eastern building line, while urban planner Maarten Schmitt projected an elongated, abstract volume between the (existing) eastern building line and Schoolstraat, which can only be understood as a herald of the current Forum building.[20]

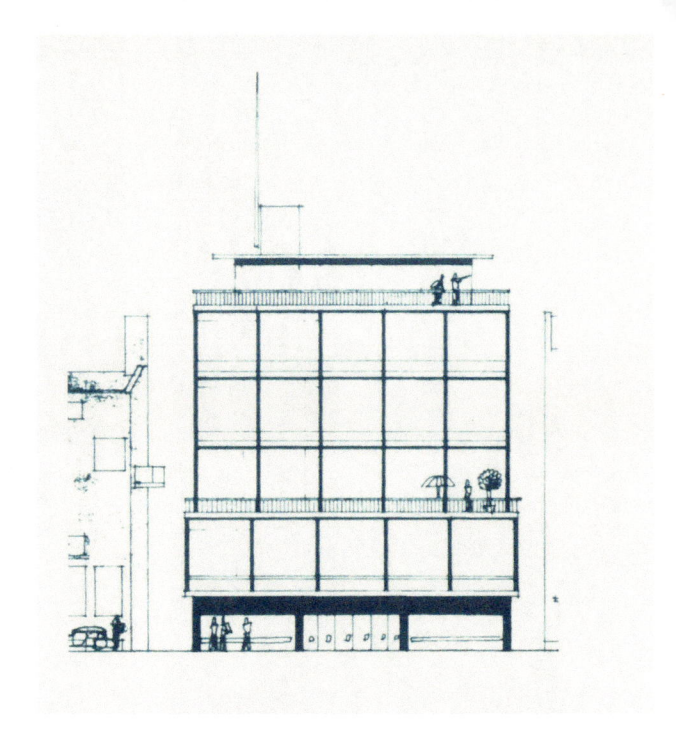

Entrance building of a cultural centre on the east side of the Grote Markt, after a design by Marius Duintjer (1959).

Further on, we devote a few words to the Forum as a vertical urban plaza – here we draw attention to the functioning of the building as a catalyst for the urban development that culminated in a new east wall and a small, new city square: the Nieuwe Markt. Only after the 2005 referendum on the east side of the Grote Markt was it possible to rebuild the east wall on the historic building line and to realise a cultural forum in the space beyond.

The Forum

The use of key buildings to boost large-scale urban regeneration projects is a tried and tested method in Groningen. The Forum also played such an inviting role. The history of the Forum as a building is discussed in detail elsewhere in this volume. We restrict ourselves here to characterising it as a vertical public square. This is given form in the glass-clad atrium that zigzags through the building from bottom to top. The architects have described it as the vertical projection of a section of the urban street plan. This introduces the 'vertical' flâneur, as opposed to the horizontal urban experience that has been discussed by philosophers such as Walter Benjamin, and later Michel de Certeau, in their critique of modernity.[21] From the roof, the city reveals itself to the visitor as a wide panorama. Conversely, from a variety of locations the city offers a view of and right

19   Beno Hofman, 'Cultuurcentrum De Oosterpoort, 40 jaar geleden in gebruik genomen,' via: http://benohofman.nl/verhalen/cultuur.

20   Maarten Schmidt, Grote Markt / north proposal, in: *Naar een ontwikkelingsvisie voor de Grote Markt*, Municipality of Groningen, 1996; Adolfo Natalini, aerial perspective of the reconstruction of the north and east walls of the Grote Markt, as part of the Nieuwe Noordzijde (New North Side) urban plan, 1997-2000 (Groningen Archives NL-GnGRA_2731_7415).

through the building, while its soaring form joins the series of towers and other high-rise buildings that – according to the brief – form the "accents on the roof of the inner city" and which are of obvious cultural and historical importance.[22] The Forum clearly demonstrates that even a building that does not relate to the historic city in form, proportion and style can still enter into a dialogue with it. The vertical arrangement of (semi)public spaces on either side of an ascending foyer is thus an intelligent reversal of the original horizontal grouping of such programme components.[23]

The Nieuwe Markt

Shifting the eastern building line and cleaning up the entire inner grounds enabled the Forum to be surrounded by a public space. Connecting to the existing series of squares, this space is connected to the Grote Markt via a public street, and the cultural building interweaves with the surrounding city via streets and alleyways. The Nieuwe Markt thus satisfies the need for what the municipality described as a "valuable extension of the city's public space" that would flow seamlessly into the ground floor of the Forum.[24] The envisaged porous character of the public spaces and buildings (typical of Groningen) situated next to and one behind the other is also reflected in the hallucinatory labyrinth of escalators and elevators that zigzag through the Forum, connecting the Nieuwe Markt with the roof terrace, a public space that can only be experienced as an elevated urban plaza.

To optimise the new square's liveliness, it was desirable that as many of the new and existing buildings as possible face the new square. This meant that the buildings that arose along the east wall would, instead of a having a classical dichotomy between public front and private rear, be 'Janus-faced'.[25] The same applied to the rear of Poelestraat, which was to be transformed into a front, with mostly cafés, bars and restaurants at ground level and

apartments on the uppermost floors. In short: the Forum served as a guideline for the further course of events. This is also apparent from the linking of the competition in 2006 with the concept programme for the east side of the Grote Markt. This formulated concrete urban development preconditions for the three sub-areas in the plan area: the Forum and the Nieuwe Markt, the rear of the Poelestraat and the east wall of the Grote Markt.

The Reconstruction of the East Wall: Ideal and Reality

The draft brief from 2006 makes it clear that the city had opted for an explicit distinction between the modern design of the Forum's signalling function and a design based on the tradition of the city, both for the new east wall and the transformation of the rear of Poelestraat. To start with the latter: the partial demolition and new construction along the back of that street had to take into account the fact that this was one of the oldest structures in the city, with a largely intact size, scale and urban grain. At the same time, the wall should continue to reflect the site's 'informal' organically grown character. The image quality plan presented by the architecture practice A AS in 2009 translated these requirements into a playful, flexible design strategy. The plan was based on a careful study of the profile of the city's narrow streets and alleyways, and emphasised the (architectural) identity of each individual 'grain' through material, height, width, colour and the degree of openness or closedness. The image of diversity derived from the traditional city was further enhanced by encouraging the use of a 'vertical building line' or third dimension in the form of cantilevered higher (residential) floors. In addition, semi-public spaces or terraces (already announced in the draft brief and typical of the urban structure) were included, behind or between the buildings.[26]

21 See, for example, Paul K. Saint-Amour, 'The Vertical Flâneur: The Narrational Tradecraft in the Colonial Metropolis' in: Maurizia Boscagli and Enda Duffy (eds.), *Joyce, Benjamin and Magical Urbanism*, 2015, pp. 225-249.

22 *Grote Markt Oostzijde – Concept-Programma van Eisen Stedenbouw, Openbare Ruimte en Verkeer*, Municipality of Groningen, 27 June 2006, p. 8, and *Cultuurhistorische Verkenning Binnenstad Groningen*, Municipality of Groningen, 2014.

23 As also studied in the 'train model' by the Department of Spatial Planning & Economic Affairs as part of their urban planning study, 2002-2003.

24 *Grote Markt Oostzijde – Concept-Programma van Eisen Stedenbouw, Openbare Ruimte en Verkeer*, Municipality of Groningen, 27 June 2006, pp. 18-19.

25 This and other statements in this paragraph are based on an interview with Thomas Müller, 31 July 2021.

26 A AS Architecten, *Beeldkwaliteitsplan Poelestraat achterzijde*, commissioned by the Municipality of Groningen, 3 February 2009.

Impression of the south side of the Nieuwe Markt, as included in *Beeldkwaliteitsplan Poelestraat achterzijde* (2009), and the realised situation (2022).

The reconstruction of the east wall was based on strict requirements of representation. It was determined in advance that the building wall would consist of two contiguous blocks, separated by a new, narrow street that would not disturb the closed character of the wall. This street would have the same width as the new Waagstraat: seven metres. In order to connect the east wall with the built environment, it would have a maximum of five (six, if exempted) storeys, be vertically plotted and take into account the specific local urban grain, to which the vertical articulation of the façades would be attuned. The stately character would be further developed by raising the ground floor by a minimum of four metres or by allowing certain functions to spread across the two lower floors. In summary, the east wall had to have a "classic appearance, in conjunction with the south wall of the Grote Markt and the City Hall."[27]

Based on the aforementioned preconditions, the architecture of the east wall is the result of an image quality plan by the Berlin-based architect Thomas Müller, and the subsequent vicissitudes of that plan. It defined the urban-design integration and formulated more specific rules for the architectural appearance of the east wall. The basis for this were the "typically Dutch town houses, as found on the south side of the Grote Markt." The architecture was to be divided into a plinth, a possible mezzanine, wall and roof edge. There were maximum roof and ridge heights. The material elaboration was to be in natural stone, brick and stucco, and the windows, eaves and floor divisions would be accentuated.[28] This plan, presented with due ceremony to citizens and experts in 2007 and adopted a year later, is a key document. More than fifteen years after the east wall was designated a conservation area – and using existing descriptions and characterisations – it provided an applied analysis of the morphological, typological and material characteristics of an essential part of the historic city centre. And, perhaps more importantly, it applied the method of critical reconstruction to Groningen's situation and provided a theoretical foundation for the reconstruction of the east wall. The latter was, also in light of the failed referendum around the north side of the Grote Markt in 2001, no superfluous luxury. The image quality plan served as a "communication tool and a source of inspiration" for the parties involved in the development of the east wall.[29]

Thomas Müller and Josef Paul Kleihues had known each other since the 1980s from the Cooper Union's revolutionary School of Architecture in New York. John Hejduk was dean of the school and became involved in the urban renewal of Groningen in the late 1980s. Müller followed suit some time later when he was commissioned to transform the Albion warehouse into a housing complex – one of the city's first examples of adaptive reuse. In Groningen, Müller Reimann Architekten subsequently designed a varied series of homes in the southern part of the Hoornse Meer district, supervised the construction of Hejduk's Wall House #2 in the same area, and designed in De Linie, a residential area in the Europapark, a classic urban block with a striking diversity of housing types. During that time, the

27   This was part of the urban planning principles approved by the population in the referendum in 2005, as mentioned in: Thomas Müller Ivan Reimann Architekten, *Beeldkwaliteitsplan Grote Markt – Oostwand*, commissioned by the Municipality of Groningen and Volker Wessels Vastgoed, 18 June 2008, p. 4.

28   Nevertheless, examples from other Dutch cities and Berlin are also included as references: see Thomas Müller Ivan Reimann Architekten, *Beeldkwaliteitsplan Grote Markt – Oostwand*, commissioned by the Municipality of Groningen and Volker Wessels Vastgoed, 18 June 2008, p. 24 and successive pages.

29   Thomas Müller Ivan Reimann Architekten, *Beeldkwaliteitsplan Grote Markt – Oostwand*, commissioned by the Municipality of Groningen and Volker Wessels Vastgoed, 18 June 2008, p. 4.

Impressions of *Beeldkwaliteitsplan
Grote Markt – Oostwand* (2008)
and the two variants of the
revised version (2014).

The Forum and the City

practice was also actively involved in the critical reconstruction of Berlin, building upon the method that was also the basis for the reconstruction of Groningen's east wall. Although he doesn't necessarily want to be classified in theoretical terms, Müller situates himself within what he calls the 'narrative of critical reconstruction': attempting to build upon the existing city by fitting in new pieces that respect the historically developed structure and which are able to create public urban spaces through architecture.

In addition to being embedded in an unequivocal set of design rules, the plan for the east wall had to be economically feasible and allow for flexible programme development. At that stage, in addition to the relocation of the Vindicat student association, the programme comprised a combination of services, commercial functions and housing, though it was not yet clear precisely where they would end up in the complex. The image quality plan provided for three buildings to the north and two buildings to the south of the new connecting street. Vindicat's building, Mutua Fides, ended up on the northeast corner simply because that was the first site that could be made available, thus allowing Vindicat to continue using its old building, halfway up the east wall, during the construction. As with the existing building, the size and scale of the new association building made for a challenging brief during the design competition and the realisation (2009-14). The relatively wide plot had to be brought into line with the intentions of the image quality plan when it came to grain size, height variation and vertical articulation. Lastly, De Zwarte Hond designed a building that can be read as an interplay of two façades, the entrance and the corner part, whose volume decreases gradually in height along Sint Jansstraat, in order to fit in with the built environment.

Phase 2: Scaling Up

Because no concrete details were available for the rest of the east wall when Mutua Fides was completed in 2014, the municipality began investigating alternatives in that year. At the same time, the altered economic climate made it clear that combinations of development and programming for plots with fixed – i.e., limited – height and width dimensions could hardly be found anymore. With these starting points, an attempt was made to reconcile the traditional city's fine grain – narrow, vertically organised plots – with the economic demand for increased scale, which necessitated fewer plots. In the modified image quality plan, Müller Reimann Architekten presented two additional variants for the building

section south of the new Vindicat building. The first consisted of an enlarged building volume in the middle of the east wall and a corner building comparable to the first image quality plan, separated by a connecting street now projected further south. The second variant comprised a colossal, continuous volume in which a covered passage provided the connection between the Nieuwe and the Grote Markt. Because the outcome was more or less fixed – the preference was for the variant with the two volumes on either side of a new street – this design exercise was mainly a gesture towards the citizenry and an attempt to keep a grip on the critical-theoretical motivation behind the new east wall, namely that the city wanted "to bring back the old character of the historic Grote Markt."[30] Ultimately the issue was to what extent the originally formulated guidelines relating to height, articulation, number of floors and façade structure could be stretched to enable the construction of a hotel with a restaurant, bar and reception rooms without frustrating the original design principles. Müller Reimann Architekten demonstrated courage by not shying away from that challenge. The practice designed a building with the maximum permitted height of 23 metres which, thanks to the effect of stepped gables suggested by the brickwork, presents itself as a row of three tall, narrow town houses.[31] Visually this respected the traditional urban grain. The rest of the volume has been set back in relation to this 'façade' and clad with a darker brick. The desired verticality has been achieved with continuous brick profiles from top to bottom, doubled at the visual boundary of the three façade parts. With the abandonment of the originally set number of floors, the number of windows increased significantly with a positive effect on the building's verticality. The jump in scale to an east wall with only three volumes also enabled the realisation of a relatively large building on the southeast corner, which once again strengthens the 'closed' access to the Grote Markt from Oosterstraat. Both the expert jury and the public voted by a large majority for Powerhouse Company's design, Merckt, which has in the meantime been completed. Although it corresponds in height, structure and vertical articulation with the basic requirements of the visual quality plan of 2014, the building has a rather bold character compared to the relative

30 Thomas Müller Ivan Reimann Architekten, *Beeldkwaliteitsplan Grote Markt – Oostwand*, commissioned by the Municipality of Groningen and Volker Wessels Vastgoed, 13 June 2014, p. 6.

31 The visual quality plan of 2014 referred to the example of the Scheepvaarthuis in Amsterdam, warehouses in Hamburg, and composite buildings in Amsterdam, Gdansk, Stralsund and Rostock.

modesty of the surrounding architecture. With its high, exuberantly profiled arcades, it is a nod to Natalini's work from a quarter of a century earlier on the other side of the Grote Markt and thus seems to mock Vidler's appeal to a critical intellectual attitude towards the traditional city as a reference for urban design.

Finale: The Traditional City Completed?

With the completion of the east wall, the Grote Markt is an almost perfect example of Vidler's third typology. The urban repair was guided by the reinterpretation of elements from Groningen's urban planning history. With the help of the lessons learned from the projects around Waagstraat and the north wall, this desire was translated consciously, carefully and with great dedication into an extremely complex and sometimes risky operation. Thanks to Groningen's characteristic continuity of policy, the deployment of a 'core group' of internal and external experts and continuously monitored support among the population, it seems that this operation has been successful. The planning process with which it was coupled is well worth considering even from a European perspective and makes it clear that this was not simply a case of urban beautification. Neither was it anecdotal reconstruction, as was recently the case in Frankfurt am Main, where the Dom-Römer quarter was rebuilt in 'original' medieval style in close consultation with local residents to undo the 'mistake' of post-war modernism.[32]

It is to be feared that future interventions in Groningen's city centre will do serious harm to the ideal type. That risk is far from imaginary. While it was somewhat understandable that the reconstruction-period architecture was omitted from the designated conservation area in 1991, that is no longer the case. Like the south wall of the Grote Markt, the north wall is part of the 'third' typology. Its preservation and restoration are also in line with national and international trends in cultural heritage: early post-war buildings are sexy, sturdy, flexible and (re)usable.[33] It would be obvious to include the remaining reconstruction architecture in the conservation area and, where necessary, to promote the restoration of its original qualities. Demolition does damage to the city and would, more importantly, undo in one fell swoop all the positives mentioned above in the planning process. Should there be a need to crown the reconstruction of the Grote Markt with a powerful final flourish, then closing the gap in front of Saint Martin's Tower would be a much more obvious

choice. This would, moreover, fit in with the collection of images, drawings and proposals of what we have previously called the imaginary city – and thus fit seamlessly with Vidler's third typology.

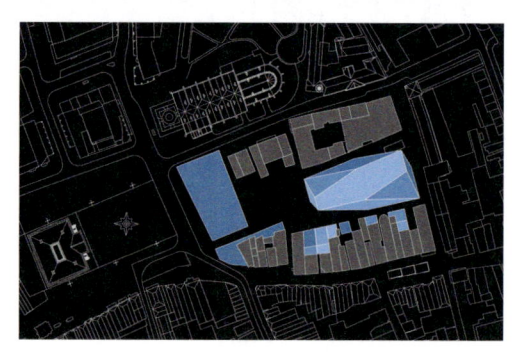

Before-and-after drawing showing the transformation of the city block to the east of the Grote Markt.

32 See: https://www.db-bauzeitung.de/diskurs/die-frank-furter-altstadt-hat-viele-muetter-und-vaeter, 1 June 2018.

33 This became apparent in 1997 when a value proposition of the north wall was drawn up in collaboration with the Department of History of Architecture and Urbanism at the University of Groningen: Wijnand Galema (ed.), *Wederopbouw in de Waagschaal. Een waardestelling van de noordwand Grote Markt*, Municipality of Groningen, September 1997.

City

City

Niek Verdonk

Urban Development as the Foundation of the Forum

How much do we value the city? As a society, what resources do we make available for public space and for public functions as the basis for urban development? After a period in which spatial planning and cultural infrastructure in the Netherlands came into question, the realisation of an entirely public cultural building such as the Forum seems to be a clear statement against selling out the city. This is remarkable considering the rich tradition of urban development in a 'design country' such as the Netherlands. Does it not go without saying that the government is responsible for what happens within its borders? And that the quality of urban space is safeguarded and that the collective guarantees the spatial and social cohesion of the design of the city?

Urban development in the Netherlands has been marked by continuous debate about the role of government in large-scale spatial developments. Certainly since the financial crisis, which reached its peak between 2008 and 2011, enthusiasm for large public buildings has dwindled and large-scale urban plans seemed to be a thing of the past. In the political and public debate about the Forum, the transformation on the east side of the Grote Markt was regularly referred to as 'outmoded'. Is the Forum indeed an anachronism, a remnant of a tradition from the previous century?

Experience with large-scale urban transformations shows that they require stamina and that they develop somewhat independently of time and trends. But public opinion tends towards impatience. In general, it seems increasingly difficult to maintain the required attention span for long-term projects, distracted as we are by a constant stream of news flashes and sound bites that keeps our attention focused on the short term. Nevertheless, we must see the Forum's realisation in the light of the constant and consistent work that has been done on Groningen's city centre since the 1970s.

The Public Domain

Pressures on spatial and cultural disciplines – with the abolition of the Ministry of Housing, Spatial Planning and the Environment as a significant low point – have limited cities' ability to initiate and manage spatial developments. A good deal of policy and the main planning regulations are aimed at permitting projects subject to conditions, at stimulating a specific spatial order and at granting permits to concrete plans. Nevertheless, one of the most direct ways to promote desirable urban development is to invest in public programmes. At the urban level, the question of which programme should be realised, where and how is crucial. It is natural that we approach large-scale public projects with a healthy dose of scepticism given that they are paid for out of the public purse. So too with the Forum, the cost and quality of the programme at that location in the city were also often the subject of debate. The development of the building withstood a financial crisis, a subsidy crisis and an earthquake crisis.

Although the road to the Forum has been marked by bumps and unforeseen turns, we see that public investment as part of urban transformation can be successful if it is worked on continuously, consistently and in an integral manner. The starting point for the building was the realisation that public investment in a site where the city was not functioning well would provide programmatic and spatial impulses that would also improve the quality and functionality of the eastern part of the city centre. With these principles, the Municipality of Groningen gave new meaning to policy that stemmed from a broad revaluation of urban life. It is actually ironic that it was precisely the completion of the reconstruction of the east wall in the 1970s with the construction of the Naberpassage – more than twenty years after the first buildings were completed – that mainly contributed to the debate – another twenty years later – that resulted in the eventual renewal of that same east wall.

Perhaps, in retrospect, we can say that it was not so much the individual buildings on the east side of the Grote Markt that were the problem as the fact that they were the sum of three decades of post-war urban development. As Cor Wagenaar convincingly showed in his book on Granpré Molière's designs for the post-war reconstruction of Groningen, *Tussen Grandezza en Schavot* (1991), discussions about the desired programme, scale and the architecture played an ongoing role in the background. The final piece in the reconstruction, the Naberpassage, went beyond typical post-war architecture. The construction of the complex heralded a new chapter in

DOELSTELLING BINNENSTAD GRONINGEN

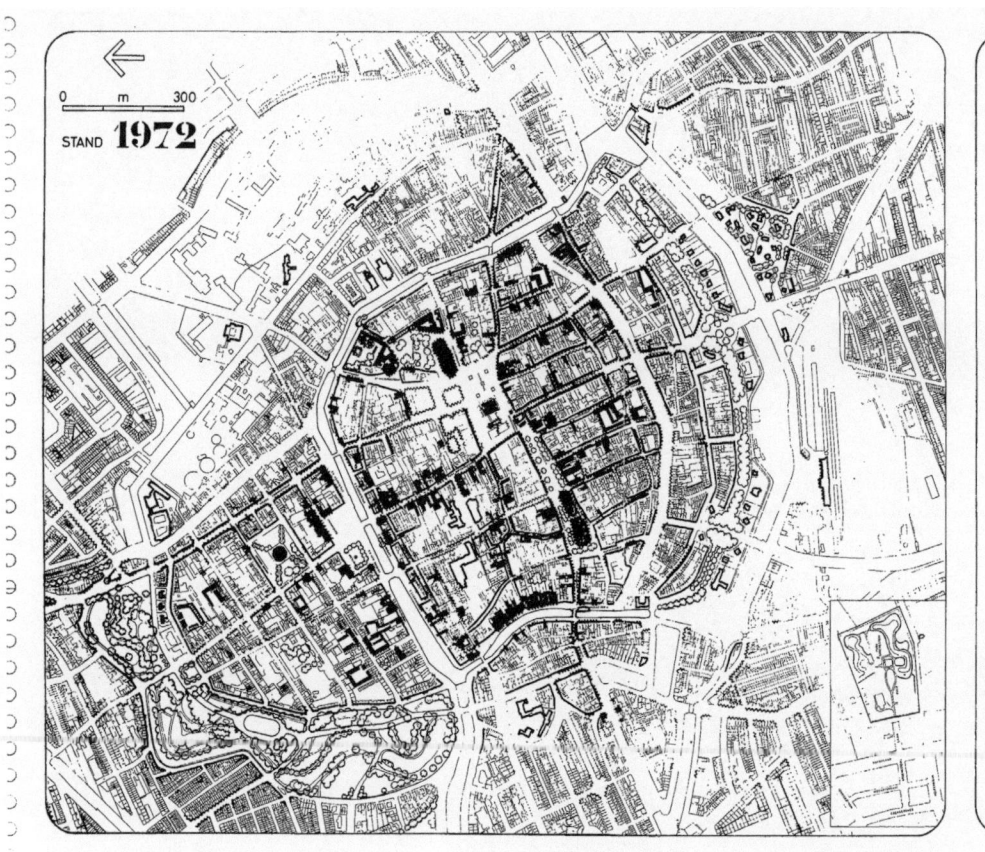

STAND **1972**

HERBERGZAAMHEID (8.5

"The hospitality of any building may be increased by fitting it with protruding and/or recessed elements, such as steps, extensions, plinths, gates, lean-tos, alcoves, which can be interpreted as a bench, table, podium or display area. A building with such facilities is useful for the elderly (resting), for children (climbing, hanging, jumping), for vendors, for meetings, for sitting in the sun, for shelter, for making announcements, and for expressing opinions." The accompanying map indicates official monuments (in black), the "affective" monuments (outlined), old trees, boundaries of valuable urban spaces, welcoming street walls (with the jagged lines), benches, seating areas and planters.

KORRELGROOTTE 6

Urban grain and diversity: "Each project and every building block must contain a sufficient variety of destinations to facilitate as many activities as possible per unit. This is most important on the ground floor, i.e., the street level. The higher floors can be used to a significant extent for residential purposes." The associated map provides an insight into the density of the urban grain size, with each unit accommodating to an activity (functional unit).

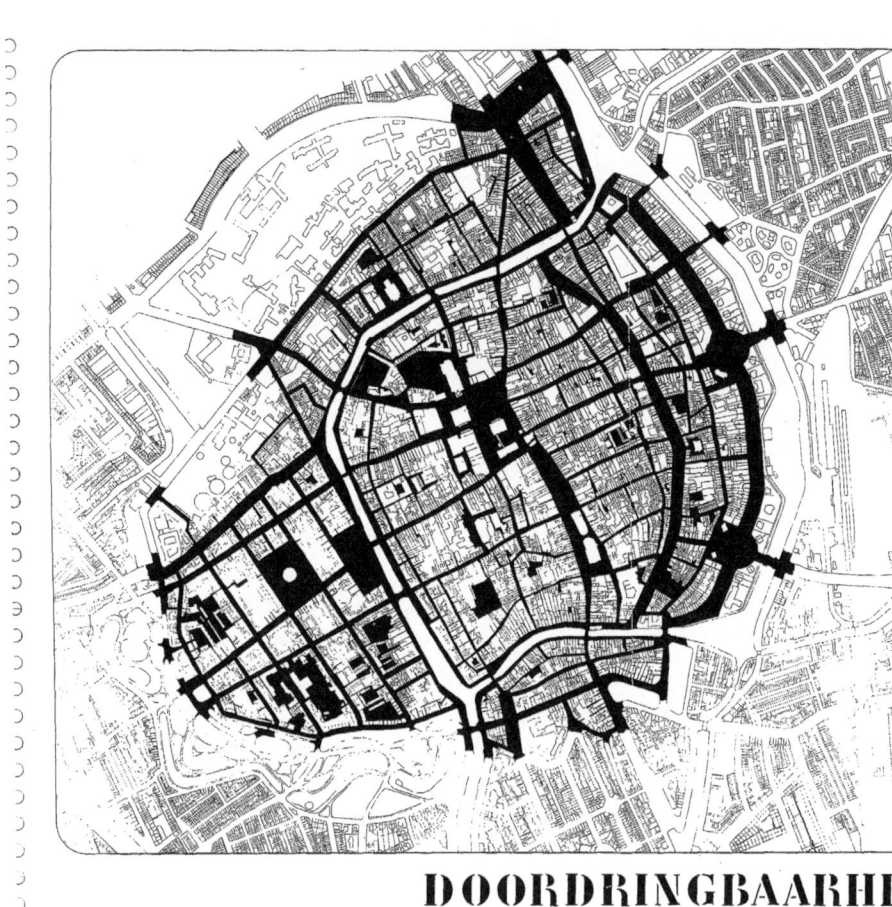

DOORDRINGBAARHEID (8.)

"For large institutions too, enclosed areas in the city centre may not be larger than is dictated by the local urban grain. In the city centre, enclosed areas are permitted only insofar as they enhance the activities of the city centre. Even then, their surface area should be limited as much as possible. It is inadmissible for individuals or groups to reserve significant parts of the city centre exclusively for themselves in such a way that others cannot benefit from them. This constitutes an unfair distribution and/ or squandering of land: the scarcest commodity in the city. The city, and especially the city centre, is a source of warmth for everyone." The accompanying map shows the intricate weave of public spaces, permanently accessible to everyone.

Niet alleen is vervanging van de bebouwing mogelijk, het kan zelfs gewenst zijn om plaatselijk inhammen of uitbouwen te maken. Deze dienen evenwel ondergeschikt te blijven aan de straatruimte als geheel. Het "model" moet er als het ware in blijven. Hiertoe moeten tenminste de hoeken (dus daar waar twee straatwanden elkaar ontmoeten) op hun plaats blijven; dat wil zeggen ook in een vernieuwde bebouwing weer op hetzelfde punt terecht komen.

In onderstaand figuur (2) wordt getracht een en ander te verduidelijken.

Cut-out of a page analysing and articulating the "interior quality of the inner city and city centre" as part of indications for designing a plan.

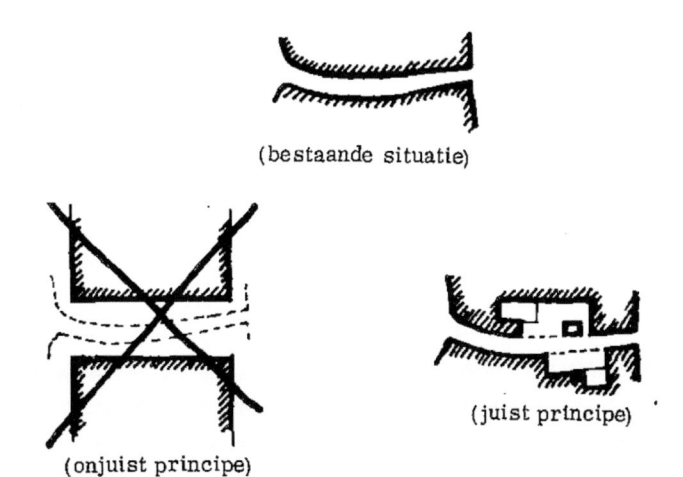

(bestaande situatie)

(onjuist principe)

(juist principe)   28

urban development that was a direct reaction to the large-scale plans that had been made for the city centre since the late 1960s. The architects of the Naberpassage, Klein and Van Linge, realised a layered sequence of small-scale and elevated urban spaces with fluid and layered transitions in which there were few clear boundaries between the private and public domains. A quarter of a century later, there seemed to be a consensus that these small-scale urban structures did not relate to the existing city. Yet, remarkably enough, the principles on which they were based, as so beautifully expressed in the *Doelstellingennota* (Objectives Memorandum) of 1972, turned out to be a timeless source of inspiration.

Although the Naberpassage was a good example of thinking about the city in the 1970s, the combination of its programme and spaces in that location resulted in a complex that was difficult to maintain and which had an inhospitable atmosphere, partly because some functions were designed in a way that was outmoded and no longer suited the use and desired quality of the public realm. But at barely sixty years old, the gradually created east wall was too recent to make way again, premises by premises, for a new generation of buildings. Furthermore, in parts the construction was far from bad. The reconstruction of the east wall was, due to the diverse nature of the plans and the extended duration of the development, more an expression of a quarter of a century of urban planning than a coherent intervention.

The recent, second transformation of the east side of the Grote Markt follows the turnaround in thinking about urban development and expansion, which in recent decades has brought renewed attention to the original structure and dynamics of the city. With greater focus on the continuity of a compact and multifaceted urban structure as the basis for the diversity of urban life, the city emerged as a 'podium' for pre-eminently urban functions. It was the Objectives Memorandum drawn up in the early 1970s that firmly anchored the ingredients of what would become the policy of the compact city in the practice of Groningen's urban development.

The Objectives Memorandum – Playing Chess with the Programme

"In order to accommodate the highlights of urban life, the city centre will have to house a coherent complex of high-quality urban facilities within a small area," we read on the first pages of the Objectives Memorandum. It was already clear at that time, at the height of suburbanisation, that the intensification of land use and mixed use of space was inevitable. Those who drafted the memorandum also noted that Groningen's city centre functioned mainly as a shopping centre and that "while taking into account the expansion and intensification of the shopping apparatus [...] a shift in emphasis towards social and cultural life" had to be achieved. The Objectives Memorandum is clear about the need for intensification and programmatic enrichment: "With the flight of institutions and residents from the inner city, the entire city can acquire an amorphous structure, in which social and cultural life is greatly impoverished. This destructive process is underway in many major Western European cities, while in the United States the disintegration has already had disastrous consequences for many cities."

There are many links to be made between the Objectives Memorandum and policy documents from the following decades. However, the plea for spatial and programmatic intensification first took concrete shape in the structural plan of 1986, the accompanying 'offices memorandum' and the Verbindingskanaal Zone Masterplan of 1987. The Objectives Memorandum also turned out to be an inspiration for the *Binnenstad Beter* (Better City Centre policy, from 1989) and the resulting *Ruimte voor Ruimte* (Room for Space policy, 1993) that arose from the structure plan. Central to these plans was the functional and spatial coherence of the city centre and, above all, the design and management of the public domain. Viewed against the standards of the times, the Objectives Memorandum was prescient in talking about the city centre's 'walkability' and prioritising public transport and cycling routes. With great foresight, the memorandum states: "The visitor's behaviour as a pedestrian is decisive for traffic relationships."

The 1986 structural plan fully embraced the achievements that gradually became part of urban development practice from the 1970s onwards. For the first time since the city's fortifications were demolished at the end of the nineteenth century, the future vision was aimed not at expanding but at intensifying the urban area. In contrast

west

kijk in 't jatstraat
visserstraat
hoge der A
vismarkt
boteringestraat
universiteit (3)
stadhuis (1)

zuid

emmaplein
a-kerkhof
vismarkt
zuiderdiep
munnekeholm
museum (5)

noord

ebbingestraat
grote markt
boteringestraat
kwinkenplein
martinikerk
V.V.V. (2)
stadhuis (1)

oost

hereplein
herestraat
grote markt
oosterstraat
zuiderdiep
politie (4)
stadhuis (1)

The so-called 'loop map' from the Verkeerscirculatieplan (Traffic
Circulation Plan, 1977) that resulted from the *Doelstellingennota*,
which shows that the inner city was divided into four quadrants
that were deliberately not connected by road traffic.

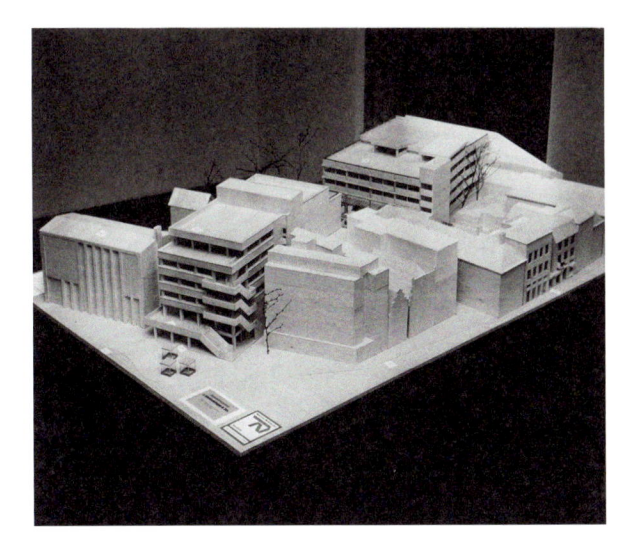

Model of the plan for the Naberpassage and garage
(1972-1975) by architects Klein and Van Linge.

Urban Development as the Foundation

Model of the Verbindingskanaal Zone (1987), that served as an intensification zone from the 1986 structural plan, and a map of *Ruimte voor Ruimte* (1993), which formed the basis for the redesign of public spaces in the city centre.

motorway. The most symbolic expression of the renewed striving for density was undoubtedly Frans Jan van Gool's PTT Headquarters, whose southern wing, with its last columns *over* the railway lines, extends to the first platform.

The revitalisation of urban culture stimulated a new conception of the city as a place for a wide range of activities, events and forms of communication, in which the connection between architecture and public space played an emphatic role in enhancing the city's functionality and hospitality. Public programmatic investments in the city centre were intended to contribute to Groningen's position as a high-quality residential, business and cultural centre in an extensive region with little urban development. The strengthening of the urban programme was deployed strategically to breathe new life into deprived parts of the inner city. For, although it is hard to imagine when looking at the current quality of the city centre, by the 1980s large parts of the heart of Groningen had become impoverished.

The relocation of the Groninger Museum to a new location in the turning basin of the Verbindingskanaal was one such well-considered intervention (although that was not the museum's preferred location). The erection of a colourful, postmodernist building on that site caused quite a stir but proved to be irrelevant for the function and the location. The museum and accompanying bridge over the canal not only enriched the city centre in programmatic terms but also contributed to refining the urban fabric and connecting the southern city centre, via Folkingestraat, with the area around the railway station. *That* was the real value of the intervention. The connection, which had already been planned by Berlage in 1928, provided an enormous impulse for the development of this side of the centre, contributed to the rediscovery of a forgotten location and strengthened the route from the station to the Vismarkt.

The redevelopment of the Westerhaven also fits in with this strategic urban development. To counteract the 'fattening' of the core shopping area around Herestraat, with its growth of large retail chains, and to prevent large commercial functions from disappearing to fields on the edge of the city, space was created for large-scale retail trade in the former fortified zone on the border of the city centre. For the western approach streets, this intervention was a functional and spatial stimulus that boosted the quality and appeal of the west side of the centre.

to the preceding decades, the emphasis was again placed on what we can call the core of more than a thousand years of urban development: proximity, compactness and connection. Encouraged by state policy, the Verbindingskanaal Zone Masterplan, under the supervision of Rem Koolhaas and Josef Paul Kleihues, was to provide space for large-scale offices and facilities, such as those of the PTT, the Groningen Archives and the Employee Insurance Agency (UWV). A little further on, along the railway, office buildings were constructed for the Tax and Customs Administration and the Office of Education (DUO). The Groningen University Medical Centre was also intensified in the zone of the former fortifications, preventing this important urban amenity from moving to a location along the

Groningen's University Medical Centre in the area of the former fortifications on the edge of the city centre.

On the scale of the city as a whole, we can see the development of the Euroborg football stadium, as part of the Europapark, within the context of this policy. Studies into potential locations showed that the final location was not the most favourable in terms of logistics and accessibility, but there were strong arguments for building the stadium there from an urban-planning perspective. It would accelerate the development of the former energy site, and the new home base for FC Groningen would give an impulse to the enrichment of the programme. The development of the stadium as part of the Europapark was in line with the principles of the compact city: the location was close to the city centre, was well connected and could be combined with a new railway station on the existing track that runs towards Zwolle. Both the sports complex itself and the Europapark lent themselves to a mixed-use development. Immediately around and adjacent to the stadium there was space for apartments, offices, educational buildings, restaurants and a large-scale supermarket, while a mixed environment of compact low-rise buildings, apartments, a residential care complex, offices and a sports facility developed in the area.

The Groninger Museum with the bridge over the Verbindingskanaal from the area around the railway station to the southern part of the city centre.

The Europapark, where the construction of the stadium provided an impulse for the development of a mixed urban area.

Groningen Grote Markt Study –
Shaping Urban Space

The transformation of the east side of the Grote Markt perpetuates a coherent policy line that dates back decades and seems to reveal a certain uninterrupted continuity in urban development. The Objectives Memorandum illustrates this once again: "In each case, one will have to ask oneself whether, in addition to improving urban life as a whole, the direct environment will also benefit and whether the development will lead to a proportional distribution of destinations and activities so that everything and everyone is served as best as possible." The contents of the memorandum even seem to anticipate the Forum's remit. "Interweaving functions is a precondition for the greatest possible encounter among people and between people and things and ideas." This sentence could serve as the Forum's motto today.

The Forum's programme was developed gradually, in a broad partnership with the Municipality of Groningen, residents, experts, entrepreneurs and interest groups, and with the aid of an open-planning process, a suggestions box and an architectural competition. Although a cultural attraction would undeniably enrich this side of the city, the question remained how such a function could make the entire block to the east of the Grote Markt function optimally again in spatial terms. The success of the Groninger Museum and the Westerhaven had ensured that the city's centre of gravity had moved, or at least developed independently of the east side of the Grote Markt. Thanks to the appeal of the Westerhaven, Folkingestraat, the markets, Herestraat and Oosterstraat, a shopping route had emerged in the inner-city street plan, of which the eastern section of the city centre was not a part.

In order to improve the cohesion between different parts of the inner city, several spatial issues had already been put on the agenda in the participation process, including shifting the Grote Markt's building line back to its pre-war position. However, the *Studie Grote Markt Groningen* (Groningen Grote Markt Study), presented by Neutelings Riedijk Architects in May 2003, formulated for the first time a convincing perspective on the spatial and programmatic potential of the east side of the square. The municipality asked the practice to translate the ideas that emerged from the open-planning process into spatial models. The designers gave the assignment a critical twist and, following a thorough analysis, turned the question around: instead of opting for a selection

The morphological transformation model included by Neutelings Riedijk Architects in *Studie Grote Markt Groningen* (May 2003).

of models, they presented a single basic spatial model that could be filled with a variety of programmes. They reasoned that the principles of a new urban plan would follow from what they called the 'morphological transformation model'.

Looking at the realised programme and its urban planning, there is little to criticise in Neutelings Riedijk's reasoning. The basic model, presented in the pre-digital era as a model series of coloured blocks, has been carried out almost exactly. It has proved capable of accommodating spatial and functional adjustments for twenty years. The study cleverly combined the main spatial considerations and insights from the ideas developed in previous years: demolishing the parking garage, shifting the east wall and realising a new cultural building. If the first years of development were focused on the joint search for the right ideas and functions, Neutelings Riedijk demonstrated that a transformation of this magnitude needed a solid foundation in urban development.

Independent of the exact programme, the right space had to be created from an urban-planning point of view. Motivated by the proposition that morphology does not equal programme, Neutelings Riedijk linked urban-design quality to programmatic flexibility. The practice represented functions and organisational principles without presenting specific designs. The study's critical approach resulted in two outcomes: programmatically it created – figuratively speaking – space to give form to the functional search for a cultural cluster, while in spatial terms, it literally sketched the contours within which that search

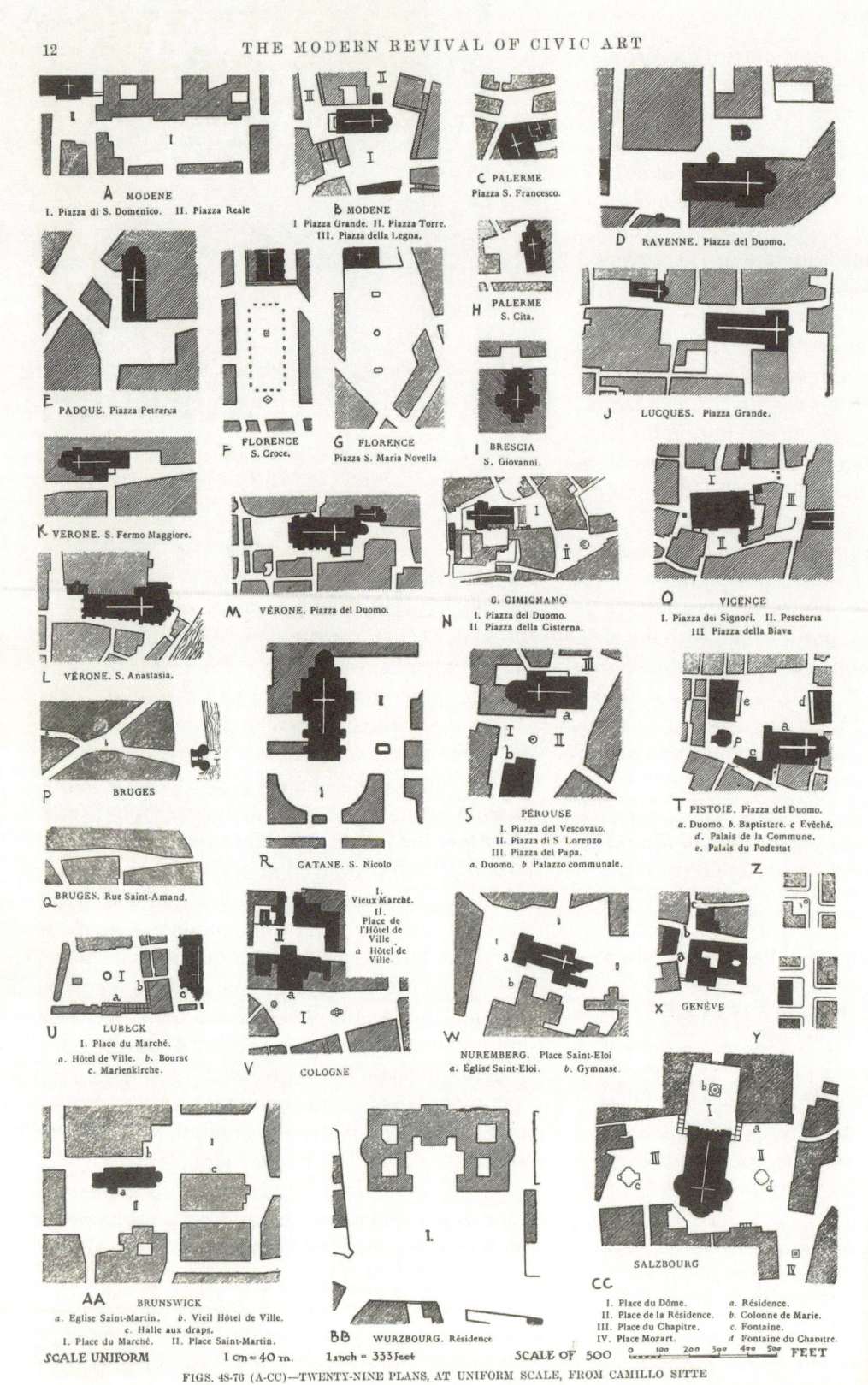

FIGS. 48-76 (A-CC)—TWENTY-NINE PLANS, AT UNIFORM SCALE, FROM CAMILLO SITTE

Fragments of city maps to scale, by Camillo Sitte, from
Der Städtebau nach seinen künstlerischen Grundsätzen,
as included in Hegemann and Peets, *The American
Vitruvius: An Architect's Handbook of Civic Art* (1922).

could take place. The model created both more mass and more public space. It fitted credibly into the historical city structure of the immediate vicinity, but also formed a new, intimate cultural square, making it a natural part of the successive, east-west oriented series of squares that determine the centre's first order of public space.

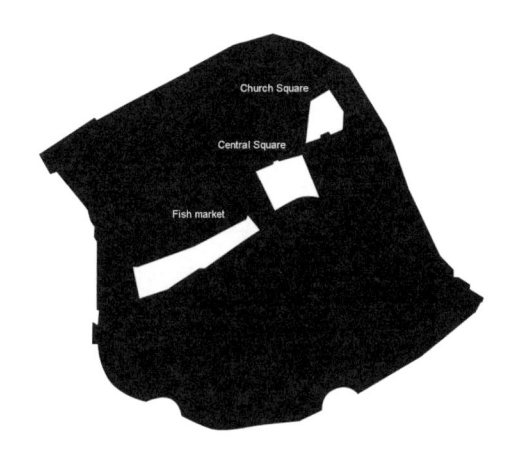

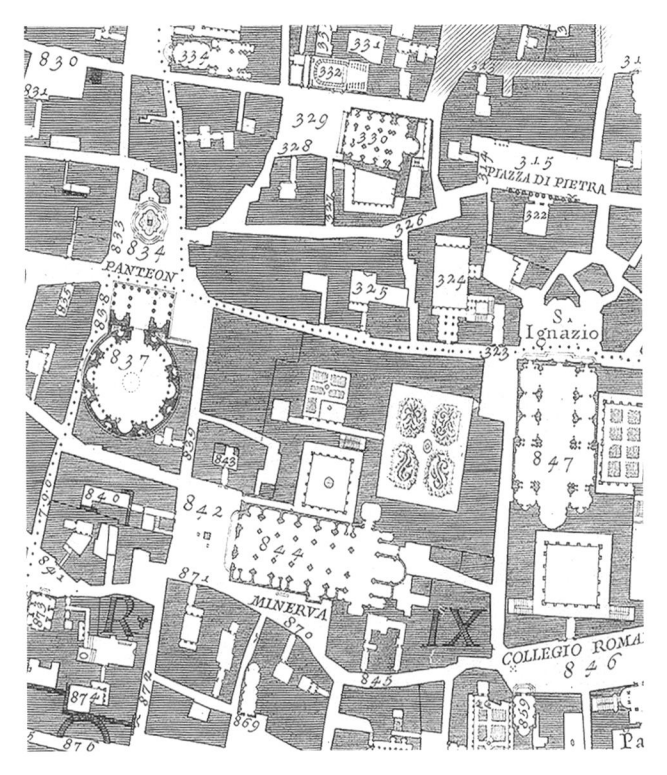

Giambattista Nolli, *Pianta Grande di Roma* (1748).

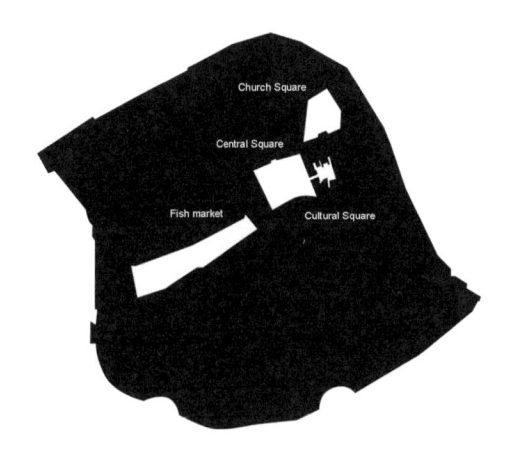

In *Der Städtebau nach seinen künstlerischen Grundsätzen* (1889), Camillo Sitte defined 'classical' spatial principles that he believed were important for urban planning. The book is both a quest for and an ode to beauty in the design of the urban street plan: the urban spaces formed by the structure of building blocks and the location of relevant buildings within them. Sitte thus explored spatial themes that had been depicted by Giambattista Nolli more than a century earlier in his *Pianta Grande di Roma* (1748), now commonly known as the Nolli map. Nolli not only indicated the distinction between built-up (black) and undeveloped space (white), but also indicated built public spaces, such as the colonnades at Saint Peter's and the interior of the Pantheon as open public urban spaces. The series of dark street plans made by NL Architects showing Groningen's main public spaces (Vismarkt, Grote Markt, Martinikerkhof) uses the same principle and adds the Nieuwe Markt to the series of squares and – following Nolli – also the Forum, in which the 'keyhole' of spaces from the Hoge Markt up to the roof represents an actual public space.

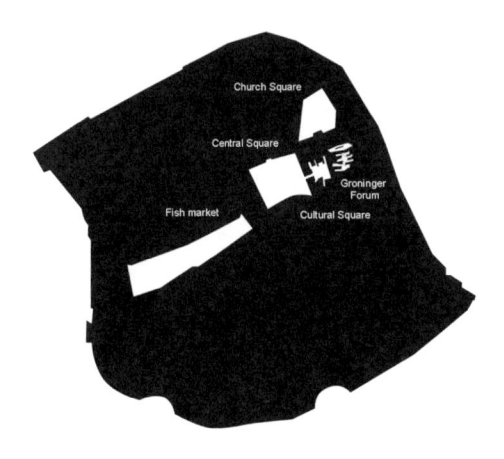

NL Architects, connection with the city: the Forum and the Nieuwe Markt as part of Groningen's series of squares on an east-west axis.

The widening of Broerstraat into a forecourt, through which the Academy building slowly unfolds into the perspective of the street (top two), and the modest Mennonite church, set back from the street, through which the building breaks free from the usual order of urban spaces.

Classical Space – Staging Urban Life

Neutelings Riedijk's research was primarily programmatic in nature. The city was advised to use the basic model to look for a synthesis of diverse cultural and economic functions of different sizes that would facilitate the creation of a vibrant cultural cluster. But despite the study's global nature, it was precisely this thorough, *actively* urban-planning approach that meant that the model addressed several classical themes at a spatial level. By the time the Forum was almost finished, there were expressions of indignation that the building had been placed not on the Grote Markt but behind the east wall. But the positioning of a cultural attraction *within* the building block, on a new square, was very deliberately chosen. The Forum has also been designed specifically for that site, attuned to its location in the urban structure.

The Forum's spatial context actually initiates a Sittean theme, namely the formation of urban spaces with building masses and the placement of important buildings within them. The idea of placing a cultural programme *within* the east wall had been studied but, given the characteristics of the location, did not yield acceptable spatial solutions. The functions would have to be arranged one behind the other in the block like a set of train compartments without the programme being accessible from different sides in an attractive way. The type of building and function envisaged in the Forum deserved its own prominent urban space.

Although Groningen has fewer urban spaces than the German and Italian cities that Camillo Sitte analysed, the city's urban fabric has several parallels with their spatial principles. The Academy Building on the square in Broerstraat is probably the best known of these. The street had already been fashioned into a square in the nineteenth century for the current building's neoclassical predecessor so that it's façade could be experienced from a sufficient distance. In contrast to its nineteenth- and twentieth-century successors, the first Academy Building was set up according to the structure of court buildings, in which the open space was not in front of or at the front, but *within* the complex. A fine, modest parallel is the ensemble that flanks the entrance to the Baptist church, around the corner from the Academy Building. With very modest spatial resources, this duo creates the same urban-planning momentum, whereby the church lifts itself above the ordinary order of streets – a composition that Giorgio Grassi utilised just as pleasingly in the entrance to the former public library. In Grassi's original proposal for the library, the entrance was much further away, so that the elongated urban vestibule would have had an even more extreme effect.

The placement of the Forum *within* the building block also stimulated the formation of the 'hidden city'. The building's sequestered character responded to the desire to be able to wander in the city centre's unforeseen spatial constellations. In the Forum we recognise the cathedrals or town halls that tower above medieval skylines, but which gradually 'hide' behind the surrounding buildings as you get closer to them. They disappear into the intricate pattern of narrow streets, alleys, semi-public squares and buildings set back from the building line. Nowhere is this experience more inspiring than at the Palazzo Pubblico in the Piazza del Campo in Siena. A mere stone's throw away, you stroll

unsuspectingly through the Via di Città, until the buildings on the Costa Barbieri give way and the square with the Torre del Mangia unfolds dramatically with a considerable sense of urban spectacle. The contrast between a compact urban fabric and the public functions of a square is here made more explicit than perhaps anywhere else.

Without wishing to make the comparison with Siena literal, the Forum offered the opportunity to create an immersive urban moment as part of the transformation of the east side of the Grote Markt. The scale and position of the east wall, interrupted only by a narrow connecting street, were intended to safeguard the Grote Markt's closed character. They also contributed to the hidden quality that arises in the building block. The east wall was moved

Original design drawings by Giorgio Grassi for the Groningen Public Library, showing an entrance set extremely far back and the realised entrance, approximately halfway between the elongated building volumes.

The Forum Groningen: vertical network of squares that culminates in the 'Hoge Markt' (High Market) on the roof, drawing the spatial and functional characteristics of the surroundings into the building.

Siena: compact building structure with the Piazza del Campo cut out as a stage for the Palazzo Pubblico.

eighteen metres towards the Grote Markt and four metres towards the Martinikerkhof. In this way, the Oosterstraat connects visually with the corner of the east wall and the Poelestraat, and links to the Grote Markt only by means of a narrow, slightly curved connection. Because the Forum is placed in the second line, as seen from the more compact Grote Markt, and is only visible to a limited extent due to the narrow opening of the Naberstraat, a sequence of urban spaces has been created. This contributes to the quality and functionality of the building block, the eastern city centre and the centre as a whole and thus serves to preserve the scale and historical continuity of the Grote Markt while allowing new spatial extremes to be sought in the building block. From the immediate vicinity, the building sometimes appears surprisingly elegant, and sometimes even disappears. Then again it looms impressively from the wings of the Nieuwe Markt.

The clever thing about the Forum design is that NL Architects has effortlessly drawn the programmatic and spatial principles of the environment into the building in one flowing movement. The context of different urban planning orders, which characterises the transformation as a whole, is continued in the building and convincingly incorporated into the design concept. Of course, it was hoped that the principles of the basic model would lead to a synthesis of the cultural programme and the public spaces. But no one could have foreseen that the building would identify with the programme and site to such an extent and would unite the cultural experiences around a public, vertical landscape in a unique way, resulting in an additional square on the roof. The architects designed not so much a building as a new type of public space in which the traditional boundaries between the city and cultural functions are blurred. The spaces and programme are carefully interwoven and unfold on a series of stacked squares that completes Groningen's principal spatial structure of markets squares. As we ascend the Forum via the 'Hoge Markt', we are constantly presented with new glimpses of the meaning and image of the city, and of the urban culture that goes with it.

KANS

RESTRAAT
RONINGEN
24000.—

GROOTE MARKT
GRONINGEN
f 22000.—

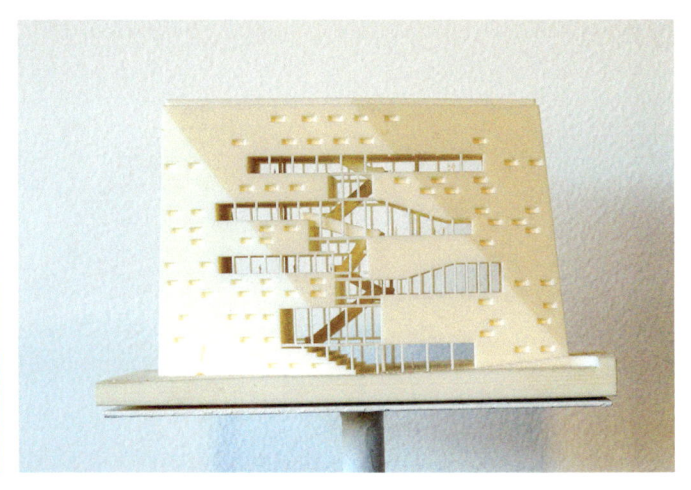

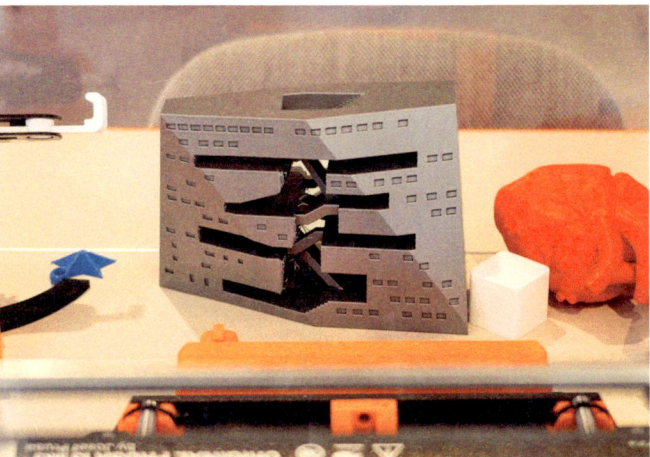
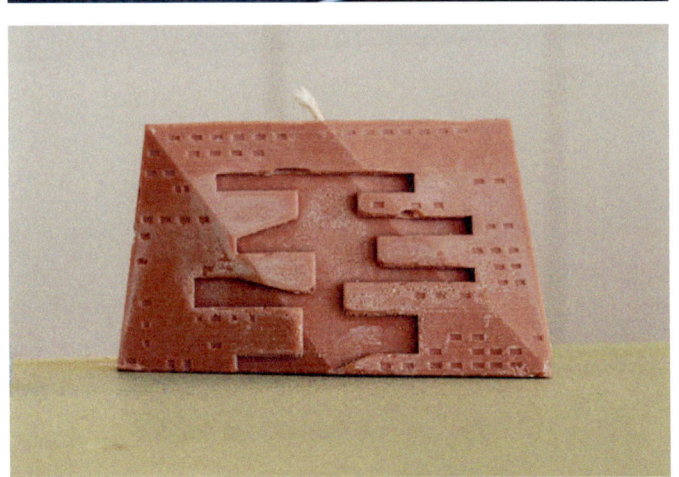

Erik Dorsman

The Design Concept Unravelled

Do we write the history of architecture on the basis of icons?
Or on the basis of a succession of often-unexposed events and
ideas, which show a development that far exceeds the sum of
modest historical moments? As historians, we tend to focus on
the built incidents: the high-quality exceptions that, while they
may perfectly express a certain period or school of thought, are
far from fully representative of what that period or movement
has produced. This may provide coherent narratives, but we
also run the risk of architectural-historical determinism based
on existing historical narratives. Viewed in this historical context, the Forum is undoubtedly the petrified image of a new type
of building: a phenomenal, solitary palace of culture to which,
decades from now, we will attribute a level of importance as if it
had come racing through history with giant strides.

To consider the Forum's specific place in our collective memory, we need to look closely at the circumstances in which the cultural complex came into being. Although the Forum has a distinctly iconic value due to its infinite silhouettes, it is significant that the architects see it as a logo: as an emblem that – more than as an image – symbolises the cultural and social significance of its programme. After decades of 'starchitects' in a globalised visual culture, the word 'icon' scarcely seems capable of evoking positive connotations, apart from its religious meaning and the art-historical baggage that goes with it.

Forum's selection in 2020 as the BNA's Best Building of the Year – submitted not in the category Identity & Iconic Value but in the category Liveability & Social Cohesion – underscores this trend. It would seem that we require a more nuanced view of image-defining and momentous spatial developments. We should guard against granting too great a place in history to these grand gestures, just as the Guggenheim Museum in Bilbao, the 'mother of all contemporary architecture icons', was wrongly given full responsibility for what has come to be known as the 'Bilbao effect', as if the building single-handedly breathed new life into the city when, in fact, it was merely one element within a two-decade-long restructuring programme for the Basque city's waterfront.

Yet there is a small series of abstract illustrations, almost icons, that symbolises the search for small steps that gave rise to Forum Groningen. In *this* historical reality, NL Architects' new type of cultural building is not the grand gesture of the architect as artist, but rather the most surprising, convincing and indisputable interpretation of its programme. Its implementation and design were postponed for as long as possible in order to explore new ways of using space in the public domain. In retrospect, NL Architects was the obvious winner with its plan. The exploratory and unconventional design method for which the office is known resulted in a logo that seemed to fit perfectly with what Groningen was looking for. No matter how abstract the pictograms are, without those striking images, Forum as we know it would probably not exist.

Abstract Images for a Boundless Exploration

Like all the other entrants, NL Architects presented its design in November 2006 to the assessment committee chaired by Wytze Patijn. The office used four powerful images as an introduction to its concept:

1) a silhouette based on the contours of the design, with the main structure of the inner city's public spaces cut into it;
2) a silhouette based on the contours of the design, with an amoeba-shaped cut-out through which a map of part of the inner city was visible;
3) a silhouette of the building including Forum's 'keyhole' with another amoeba-shaped patch derived from the Dadaist artist Jean Arp's 1961 lithograph *Plakat Basel*;
4) and a silhouette of the building including Forum's keyhole, through which a slightly larger section of the map of the inner city could be seen.

With these four images, the office provided a strategic response to the city's desire to undertake a spatial and programmatic exploration. After all, what exactly was the city doing commissioning a building whose function was not yet clear? The municipality's and the participating cultural institutions' ideas about the new functional constellation to be created and the appropriate type of building to house it, were boundless rather than clearly defined. NL Architects perceived this not as a defect, but rather as the potential of the multifaceted assignment. The designers were expected to contribute to Forum's conceptualisation and development through analysis of the brief, their own conceptual capacity and interaction with the client. NL Architects was already known for taking assignments further than anticipated. While not experienced with

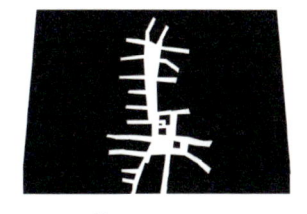

1)

2)

3)

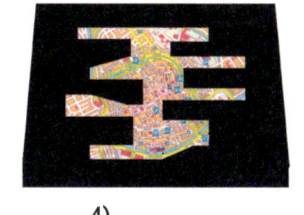

4)

The first images of NL Architects' Forum presentation (November 2006).

large-scale, cultural complexes, the office had demonstrated its ability to think independently and to push the boundaries of a brief, frequently combining requested elements with functions that were not part of the brief at all, while ensuring that their synthesis amounted to much more than the sum of its parts, often resulting in an enrichment of public space.

What followed those first images in the presentation was a memorable story about an extraordinary building. The office successfully used form and function diagrams, drawings, simple visualisations, and photographs of models to reduce the unusual structure and organisation of the inventive design to a clear and powerful logo. It also devoted a great deal of energy to the spatial exploration of the potential of the functional assembly in the so-called 'domains', which were later redubbed 'spheres' and ultimately 'squares'. The design concept and the presentation seemed to coincide. That we were dealing with a memorable moment here was not something that everyone was aware of. Looking back, it is clear that the four 'iconic' images revealed the design's substantive foundation, namely the study of the overlap of urban space and a multifaceted cultural programme, but *within* a building. This uninhibited quest was preceded by two documents with a strikingly comparable visual language.

The Morphology as a Starting Point

No matter how successful NL Architects' presentation was in explaining the organisation and design of the mixed programme, few would have been able to imagine exactly how Forum would turn out, or indeed even what the plan entailed. The design was difficult to imagine because of the as-yet-unknown mix of cultural programming and its ground-breaking spatial interpretation. For many, the plan remained just as abstract as the icons with which the architects had introduced their story. For a long time, one criticism levelled at Forum was that its layered and multifaceted organisation was not sufficiently tangible. There was a notion that it was 'nothing but' a building, even during its construction. Because the development of the brief and the building happened simultaneously, these concerns were understandable. However, we can also see this thorough exploration as the core of the assignment, from which a coherent spatial and functional concept emerged.

The fact that the new cultural attraction was not clearly defined was certainly seen by critics as a weakness. Nevertheless, the assignment's open and unprejudiced perspective followed logically from the *Studie Grote Markt Groningen* (Grote Markt Groningen Study) of May 2003, with which Forum's spatial history began. After two years of collecting ideas and advice about the future of the east side of the Grote Markt, the municipality asked Neutelings Riedijk Architects to translate the resulting concepts into spatial models. The essence of the study was to ascertain the urban-design consequences of a new, public, cultural building on the east side of the Grote Markt. The thinking behind the building's composition was determined by five distinct functions: a theatre and music venue, a library, a history centre, a commercial development

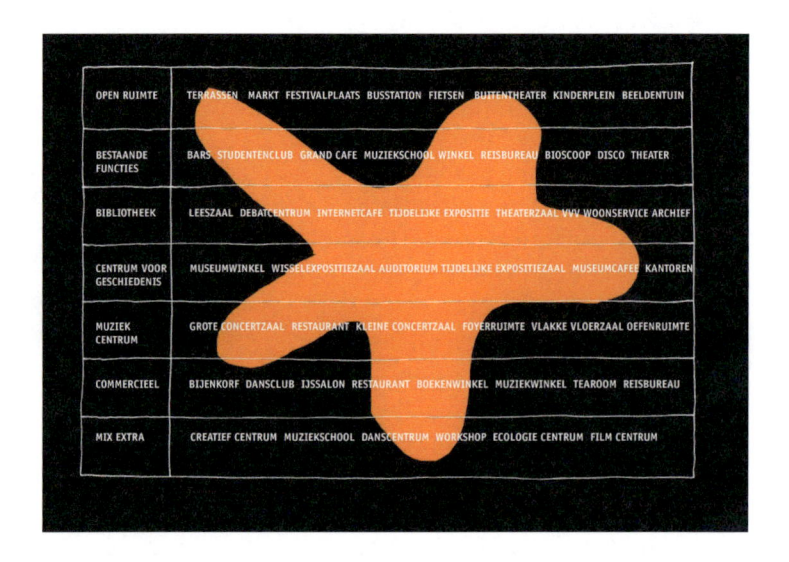

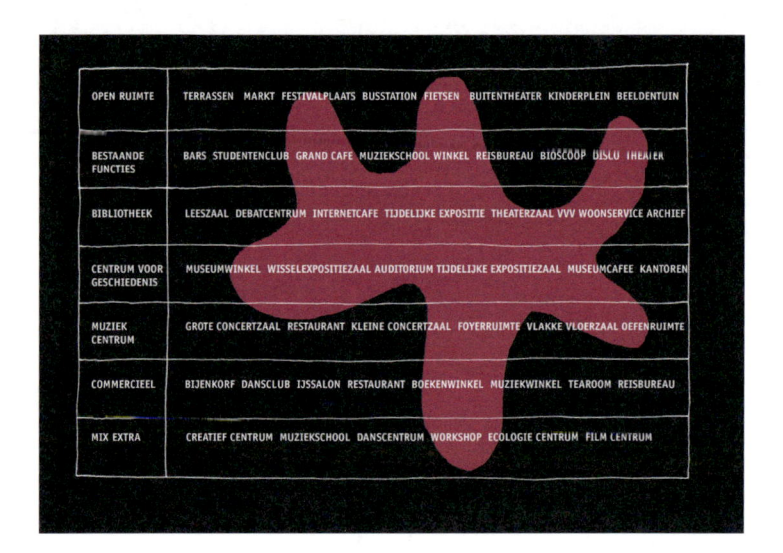

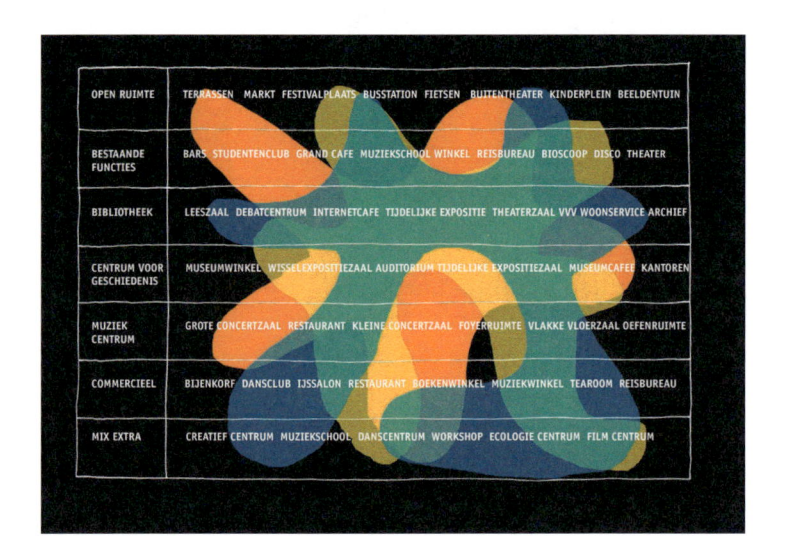

Function diagrams and proposition from *Studie Grote Markt Groningen* (May 2003) by Neutelings Riedijk Architects.

with a department store or a mixed-use development with smaller units. In short, an assignment that was, at that stage, far from precisely defined.

In addition to addressing the main question, the architects undertook a thorough spatial study of the structure, form and functioning of the city centre and the site within the context of its historical development. After collecting data about the site and undertaking a schematic study of the functions, they postulated the following: morphology ≠ programme. A brief exploration of site references on the location then paved the way for a comprehensive morphological investigation, which formed the prelude to what they termed the 'morphological transformation model'. In response to the commission, instead of presenting several models, Neutelings Riedijk presented a single, basic, spatial structure within which various elements could be given a place in the building block that they designated as a culture cluster. The office thus developed a spatial strategy for the Grote Markt in general, and for the east side in particular, without necessarily leading to distinct spatial plans.

The Grote Markt Groningen Study was the first concrete representation of the idea of transforming the east side of the Grote Markt. But this vision immediately called into question the project's planned timeline and phasing. At the end of the study, the architects stated that the eastern block should not be limited to one of the five possible functions but should instead provide a synthesis of functions, an unexpected composition of functions, a programme with components that complement and reinforce each other. A new constellation would raise Groningen's profile, strengthen the city centre and increase the vibrancy of the area around the Grote Markt. The urban-design principle that emerged from the transformation model offered much more space than was initially thought possible.

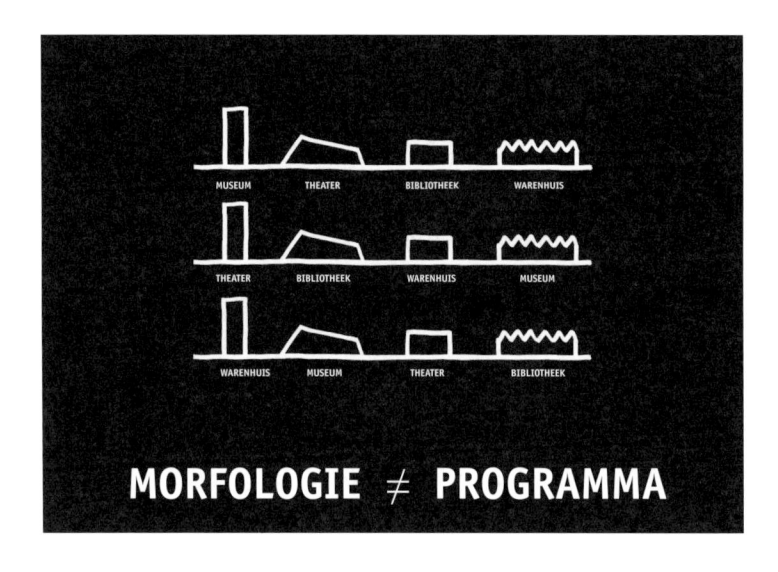

MORFOLOGIE ≠ PROGRAMMA

It would be easy to combine a mix of diverse functions, varied in size and type. The study came at the right time and went much further than envisioned precisely because it was not based on a narrowly defined assignment. Neutelings Riedijk's research was met with enthusiasm and gave the municipality new ideas about the project's scale and time frame. The study had united so many ideas and insights that a 'trend break' was acceptable and changes of course in the process were inevitable. But of greater interest for Forum, in retrospect, than the basic morphological model, test interpretations or the exploration of the variants, were the functional diagrams with amoeba-shaped spots that reinforced the principles of the urban model.

A New Functional Concept

It takes little effort to see in Neutelings Riedijk's functional diagrams a harbinger of what would become the Forum logo. Looked at through squinted eyes and with a little imagination, one can even see a cross section of the building, expressing its principles in an immaterial yet unambiguous manner. It is significant that the schemes of Neutelings Riedijk and NL Architects appear to tell a similar story, although the designers of Forum were not given the Neutelings Riedijk study as context for the competition. Apart from the spatial model, the results of the functional research eventually seem to have been condensed into a single existing, non-figurative reference image.

Neutelings Riedijk's study ended with several almost rhetorical questions that summarised the crux of the study and which could serve as a guide for subsequent studies.

¿ Do we want a lively, yet still compact city with the most important public and cultural functions at its centre, or do we accept a more sprawling city with several important public and cultural functions on the periphery?

¿ Do we want a lively eastern block to strengthen Groningen's centre, or do we want to implement only limited spatial and functional changes?

¿ Do we want a single, inspiring complex that draws upon the five different programmes, or should we limit ourselves to one of the five?

In a city that had actively embraced the compact-city policy since the 1980s, these were not difficult questions.

Using Neutelings Riedijk's study, over a period of about three years the municipality worked on the urban-development plan and a concept brief for the Forum. The principles of the urban plan followed the study's transformation model and were supplemented in the appendix by a representation of the *Concept Programma van Eisen ten behoeve van de meervoudige opdracht voor het Groninger Forum* (Forum Groningen's Urban-Design Principles). The principles served as a framework for the competition and illustrated the desired spatial properties of the cultural complex within the context of the site and the city centre. Unlike Neutelings Riedijk's study, the cultural programme had not bled across the site like a stain. In the urban development plan, a broad functional composition was still the starting point for the transformation as a whole, but a new configuration of the culture programme had become concentrated in the main volume of the basic model in the eastern half of the site.

In the run-up to a referendum on the entire intervention, Neutelings Riedijk's suggestion to create a complex that housed various functions had developed into the House of Information and History, later renamed Forum Groningen. More than an accumulation of cultural functions, it should become a place that centred on the exchange of knowledge and information. The overlap of different functions and facilities would allow for a diverse range of activities: from consulting and borrowing books and studying to attending conferences, lectures, debates, film screenings or exhibitions. This represented a new functional concept, whose partners from the outset were the Groninger Museum, the Public Library, Filmhuis Images and the Groningen

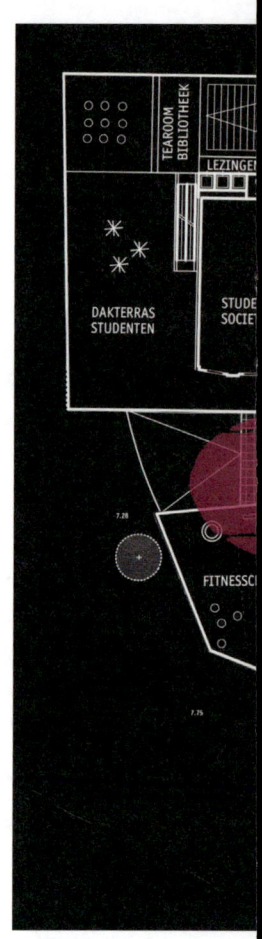

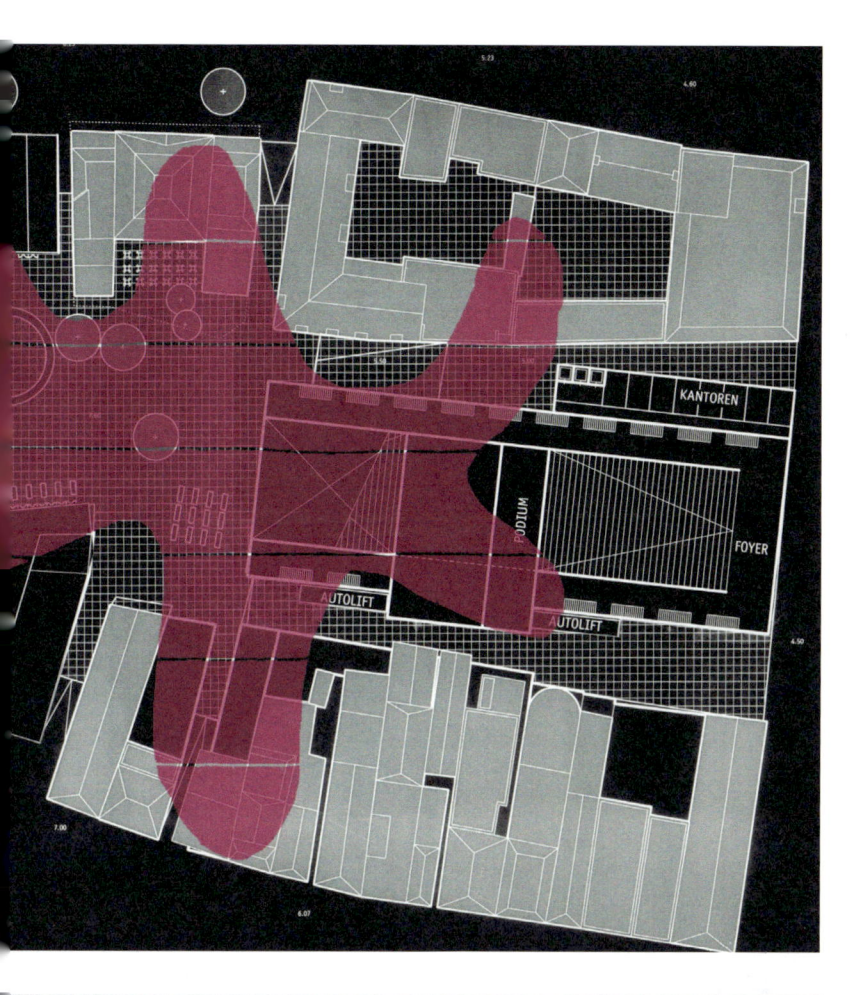

The morphological transformation model from the study by Neutelings Riedijk Architects.

Archives. In addition, the city's Maritime Museum, the University of Groningen, the Hanze University of Applied Sciences, and debating and knowledge centres such as Studium Generale and Dwarsdiep were mentioned as participants. The mission statement outlined in the brief for Forum called for a carefully combined and integrated programme that must transcend the individual functions and make them accessible to a wide audience.

The otherwise rather dry and business-like brief posited an as-yet-undefined idea about the synthesis of functions while paying detailed attention to the descriptions of the partners, possible participants and the composition of the individual collections. The document discussed the joint operational management, Forum's identity, its role as a driver of the redevelopment and the desire to employ the building to increase Groningen's international architectural profile. Perhaps the best expressed ambition in the brief was that the building should not become the sum of the accommodation needs of the partner organisations, but should be an international example of integrating multiple functions within a single building: a new archetype in which the organisations not only shared accommodation but actually cohabited. While considerable attention was paid to the description of the functions to be accommodated, the 'domains' remained mere suggestions. This was, after all, unknown territory. The philosophy was illustrated by means of international examples, such as the Guggenheim Museum in Bilbao, the Seattle Public Library and the Centre Pompidou in Paris: all interesting references in one respect or another but not really indicative of what Forum was supposed to be. Among these scant images, Jean Arp's amorphous *Plakat Basel* was particularly striking, an image that, in addition to the cautious, tentative description of the mission, was also used to depict the functional principle (it is the only image that appears twice in the brief). As an illustration of the mission statement, the artwork is captioned: *'Multiple individuals create a new identity.'* The functions to be accommodated are illustrated by the single word *'integration'*.

The Immaterial Foundation

It is perhaps telling for the development of a new type of cultural building that an abstract artwork from the 1960s, made for an exhibition in the Kunsthalle Basel, forms the most exemplary representation of the relationship between an urban-design study, the architectural brief and the final, realised design. Seeing the images side by side, it is not readily apparent that we are witnessing the development of a ground-breaking building. Rather, we imagine ourselves back in the Kunsthalle, attending a revival of Dadaism, with the dry humour that goes with it. It was not yet apparent at the presentation of the competition design, but when considering the preliminary phase, it is striking how the visual language and the schemes used in each phase eloquently represent the envisaged spatial principles. Through the power of the image, it is striking how pointedly the NL Architects' design answered the competition brief and how constant is the line between the urban-design study, the brief and the finished building, despite the occasionally intangible ideas and descriptions that accompanied the process.

The series of artistic images also represents, both at an urban-design level and a functional and typological level, the genuine research into the right development on the right site – a task that has, in a sense, played tricks on the location since the period of post-war reconstruction. It shows a certain audacity to continue searching for such a long time in terms of abstract images and concepts so that, initially, the answer to a question is no closer to hand, but the possibilities of the assignment are advanced. How long does such a process take? How credible is that search? Not everyone commits themselves to an assignment with such dedication, wants to keep exploring, wants to search for what's behind the curtain. Most people probably love the curtain because it gives them stability and definition. But NL Architects' design pulls back the curtain – and the curtain behind that curtain.

The search for the right cultural programme and its spatial interpretation had inspired Neutelings Riedijk to create a solid urban-design foundation, which showed that a combination of different cultural and commercial functions was possible. If the series of iconic illustrations represents anything, it is that the intelligent connection between the study's spatial and functional principles seems to have had a direct influence on the Forum's programme and design. NL Architects adopted Neutelings Riedijk's basic model as an urbanist set-up, although the functions within the block are somewhat more strictly separated from each other. NL Architects' plan essentially uses the same organisational principle, whereby the stain in Neutelings Riedijk's study has shifted from the plan to the elevation to create Forum's famous 'keyhole'. The amoeba was to become the 'counter-mould' of the atrium and the study's superlative degree, whereby the anticipated functional interaction at the urbanist level was brought inside the building. This clever reversal not only resolves the boundaries between functions, but also creates a continuous line between city, square and building: the street life has convincingly been pulled into the building.

The design concept allowed various functions to be brought together around a series of squares that transcend the brief, while at the same time preventing the building from becoming merely a collection of different cultural venues. The Forum emerged as a dynamic stack of programmatic components arranged around a central void that, as an extension of street life on the Nieuwe Markt, ensures both the opening up and overlapping of the rich cultural life. It seems that NL Architects has implemented the principles as laid

down in the urban-design study extremely clearly and consistently – much better than Neutelings Riedijk did with its competition entry for the Forum itself. NL Architects took the advice from the study not to choose one specific function but to look for a synthesis of functions and made it the quintessence of their design. It breathes the principles of the urban-design plan. And it is perhaps this fact that makes those first images from the competition presentation so powerful, as if they were an advance on the perfect interpretation of the urban planning and programmatic principles. NL Architects' proposal was not only a beautiful spatial interpretation of the assignment, it was the only design that really responded to the concept of the Forum and could therefore clearly contribute to its development.

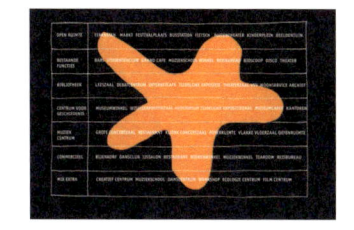

NL Architects made the desired interaction between functions and between the building and the environment the heart of the assignment, whereby the programmatic elements could be spatially interwoven with a public atrium – a vertical 'Hoge Markt' stretching up to the roof – as a natural continuation of the urban space. The building had indeed become a logo for the Forum through a series of small, abstract steps that NL Architects has navigated in a masterful fashion.

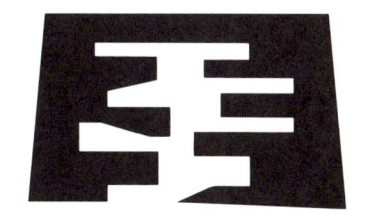

Micha Wertheim

"No higher than St Martin's Tower!"
my brother began to cry
as our plane took off into the sky

The flight attendant said that she would try,
and then returned
with a cup of water,
a bag of almonds
and some lies

Comforted, by what we knew
not to be true
we saw the world below, reduced in size

Staring down, and drinking from that plastic cup
we thought, perhaps this is what they mean
when they speak of growing up?

Illustration: Cristina Garcia Martin

City

DESIGN

Jola Meijer & Erik Dorsman

The Competition — A Reflection on the Submissions

In April 2006, the Municipality of Groningen held an international competition for the design of the Forum, including the underground parking garage and the public space of the Nieuwe Markt. Of the thirty-five submissions, seven architects from the Netherlands and abroad were selected to develop a draft design: Erick van Egeraat Associated Architects, Foreign Office Architects, Neutelings Riedijk Architects, NL Architects, UN Studio, Wiel Arets Architects and Zaha Hadid Architects. Between November 2006 and February 2007, the seven proposals were assessed by a committee made up of representatives of the Municipality of Groningen, the Public Library and the Groninger Museum, led by an independent chairperson. Members of the public could also indicate their preference via a survey. The design by NL Architects emerged victorious both with the expert judges and the public. But what did the six 'non-winning' designs look like? How did the other practices interpret the challenging brief and how did their approaches differ? And what set the winning design apart from the six non-winning plans?

1   The 'evaluation committee' comprised chair Wytze Patijn (former Chief
     Government Architect, Dean of Delft University of Technology), Kees
     van Twist (director of the Groninger Museum), Rob Pronk (director of the
     Public Library), Arie Wink (general director of the Department of Spatial
     Planning and Economic Affairs, Municipality of Groningen) and Niek
     Verdonk (Chief Municipal Architect, Municipality of Groningen).

Spatial and Functional Ambitions

Two ambitions outlined in the brief and the urban planning principles leave no room for misunderstanding in terms of the Forum's aims and are therefore a good starting point for an analysis of the submitted designs. Firstly, an important challenge was to site the building carefully on the new square and give it a convincing relationship with its surroundings. The intention was that the Nieuwe Markt should become a high-quality extension of the city's public space, a lively square that would connect the Forum with the city's public domain. With an envisioned area of approximately 17,000 m², an average height of 33 metres and a maximum height of 45 metres, the municipality drew up seven urban development principles for the Forum.

1. At the ground-floor level, the building should respond to the immediate surroundings in terms of scale, size and building plots.
2. The building should have more than one entrance and no closed sides.
3. A substantial part of the ground-floor space (the foyer) should function as an extension of the public space of the Nieuwe Markt.
4. The building's façades should have an open character.
5. The building's roof should be publicly accessible (restaurant and public space).
6. The building should vary in height, thus referring to the city's varied roof landscape.
7. The building should add a new height accent to the city's skyline, thus emphasising the significance of the centre as the heart of the city.

Secondly, it demanded a ground-breaking spatial concept within which the Forum's varied functions were to be interwoven. The brief was based on the needs of the building's principle partners: the Public Library, the Groninger Museum, the Groningen Archives and the Images cinema. The combination of these parties had to be more than a simple sum of functions. The Forum should become a national or even international example of how multiple cultural organisations can be integrated within a single building: a new archetype in which these parties would not just *share* a building, but would actually *cohabit*, allowing for interesting instances of cross-pollination. The architects were expected to develop the Forum's vision further by analysing the brief and bringing their conceptual capacities to bear on it. During the design process, after the selection, the brief would be gradually refined further.

Two concepts were central to the Forum's content: domains and programming. In addition to a classical conference centre for lectures, symposiums, films and exhibitions, the domains had to house the permanent collections of the museum and the library. This is where the synthesis of the brief had to be expressed: within the domains, it should be possible to mix the collections in a variety of ways – temporarily or permanently and displays of varying size – spread across the building on the basis of current or historical themes, trends or specific objects from the collections. In addition, the domains must provide spaces for study and educational events. In line with the building's urban-planning principles, the Nieuwe Markt was also regarded as a domain. Because the programming and presentation of the collections and the exhibitions

policy had to have a continuously innovative character, the building had to be flexible and be able to accommodate variety. So, although the brief demanded a completely new building typology, the design should not deliver a tailor-made suit. The domains had to have an open atmosphere, but also allow for intimacy: they should be experienced as a single space, even if they were housed on different floors. This spatial effect could be attained through the use of voids, atria and sightlines.

To promote the formation of knowledge and opinions, the Forum must become a place where the exchange of information and culture was central. The overlap of a variety of facilities should provide a diverse palette of activities: from borrowing books, searching for information and studying to attending conferences, lectures and debates, participating in courses, workshops and tours, seeing films or visiting exhibitions. Such a mixed programme would provide dynamism all day long. With such a broad scope of functions, it was anticipated that the building would attract more than a million visitors each year.

How did the architects incorporate these ambitions into their plans? And how did their designs match the brief and the urban planning principles? What parallels and differences can we discover if we analyse the submissions in detail, looking at their relationship with the environment, the influence this had on the shape and appearance of the building and on how the architects organised the various interrelated functions?

1. At the ground-floor level, the building should respond to the immediate surroundings in terms of scale, size and building plots.

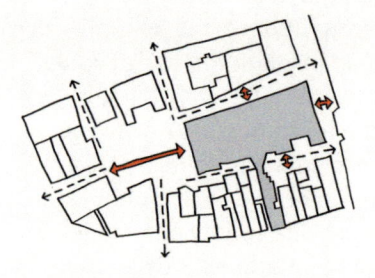

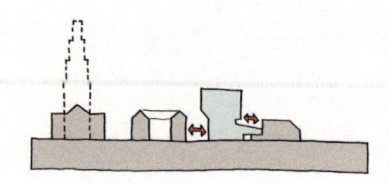

2. The building should have more than one entrance and no closed sides.

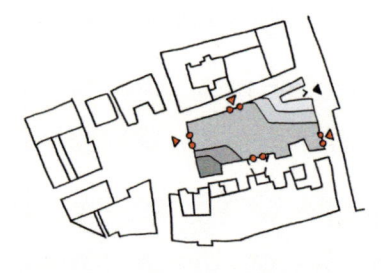

3. A substantial part of the ground-floor space (the foyer) should function as an extension of the public space of the Nieuwe Markt.

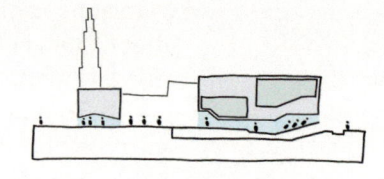

4. The building's façades should have an open character.

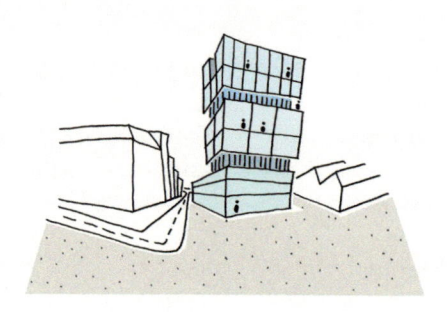

5. The building's roof should be publicly accessible (restaurant and public space).

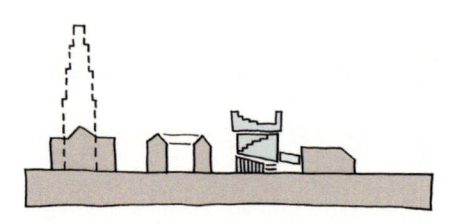

6. The building should vary in height, thus referring to the city's varied roof landscape.

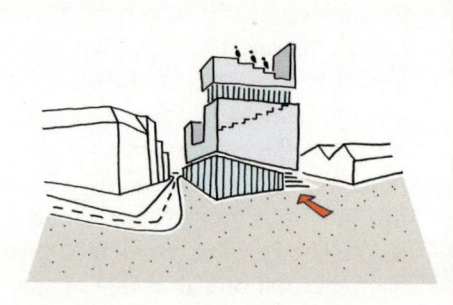

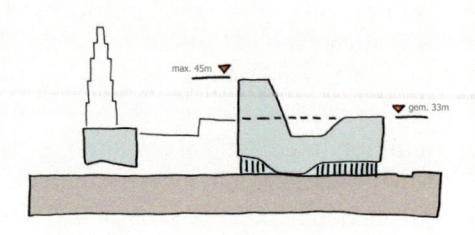

7. The building should add a new height accent to the city's skyline, thus emphasising the significance of the centre as the heart of the city.

'Illustrations for explaining the urban planning principles of the Groninger Forum,' as included in *Grote Markt Oostzijde – Concept-Programma van Eisen Stedenbouw, Openbare Ruimte en Verkeer* (June 2006).

Erick van Egeraat Associated Architects

Foreign Office Architects

Neutelings Riedijk Architecten

UN Studio

Wiel Arets Architects

Zaha Hadid Architects

The Competition

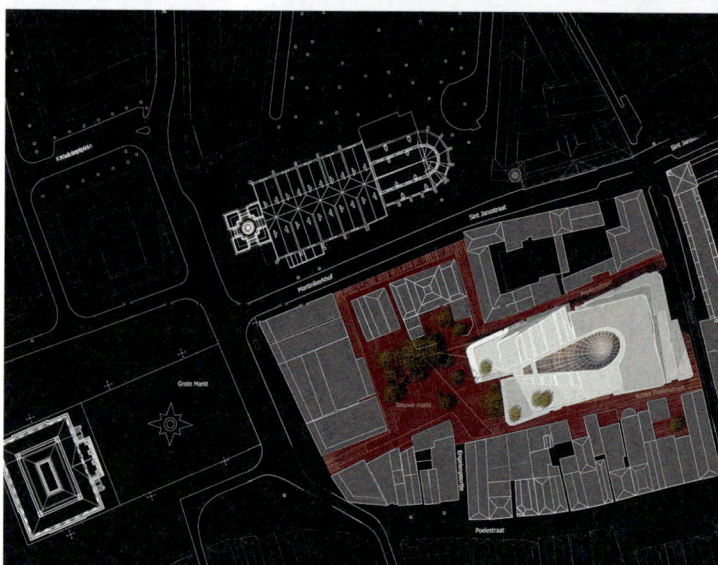
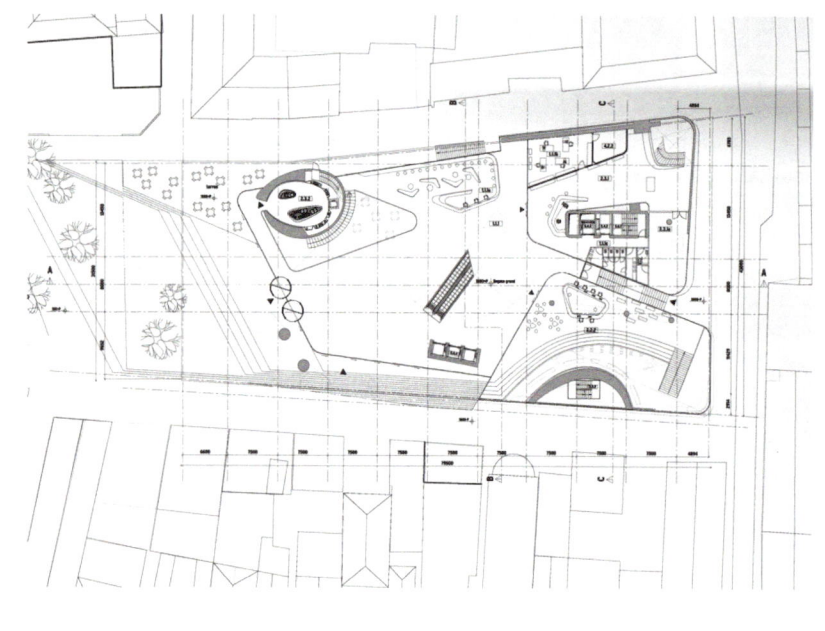
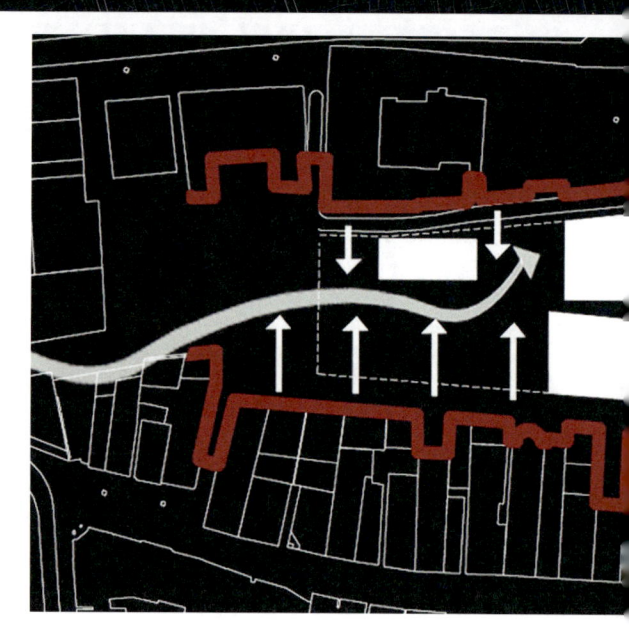

"An earthy, urban building with a very quiet exterior" was Erick van Egeraat's aim.[2] To connect the Forum convincingly to the urban context, he not only modelled the building but also immediately refined the urban model. In a visionary move, he shifted the planned connecting street between the Grote Markt and the Nieuwe Markt one plot to the south – exactly as in the ultimately realised design. Van Egeraat did this to create a smooth connection with the existing series of squares in the centre: Vismarkt – Grote Markt – Martinikerkhof. He carefully tuned the shape of the building volume and the location of the entrances to this city structure: the open space of the ground floor appears to have been carved out of the building mass and is continued with a cavernous atrium at the heart of the building. Because the foyer rises slightly in relation to the sloping square, there is room for a basement with a café. This relates to the foyer through voids but connects to the level of the adjacent Schoolstraat. Van Egeraat extended the Nieuwe Markt fluidly inside the building by allowing the glass frontage on the side of the square to be fully opened. The building thus interacts with its surroundings both on the ground floor and at the basement level.

Van Egeraat's Forum is a softly sculpted rock, calm and massive, narrowing towards the top, surmounted by a transparent glazed Art Deco roof closing off the atrium. The building's stepped structure and articulation alludes to the building volume of Saint Martin's Church and Tower. As the building narrows towards the top, it creates room for terraces in various places. The resulting varied roof landscape is supported by the façade, which is divided into facets, creating a "layered dialectical interplay between robust mass and transparency, weight and weightlessness." The glass façade, screen-printed with an alabaster-like print, enhances the interaction between diffused light and shadow, making the building an illuminated beacon in the heart of the city at night. Like a carved glass sculpture, the building is folded around the cave, with vertical cuts here and there revealing something of the brick inner world. Like the square, the foyer and atrium are covered with vaulted red brickwork typical of Groningen. "From a distance, the building [...] appears impenetrable, while up close it is open and accessible."

The elliptical atrium provides an overview of the interior, and spatially connects the various functions within the building. An elongated, spiral staircase follows the contour of the atrium and provides access to the floors at ever-changing locations, supplemented by a double escalator and an emergency staircase at the edges of the building. There is a diversity of open and closed spaces, some with a contemporary feel and others, such as the library, with a classical atmosphere. Van Egeraat envisioned an unforgettable "insane space" that would create an "unprecedented visual spectacle." Although the sculpted heart forms an exciting route through the building's various functions, the programme appears to be largely divided per floor. As such, the question remains to what extent the spatial design meets the building's stated need to foster cross-pollination. Almost nowhere do the floors – arranged as domains – connect directly in spatial or visual terms to the atrium or to functions on other floors, which makes it difficult to experience the building's structure. The individual floors are open and flexible, offering space for functional interaction but they provide little connection to each other. Due to the specific position of individual functions within the building, the question remains whether, given the transparency provided, the programme radiates sufficiently within its surroundings, except as a light beacon. From an organisational and functional point of view, the design mainly looks inwards, making it difficult for visitors to orient themselves to the environment from inside the building. Perhaps Van Egeraat should have used the interplay of contrasts – inherent in the brief – in a different way. Perhaps the relationship between the building, the city and the mutual functions could have transcended this interplay.

2   All quotes about the sketch designs come from the planning material submitted by the architectural practices or from presentations given by them as part of the assessment process.

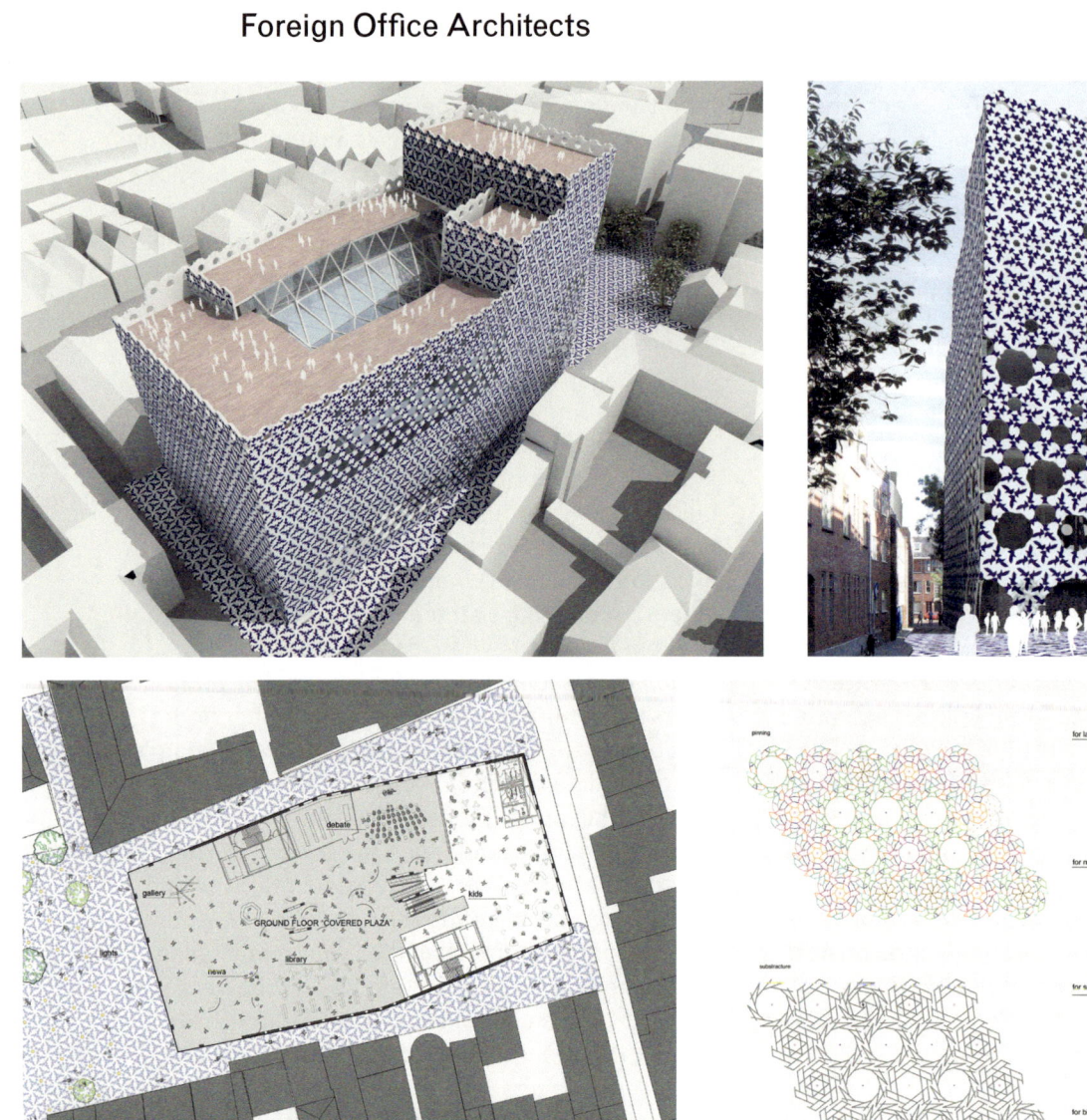

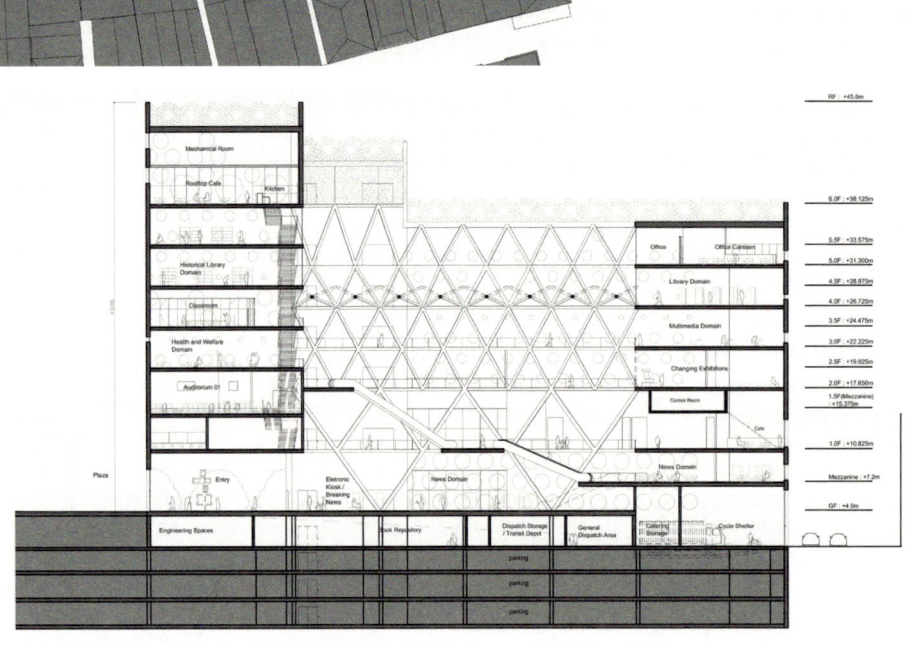

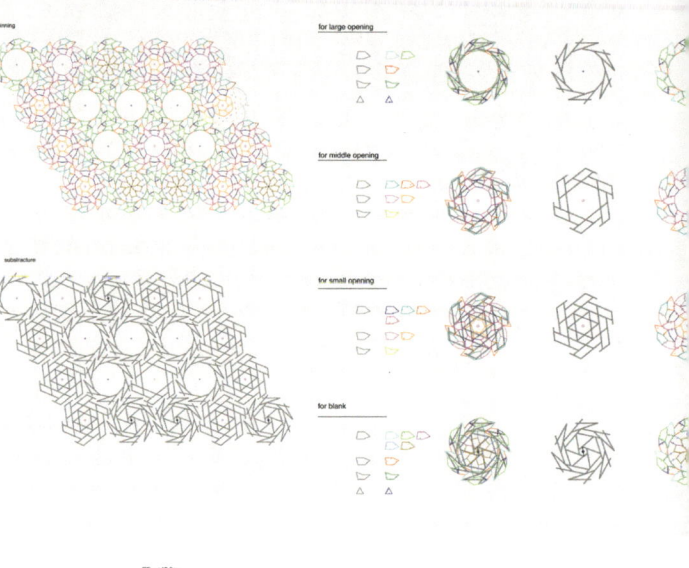

west facade (A)

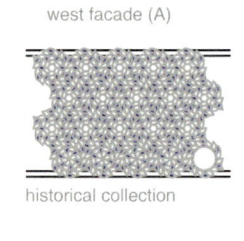

historical collection

rooftop c

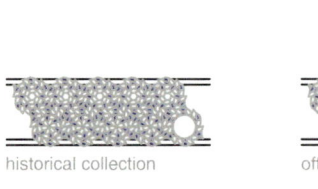

historical collection

offices

the body and health

instructio

Foreign Office Architects proposed a building volume based on the compact, resilient and unambiguous building structure of the existing city. The architects sought a "synthesis of the rich urban heritage and the innovative character" of the programme to be housed. Based on building lines in the area and sight lines to the surrounding buildings, they modelled a diamond-shaped block from the two main directions. The typology of the urban block is continued in the atrium, which functions as a covered internal area that becomes more spacious as it rises. The use of a consistent structural pattern creates a clear basic structure within which the programme can be flexibly accommodated, also in the future. With a flexible building structure and a range of functions that could be developed, the designers envisioned an "information container" whose diamond-shaped floor plan creates extra space in the narrow neighbouring streets. Although Foreign Office sought a direct relationship between the building and the square in terms of character, the spatial connection is limited to the west side of the building. The ground floor therefore acts only to a small extent as a continuation of the Nieuwe Markt: the entrance side provides a fairly classical transition between outside and inside.

To connect with a local urban tradition, the architects looked at the compact building blocks with a "perforated ceramic skin" that are typical of Groningen. They covered the façades with a pattern of blue and white tiles – familiar from Dutch porcelain – arranged in a symmetrical Penrose tiling pattern. A connection to the Nieuwe Markt and the surrounding urban fabric is created by continuing the tile pattern – for maximum visual effect – on the square, as if the building is spreading its tentacles towards its neighbours. The pattern of the tiles results in perforations of various sizes and shapes for different functions, but the façade nevertheless gives the building a fairly closed character. Even the view of the city from the roof terraces is framed by the architects with the systematically applied peepholes.

Foreign Office conceived the entire building as a continuous route. They accommodated the programme in a single long, spiral-shaped split-level construction. From the third storey, the floors are always half offset from an east-west diagonal that runs through the building, creating hook-shaped floor plans. They employed the split-level principle to promote the vertical route: in essence the building forms a 15-metre-wide street that ascends with a constant offset of half a floor. Even so, this design seems to limit the interweaving of the programmes. The ground floor is conceived as a foyer and an open floorplan for the news domain and café, a children's library and other supporting functions related to current affairs. At successively higher levels are the cinemas, the auditorium and the activity rooms, then the exhibition spaces and the domains, and finally the library and offices. The roof is accessible via the last domain, with the historical collection and the Groningana, followed by a rooftop café. In a sense, the spiral split-level creates a fluid cohesion between space and functions. But this barely hides the fact that the programme is mostly laid out on the route in a specific sequence, without creating spatial or functional cross connections. The principal seems to have been used in the first place to unlock the programme in an exciting way, but it does not directly enhance the programmatic versatility. Like Van Egeraat's plan, the building is insular and is limited in its openness to discovery. The question remains whether the chosen organisational principle would have provided an adequate solution for the desired spatial use and whether it would have promoted exchange between its diverse functions.

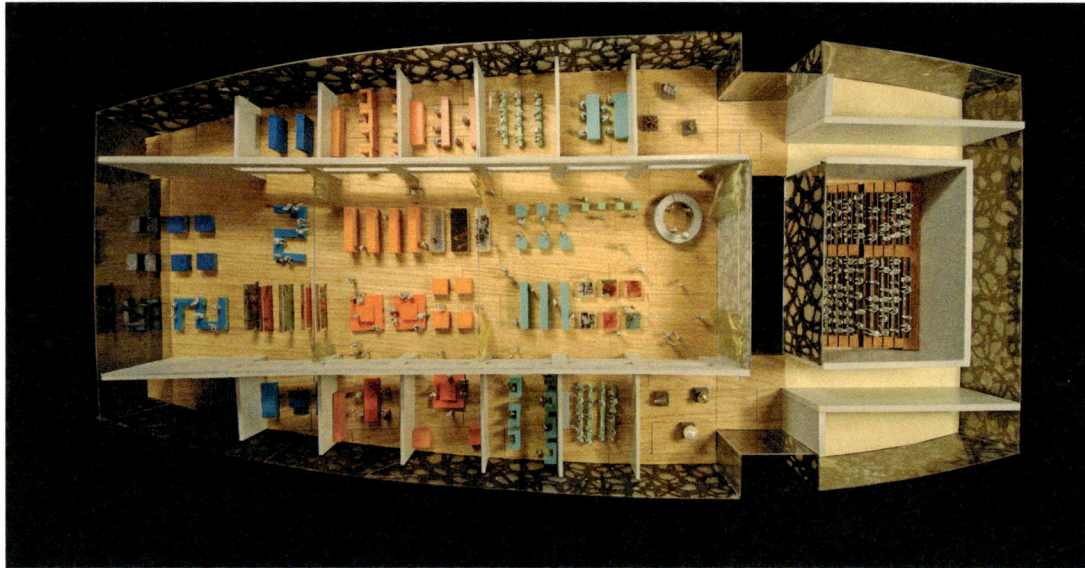

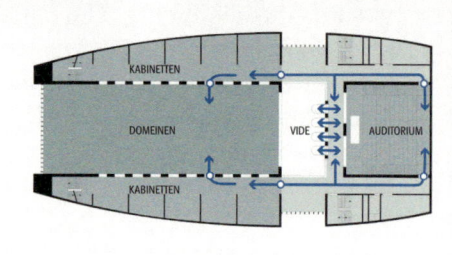

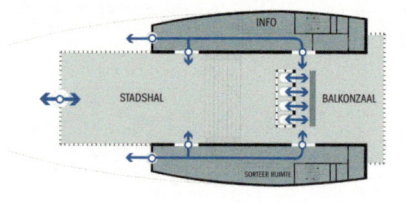

The Forum envisioned by Neutelings Riedijk Architects is an expressive sculptural building made up of two clearly defined building volumes: the nave, or front house, and the tower, or back house. A monumental void connects both volumes and ensures the spatial continuity of the urban hall, the balcony and the roof terrace. The practice conceived the Forum "as an inseparable part of the urban public space that flows smoothly from the city" that forms the "culmination of a series of meaningful public spaces" in 'Groningen's close-knit system of squares, streets and alleyways." By means of a natural stone 'carpet', the architects allow the public space literally to continue within the building "via the covered square, over the monumental stairs to the city balcony, up through the open void into the domains" ending in a "panoramic view of the city and the Ommelanden [the environs]" on the roof. The building volume has a striking appearance but blends into the existing city due to its articulated character. The building becomes narrower towards the bottom, creating ample space at ground level and admitting sufficient light and air to the surrounding streets. The designers played with the modelling of the volume: the building also narrows towards the top, accentuating the city's four-storey skyline. In addition, "cuts, recesses and oriels" reduce the large-scale volume to an urban scale. To strengthen the connection between the Forum and the surroundings, the architects moved the entrance *underneath* the building and made the ground floor – except for the side aisles – as transparent as possible. The façade facing the square is designed as a large window on the city – making activities visible – which also serves as a projection screen.

Neutelings Riedijk's Forum is designed as a neutral structure that can be furnished, programmed and used in various ways. This basic spatial structure creates distinctive spaces in which opposing concepts such as "high-low, large-small, light-dark, horizontal-vertical, introverted-extroverted and intimate-generous" play a role. The programme is clearly divided over the two volumes with the domains and exhibition spaces in the front house and the cinemas, lecture halls, course rooms and offices in the back house. The front house has a classical design with three naves, in which a wide double-height central space is flanked by narrow two-storey naves with cabinets. The heart of the back house is formed by the double-height spaces of the cinemas and the auditorium, surrounded by the other functions. Logistics facilities and infrastructure are clustered in the side aisles along the void, while the vertical open space has transparent lifts with views of the entire building. In addition to the transparent parts of the urban hall, the balcony, the void and the window on the city, the outer façade has a "fine-mesh, open filigree structure" of sand-coloured ceramic elements that drapes like a veil around a fully glazed curtain wall. The façade refers to the tradition of openwork stone buildings but also forms a translucent screen that creates a "play of light and shadow on the outside and filters light on the inside."

The design and appearance of the building are carefully attuned to the environment, while the internal organisation allows for various zoning and routing patterns. The building is carefully considered, provides clear access to the various functions and offers a variety of programming options. There is room for a variety of different functions and spatial arrangements, especially in the large and small spaces of the front house, where the main rooms measure no less than 18 x 45 metres. This flexibility is enhanced by the fact that, in addition to the main access, these spaces connect to each other on the west side of the building. Neutelings Riedijk paid a good deal of attention to various usage scenarios for the building, an approach that was shared only by NL Architects. An impressive number of floor plans and photographs of models paints a convincing picture of the possibilities of the urban hall and the domains. However, the connection between the urban hall, the balcony, the domains and the other functions seems limited. There is sufficient potential on the floors themselves, but the spatial structure barely supports interaction between the functions and the domains. Instead of providing an open connection, crossed vertically by the lifts and from which there is a view of the programme, the void is an empty space around which the connections run. This does not give rise to spatial or strong visual connections. This omission also means that the cinema and news café are somewhat 'tucked away' on the flanks of the city balcony on the first floor, while the roof terrace is semi-submerged in a rising roof contour and offers visitors a view only to the west.

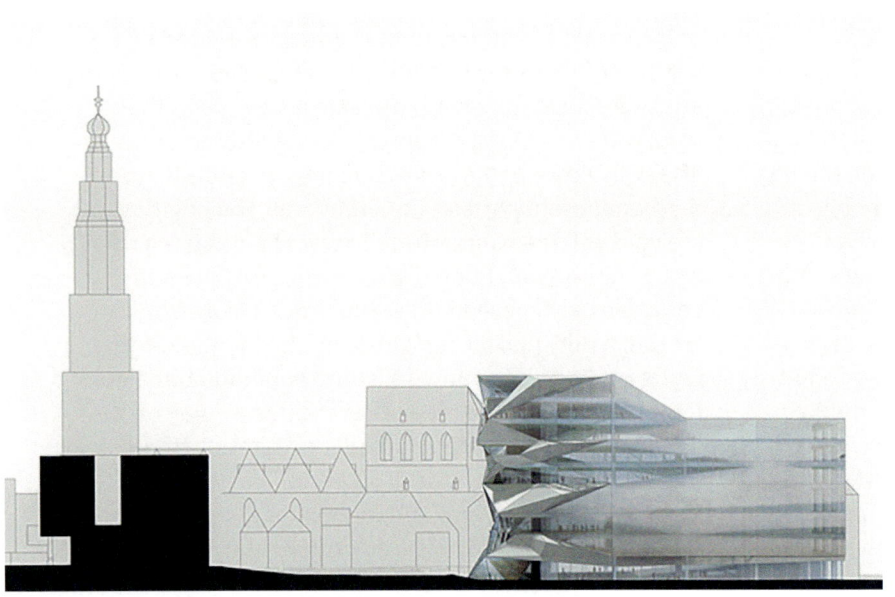

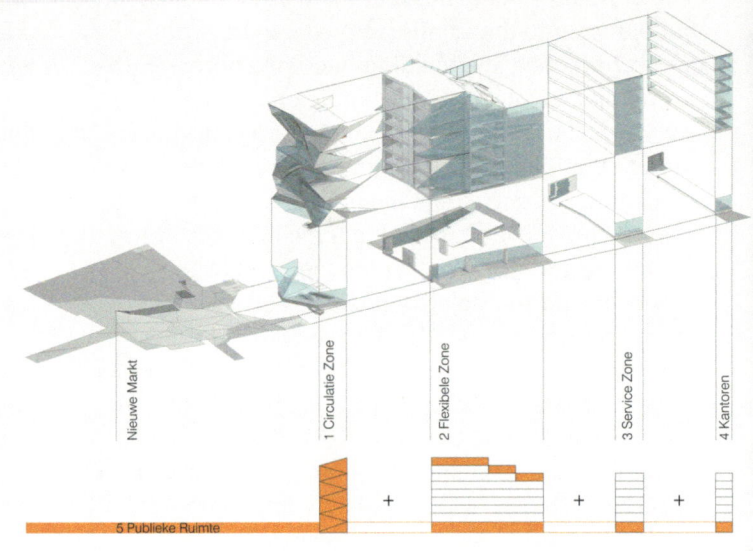

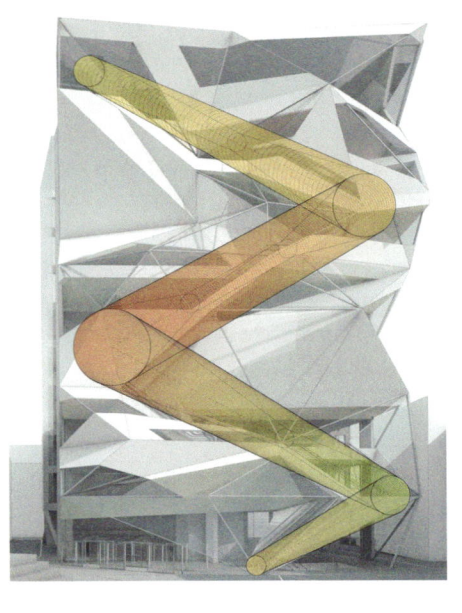

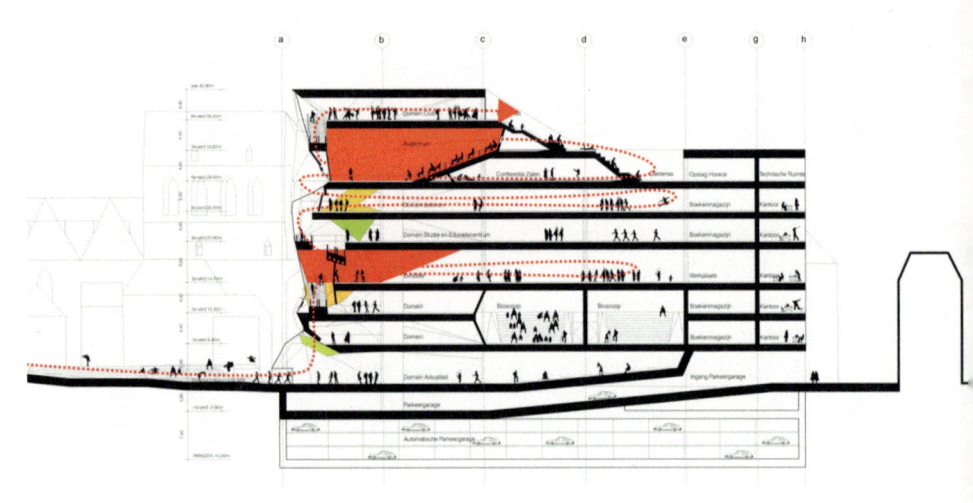

UN Studio's plan focuses entirely on the Nieuwe Markt with an expressive, fragmented, facetted glass façade. The design of the square follows the same line and seems to be its horizontal continuation. Immediately behind the largely transparent façade is a multiform void structure with escalators: the so-called "circulation zone." This circulation spectacle connects the surroundings with the domains and the main foyers: from the entrance to the cinema, the exhibition space, the auditorium and the sky lounge on the top floor. Although the ground floor has several entrances, is transparent in character and public in its programming – including the current affairs domain, the news café and a shop – only the emphasis on the west side of the building seems to ensure cohesion with the urban context. The building does not present itself clearly in all directions. On the west side it is slender and opens up, while towards Schoolstraat it is wide and reserved in appearance. The proportion of the volumes is in line with the surrounding buildings, but the differences in expression enhance the feeling of a building with a clear front and back, which does not promote accessibility.

In a certain sense, the building's main layout supports this distinction between front and back sides. Seen from the Nieuwe Markt, the plan is divided into four zones: the aforementioned circulation zone; a "flexible zone" for the domains, the cinemas, exhibition spaces and the auditorium; a "service zone" with storage, book stacks and workspace; and an "office zone" including technical areas. The deeper you venture into the building from the circulation zone, the less public it becomes. The façades provide a fairly literal expression of this distinction. Although the building has glass façades, it is not very open: on the sides and back, the first layers contain 'closed' functions that negate transparency. By contrast, to the west the building opens up to the maximum: UN Studio conceived the facetted circulation zone as an interactive, three-dimensional media screen. Blocks of elementary colours refer to different programmes on the floors, making it clear from the street what is happening in each part of the building. This 'Centre Pompidou effect' ensures maximum dynamism and exchange on the west side, although this 'signboard' also limits orientation and the view of the surroundings.

Although the organisational principle of zones seems to play tricks on the building, in a vertical sense the various functions are well distributed and mixed with the domains over the floors. The choice to place the cinemas, the exhibition space and the auditorium far apart guarantees the presence of the public throughout the building at different times. Striving to future-proof the building through a flexible structure, however, comes at the expense of a characteristic and specific layout that could have given shape to the interaction between the various parts. The architects could have better interwoven the ability to roam through the building – as concentrated and symbolised in the circulation zone – with the plan's basic flexible structure. The choice not to do so seems like a missed opportunity. Perhaps the most telling outcome of the distribution of the programme is that the terraces, created by the articulation of the volume of the middle section, are oriented to the east, and the building – at its peak – seems to turn away from the inner city.

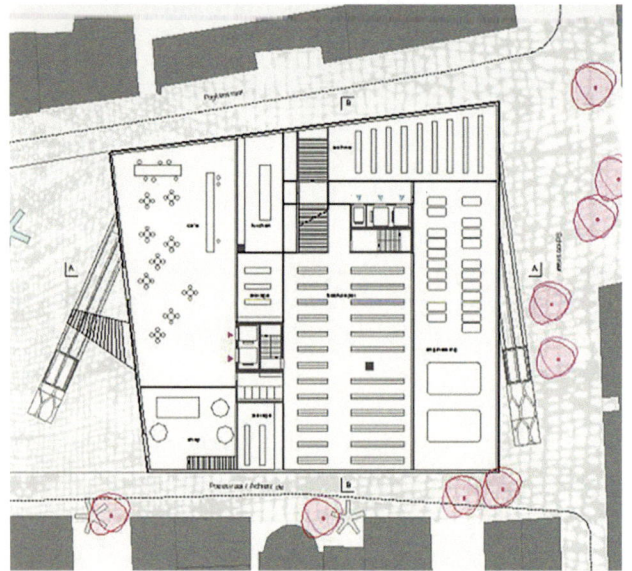

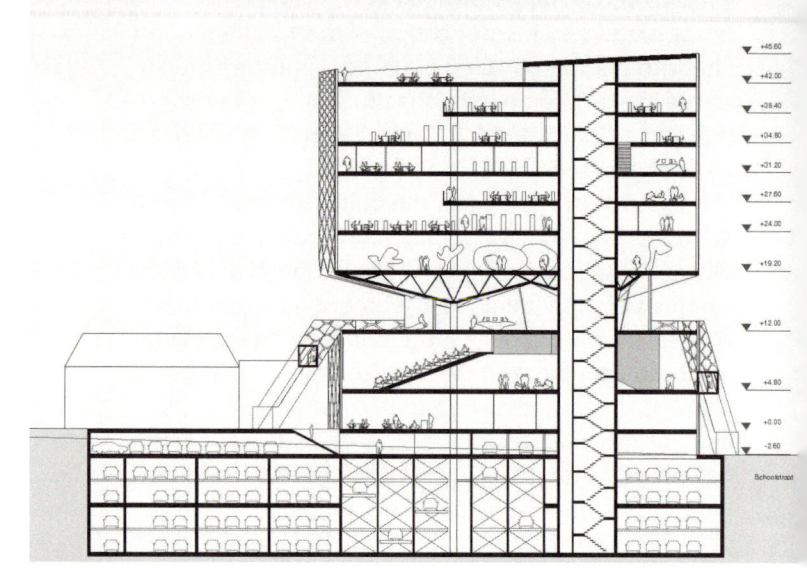

Wiel Arets chose to minimise the Forum's footprint so that the Nieuwe Markt could remain as spacious as possible and connect convincingly to the sequence of squares in Groningen's city centre. In this way he created space for extra quality: half of the square in his proposal is filled with trees, a reference to a forest. In addition to the principle of reducing the footprint, Arets made another radical choice: he placed the access to the building on the third floor, level with the roofs of the surrounding buildings. His Forum is divided into two volumes, slightly rotated in relation to each other, thus creating an "inverted silhouette." On the elevated level is a public space with a central foyer, from which the cultural and commercial activities can be reached. Its ceiling inverts the form of surrounding roof landscape.

In Arets's proposal, the accessibility of the Forum's functions and the way it relates to its surroundings therefore literally have a layered character. An escalator on the Nieuwe Markt and one on Schoolstraat establish the link between the raised ground level and the immediate surroundings. Although the access level is supported by entrances on the ground floor, there is only a limited direct relationship between the street level and the functions on the lower floors. This is partly due to the closed appearance of some parts of the programme: cinemas, auditorium, shop and café. The compact form allows for an intense but simple stacking of the programme. The top floors house the library, the domains, study areas, exhibition spaces, offices and restaurant. Because the building has load-bearing façades and is structurally supported at only four points, the floors here are virtually free of columns and can therefore be arranged flexibly. The floors are linked by a vertical route and the staggered voids are also intended to promote "social interaction." Arets's Forum is a compact volume, forty-five metres high, with an eye-shaped grid as the basic structure for the glass façade. The load-bearing transparent skin gives the building a distinctive appearance and projects the activities and atmospheres from within the building onto the city.

Arets called his Forum a "public palace," but some of his design's fundamental principles seem at odds with its public and accessible nature. Apart from the interesting access, the interaction between the Nieuwe Markt and the elevated ground level appears minimal and the difficult relationship between the functions on the lower floors and the surrounding urban fabric also produces little life around the building. Internally, the spatial exchange between the domains and the exhibitions feels limited. The access and the void structure of the floors function independently of each other and it is unclear how the domains benefit from the flexible basic structure in relation to the other functions. The compact layering and the elevated ground level may provide the building itself with interesting features but the question remains whether they contribute to the urban context: because of how one ascends the building, this Forum turns, in a sense, away from its surroundings.

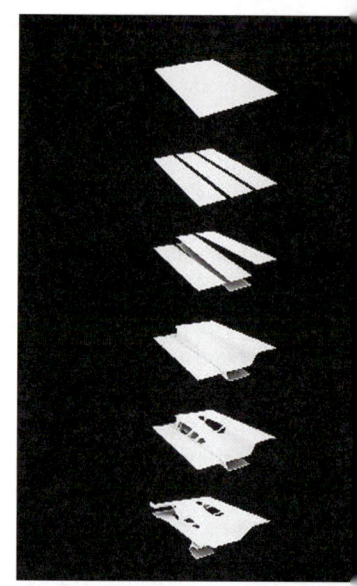

Zaha Hadid's Forum is perhaps the most far-reaching of all the designs, both in its organisation and appearance. The building is designed as a "graceful volume that floats above the roofscape" with sharply defined shapes and rounded curves. Hadid thus anticipated the innovative character inherent in the commission. By largely lifting it up on columns, the design extends the Nieuwe Markt beneath the building. The "square landscape is animated by a whole series of integrated programmes: the Groninger Forum shop, the news café, the entrance to the underground parking garage, the street furniture, the visually hidden bicycle storage and the loading bay. The ground floor of the Forum is literally an extension of the public space." Although the Forum shop and the news café are located directly on the extended square, the building is connected only laterally to its surroundings. The functions are 'raised' above ground level, accessible via escalators and lifts, but disconnected from the city's streetscape.

For the internal organisation, Hadid designed the domains as a slightly sloping continuous circuit, allowing them to be experienced as a single continuous space. They form a "continuous public connection between the new square below the building and the roof landscape above." For Hadid, the demand for versatility, flexibility and cross-fertilisation between the domains was best served by a continuous route, rather than several floors. She set up the circuit as a multi-storey roller coaster, made up of three parallel floor fields, the outer ones of which slope upwards or downwards. This sloping system generates spatial diversity: several single-height storeys in the central floor fields combine with double-height spaces on the sides. The different functions are organised vertically in such a way that combinations of programmes are possible at any level. In the open, flowing spaces, the domains must be flexibly arranged in relation to the exhibition spaces, cinemas, study spaces and the auditorium and give rise to exchange. Depending on the need for peace and quiet, or dynamics and interaction, functions are respectively situated further away or closer to the 'rollercoaster'. Hadid placed the closed functions mainly on the south and east sides of the building and the publicly accessible ones mainly on the north and west sides.

The façade reinforces the distinction between the open and closed functions. The west and north sides are largely glazed, which reinforces the visual relationship between the programmes and the environment. The south and east sides have minimal apertures and are therefore less transparent. The building thus opens up to the Nieuwe Markt and the Martinikerkhof but has its 'back' to Schoolstraat and Poelestraat. The building's curvilinear flowing façades symbolise the "fusion of programmes, which leads to continuous activity and encounters." Several design principles have been implemented so radically that they appear to give rise to a building of extremes. The ground floor does not function as an extension of the public space: it becomes the public space. But this lacks a convincing connection between the building, its functions and its surroundings. The fusion of the programme components is so substantial that the building and the route through it have themselves become a flowing mix. The question remains whether this would have benefited the functionality. As the designers themselves put it: "We offer not division and hard boundaries, but transparency and continuity." If everything is flowing, will specific and meaningful places still arise?

Route Versus Place

Comparing the unrealised plans and examining them critically, we notice, in addition to a large number of differences, the extent to which certain design principles and suggestions recur in the six designs. This says something about the thorough way in which the competition was prepared. One can discern a clear difference in how the various architects sought to connect the building to its surroundings. In the plans by Van Egeraat and Neutelings Riedijk, the lower levels are emphatically oriented towards the square and the surrounding urban structure, while those by Foreign Office, Arets and Hadid function more as internally oriented 'islands'. UN Studio's design is somewhere in between, but again shows parallels in its massing with those of Van Egeraat, Foreign Office and Neutelings Riedijk. Like NL Architects, Arets and Hadid opted for an unambiguous volume, without variation in height or a clear distinction between different building volumes. NL Architects' Forum sits perhaps precisely at the centre of the sliding scale between a homogeneous and a composite volume. Because of the cut corners the building volume does indeed vary in height, albeit to a smooth extent.

NL Architects' plan also appears to sit at the centre of the other designs in terms of its internal organisation. It is as if it convincingly concentrates all the spatial principles arising from the brief, which the other plans also contain to a greater or lesser extent. In short, the essence of the brief lay in the way in which a striking relationship was created between an accessible, challenging route along the programme, a series of open, transparent and flexible spaces for the desired overlapping of functions, and a sequence of intimate, recognisable places. We see the basic spatial principles as they emerged from the brief and the urban development conditions in a variety of compositions and connections. The split-level, the spiral route and atrium, for example, are reflected in the plans of Van Egeraat and Foreign Office, where the former presents a spiral staircase upgraded to an atrium as an excellent route at the heart of the building somewhat detached from the programme, while the second presents the building itself as a route through the use of split-levels. Although, at first sight, these two plans may seem at opposite ends of the spectrum, in both cases the chosen organisational means primarily represents an *accessibility principle*. The relationship with the functions on the floors is minimal. In Hadid's plan, in which the building has also become the route, this interweaving between route and floors has been taken to the extreme – so much so that space and access seem to merge completely.

The route is also explicitly presented as a spectacle in UN Studio's plan but has been completely separated from the programme. The circulation zone serves as a link between the building and the city. Simultaneously, the division of the domains and the specific position of the closed functions such as the exhibition spaces, the auditorium and the cinemas appear to promote a good route through the building – as is, in fact, also the case with the realised plan by NL Architects. This seems to be much less the case with the plans by Foreign Office, Neutelings Riedijk and Arets, although this principle is most symbolically implemented in the latter plan in which, in order to reach the various functions, visitors are first raised to the level of the surrounding roof landscape at the heart of the building.

The fusion of route, functions and domains has been implemented most extensively in Hadid's plan. The ingenuity of this design is that the functions are organised vertically in such a way that they allow a multitude of points of contact and cross-fertilisation. Nonetheless, it is striking that, despite the various plans' differences, when it comes to access and route, comparable spatial structures arise. Neutelings Riedijk's plan is classical in design and route, with the lifts at the heart of the building as the main movement. Hadid's, on the other hand, is a succession of sloping 'figure of eights', in which the distinction between horizontal and vertical movement has essentially been removed. The double-height spaces that arise along the single floors of Hadid's rollercoaster route are reminiscent of the domains in Neutelings Riedijk's front house, which are flanked by the narrow aisles with two layers of cabinets. The practice convincingly demonstrated the added value of this through endless scenarios. They make us curious about the possibilities of this spatial structure in Hadid's plan, which, despite the versatility of the design, gave hardly any insight into the potential of the space.

In terms of spatial and functional requirements, the plans by NL Architects and Hadid undoubtedly exhibit the greatest similarities, apart from their fundamental differences in appearance and their diametrically opposed relationship with the urban context. The plans by Arets,

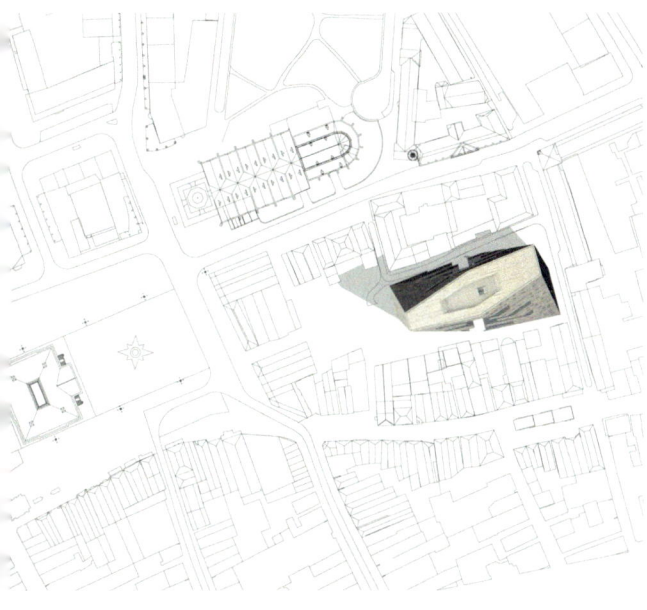

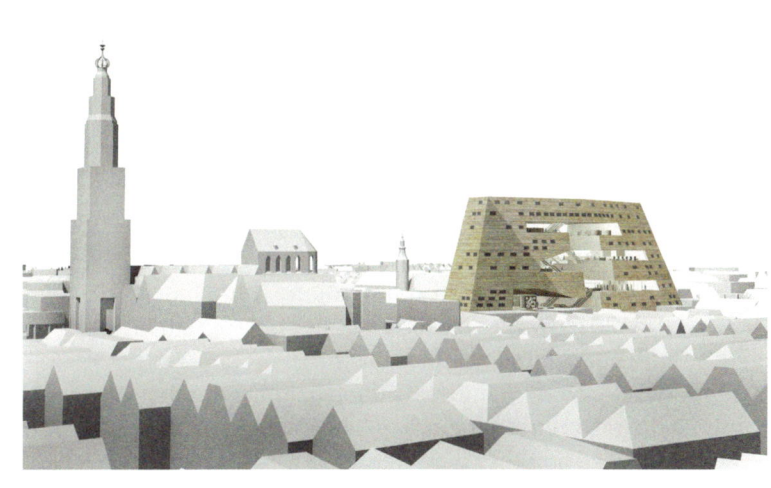

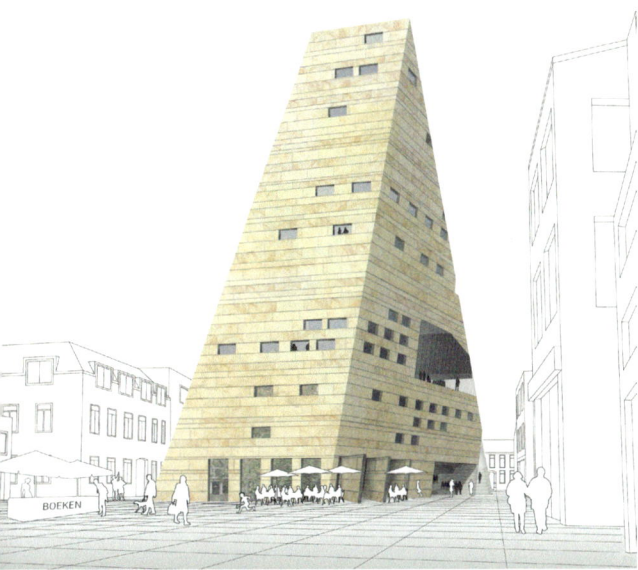

Foreign Office and UN Studio present fairly conventional spatial ideas when it comes to the composition of routes, domains and places, although they have distinctive features in parts. Van Egeraat and Neutelings Riedijk introduced several spatial and architectural principles that ensure very specific and handsome buildings: in both plans, the central role of the atrium is particularly striking, which can be considered as a simplified variant of NL Architects' 'keyhole'. Even so, in these plans the interweaving of route, domains and places remains limited, certainly when compared to the designs of Hadid and NL Architects. In both these designs, everything is done spatially and organisationally to fuse access, movement, overlapping and experience into a convincing whole.

What mainly sets the two apart is a distinct difference in approach. Hadid seems to follow an almost postmodern concept, in which the desired fluid coherence of route, domains and functions apparently results in fluid forms. In NL Architects' plan, the principles of split-level, atrium, spiral route, domains and places are convincingly intertwined without losing their spatial characteristics and quality as a whole – on the contrary, they are arranged in such a way that they reinforce each other. What in NL Architects' scheme has become the keyhole – the system of squares connected by escalators that criss-cross the atrium – Hadid conceived of as a flowing, double loop with very modest voids. This design concept has been implemented so hermetically that the continuity of the route not only provides connection and interaction, but also limits the overview and the mutual coherence between functions. The two plans' routing is essentially not that different, but the experience of that route and the relationship with the squares and functions – the 'architectural promenade' – differ considerably.

Having studied all the non-winning entries, the design by NL Architects emerges as the only one that in no way compromises the requirements and desired spatial principles set out in the competition brief. Foreign Office's split-level, UN Studio's circulation zone, Neutelings Riedijk's flowing urban hall and balcony room, Van Egeraat's amazing atrium space, Hadid's spatial interweaving of route, squares and places, Arets's homogeneous distinctive volume: all are contained in the winning plan. In the completed Forum, the promenade is spatially and visually linked to the atrium and the squares but organised in such a way that flowing routes are created through the domains. Because various functions are also provided internally with a special staircase, the diverse use of what NL Architects calls the "Hoge Markt" (High Market) is guaranteed. As was the programmatic intention, the winning design ultimately brought together the most striking spatial principles in a single scheme.

3   *Promenade architecturale* is a term coined by the Swiss-French architect Le Corbusier (1887-1965), meaning a processional route through a built space.

Lighting is an essential part of the spatial experience. Is it possible to create a 'homely' atmosphere in a public building? Model maker Made By Mistake provided the competition model with festive variable lighting. In the completed Forum, every light fixture has its own IP address, which enables each LED lamp to be controlled individually. The basic lighting colour is tunable white, which means that the colour temperature and intensity of the lamps can be easily adjusted. Pre-sets make it possible to create light conditions for specific occasions. With additional light sources such as spots and screens, light technicians can add colour and create accents.

Design

Ronald Hooft

Anyone in the Netherlands or Flanders with a typing diploma and an abusive mother or father – or both, those are the really lucky ones – has a chance of winning a tidy half a million euros in prize money every year as a novelist. And if you can speed-type 120 words per minute, you can publish a book every two years, greatly increasing your chances. And if you're down on your luck and the prizes keep passing you by, then regular talk-show appearances might eventually land you a lucrative TV contract.

Things are a little different in the field of architecture, where around ten thousand qualified architects battle it out annually for a single engraved Plexiglas plaque: the trophy that goes with the Building of the Year award. Nowadays most books, even the really good ones, are offloaded in the bargain shops within three years, whereas even the most hideous buildings remain in the public realm for half a century. Well, I guess there are pros and cons to both professions.

At the end of 2019, the Forum Groningen, designed by NL Architects, was completed on the site of a run-down parking garage that had been used by successive generations of students as a public latrine. The following year, the building was rightly awarded the aforementioned architecture prize. The majority of Groningen's residents who voted for NL Architects' design over the plans of a group of internationally acclaimed architects did so – on the basis of a shiny wooden model – on the assumption that a wooden building would be constructed in the heart of the city.

The completed building is clad with sand-coloured natural stone panels and will be around for much longer than fifty years. In all that time, an enormous number of books – whether or not crowned with generous prizes – will be lent out by the library housed in the Forum. But no one can take away that thick slab of Perspex on NL Architects' mantlepiece.

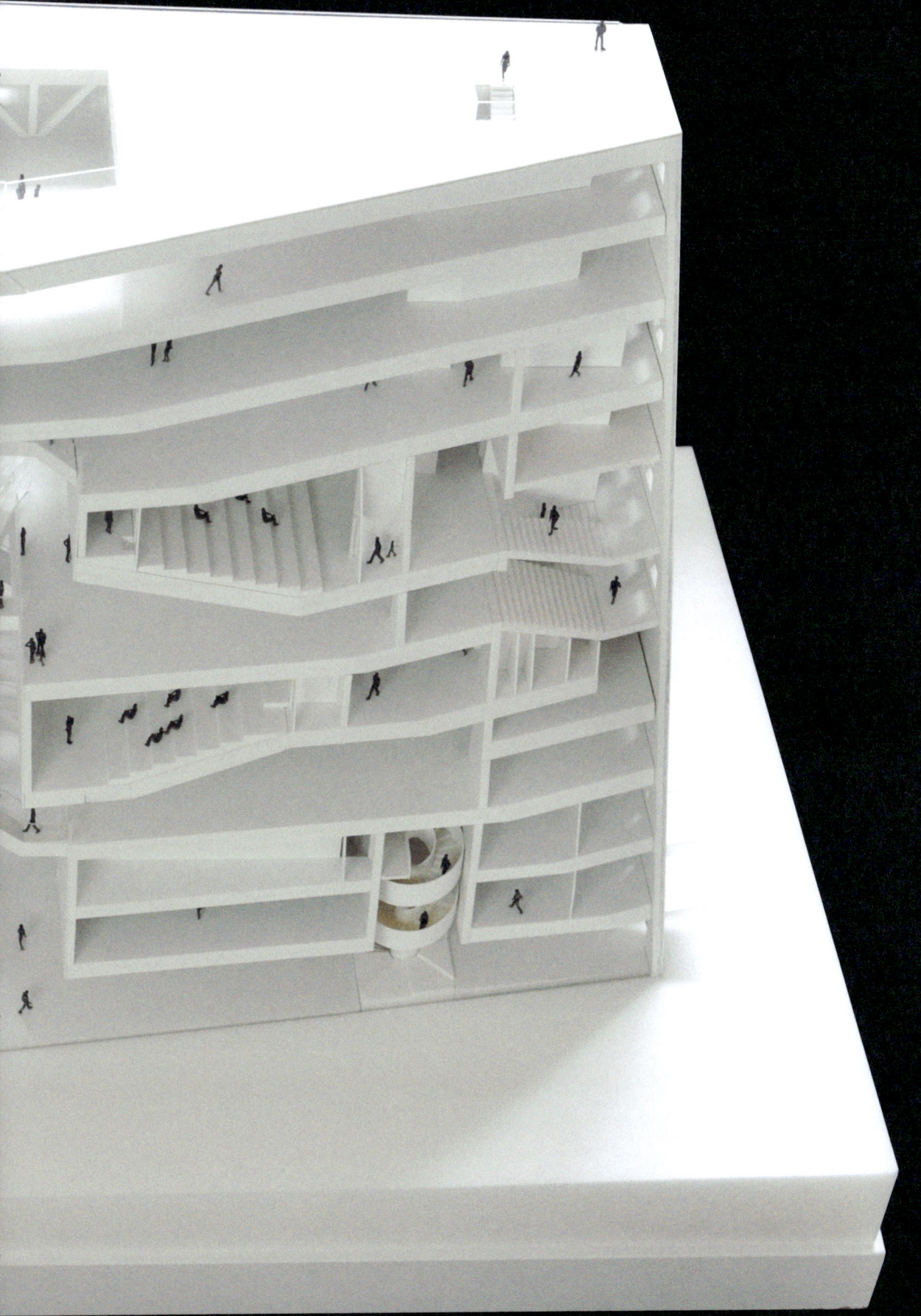

Anneke Bokern

A Gentle Giant in the Shade

Anneke Bokern spoke with Kamiel Klaasse and Pieter Bannenberg of NL Architects about the motivations underlying the design of Forum Groningen. What models did they work on for the competition, how did they develop them and what factors were decisive in the choice of the 'keyhole model'?

Your design for Forum came out of an international competition. What were the requirements for the scale and shape of the building? Is it true that you were not allowed to exceed the height of St Martin's Tower?

Kamiel Klaasse, laughs — "The starting point was an urban planning vision from 2003 for the east side of the Grote Markt by Neutelings Riedijk Architects. One of the definitive planning principles for Forum was variation in height, represented by a volume comprising a lower and a higher part, resulting in a composite contour, a kind of cathedral with a nave and a tower with a height limit of forty-five metres. This height difference may have been appropriate from an urban planning perspective, but we didn't think it worked in terms of the building's brief. We thought it was very important that the building should form a cohesive unit, to make it clear that Forum is a single institution and not a collection of cultural enterprises."

Pieter Bannenberg— "What the municipality proposed was almost a church typology. We didn't think that fitted the brief at all. We apparently felt at that time that the organisations still needed to come together and that it was therefore important not to introduce a hierarchy. The big challenge was to realise the entire building within the permitted height of forty-five metres, while meeting the requirement that it should remain below thirty-three metres on average."

Kamiel— "And there was another aspect. For us, the roof terrace was the greatest benefit of levelling the height of the volumes because it enabled us to create a public square in the sky: a kind of mountain plateau with clear views of the city."

So, it was clear that it had to be a single volume. How did you proceed? Did you then hollow out the block like sculptors or did you start designing from the inside out?

Pieter— "We started from the inside out, with the brief. During the first analysis it was immediately obvious that we could make a clear distinction between the open and closed spaces. This could create a kind of yin-yang of extravert, transparent spaces and introvert spaces with less need for daylight, such as the cinemas and museum galleries. This coincided neatly with the distinction between the freely accessible zones and the areas for which an admission ticket is required. Many of the spaces, mostly the closed functions, were typologically familiar territory and we could simply look up the dimensions and characteristics in Neufert's *Architects Data*, the design guideline for architects. What gradient should the floor of a cinema have? What is the ideal height, width and depth? There is an enormous historical arsenal of norms and regulations for this type of space that we can draw from. The same applies to museum galleries and auditoriums. The biggest puzzle was posed by the unfamiliar types of space, the so-called 'domains': the spaces where the exchange between the various functions in the building was supposed to take place. These were completely new. Which typology do they correspond to and what kind of spatial experience?"

Kamiel— "The brief was very adventurous. In Forum, the idea was that the conventional boundaries between museum, cinema and library should disappear. There had to be much more interaction between the disciplines. Conceiving an interface for this was the main challenge. It was totally unknown terrain and a crucial part of the brief. In the end, we designed the closed parts of the building so that they are the 'bearers' of the public spaces: a mutual embrace."

A Gentle Giant in the Shade

Still from a video by the Club House for the Deaf showing the sign for the Forum.

You have described the building's internal layout as an 'atrium with tentacles'. What exactly are those tentacles? The escalators, the squares or the spaces connected to the atrium?

Kamiel— "There's an online video about Forum with sign language for the deaf that proposes a brilliant sign for the building: two hands with spread fingers, which literally depicts the floors and the emptiness in between. It makes you wonder: is it about the fingers or about the space between them? The tentacles are Forum's architectural 'invention'. Normally an atrium is a vertical void in a building, but here it has horizontal branches. Together the two form a system, creating a continuous public space: a stack of connected squares."

What surprised me upon entering was that the atrium is so vertical. In photos it looks much wider, but in reality it really draws you upwards. It's a kind of vertical living room.

Kamiel— "In general, it's not so easy to entice the public to go from the ground level to higher floors, but in Forum the 'capillary action' of the atrium is very effective. We have deliberately tried to match the typology of the living room. You can see Forum as a supersized split-level house. You only have to go up half a floor to get to the next level, so there's a smooth transition between the floors. The experience of verticality becomes even more interesting when coupled with horizontality, and split-levels also always create diagonal sightlines. Our goal is to spread the visitors as much as possible over the building. I like to compare it to Super Mario: you jump from level to level. This setup makes it possible to explore the entire building, every corner of which becomes accessible."

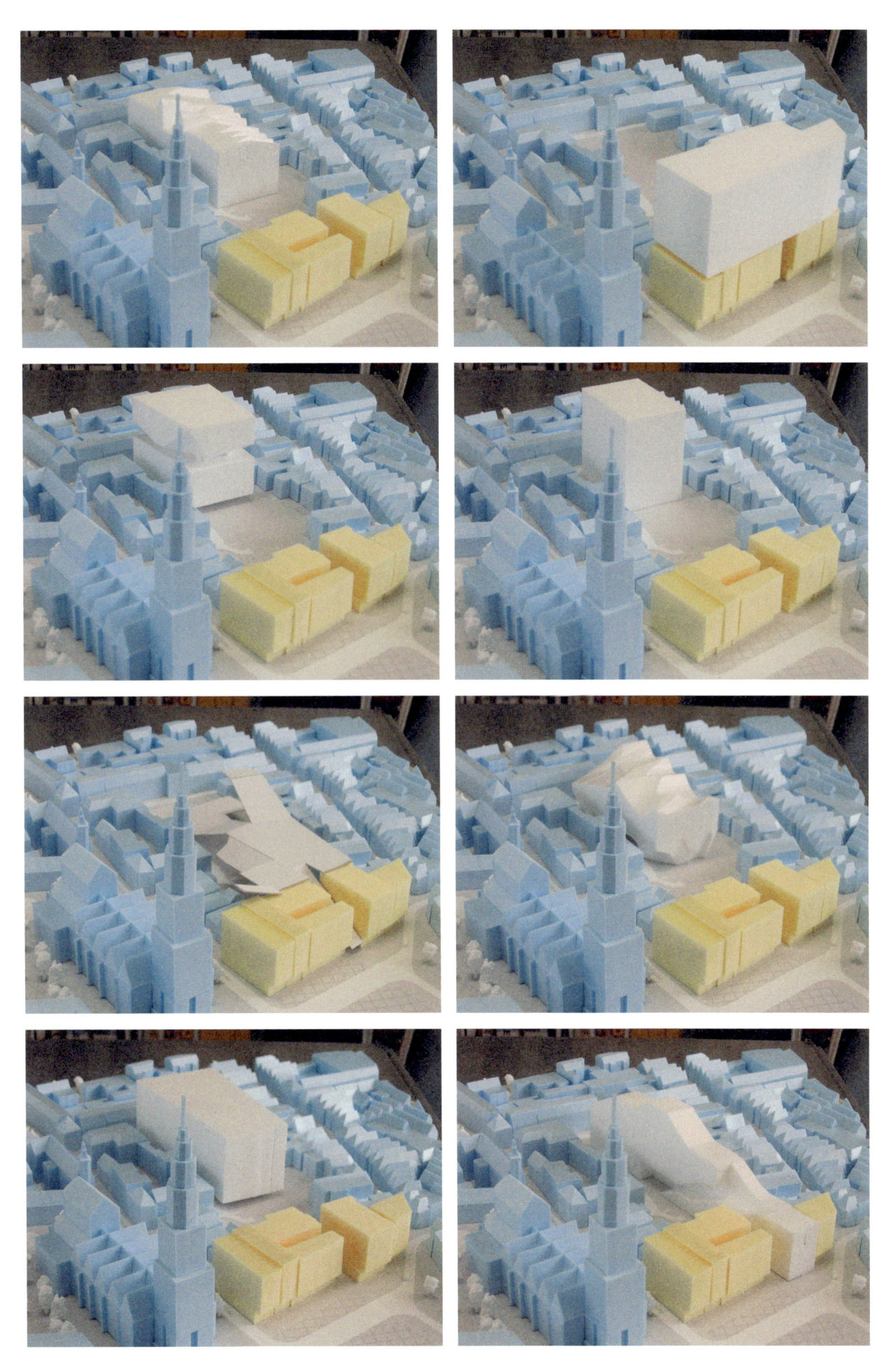

A Gentle Giant in the Shade

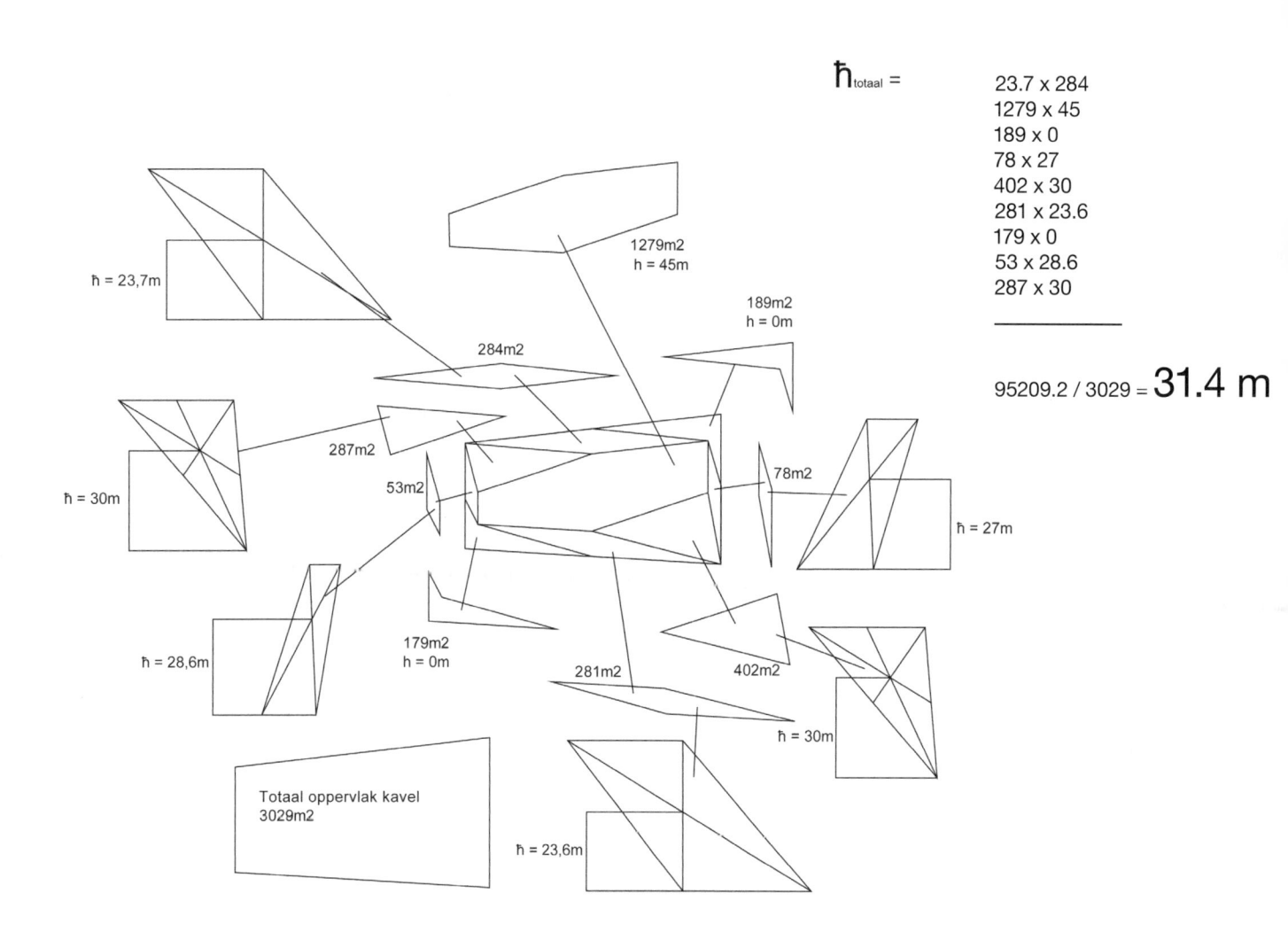

$\hbar_{totaal} =$

23.7 x 284
1279 x 45
189 x 0
78 x 27
402 x 30
281 x 23.6
179 x 0
53 x 28.6
287 x 30

———————

95209.2 / 3029 = **31.4 m**

$\hbar = 23{,}7m$

1279m2
h = 45m

189m2
h = 0m

284m2

287m2

53m2

78m2

$\hbar = 30m$

$\hbar = 27m$

$\hbar = 28{,}6m$

179m2
h = 0m

281m2

402m2

$\hbar = 30m$

Totaal oppervlak kavel
3029m2

$\hbar = 23{,}6m$

How do you calculate the average height of a tapering and slanted building? When asked whether their design was a maximum of 45 metres high, with an average height of 33 metres, NL Architects presented a careful calculation that clearly shows that, on average, the building does not exceed 32 metres.

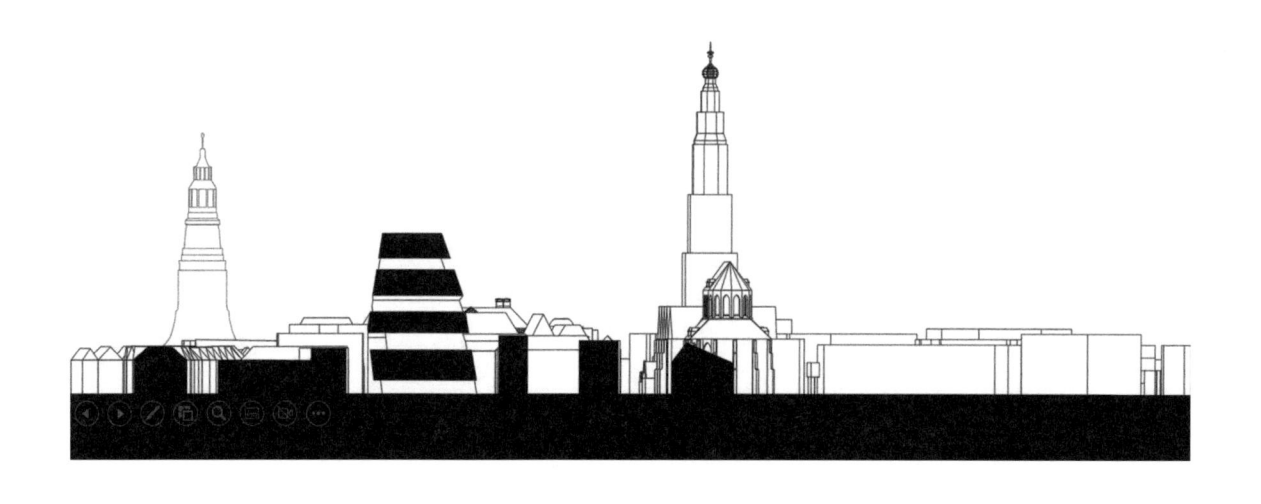

The most unusual thing about the building's structure is that all the closed functions are at the edges and the public areas form the heart of the building. When did this idea emerge?

Kamiel— "In the beginning, we also had models that worked the other way around. But in the end, we found it most obvious to hollow out the thickest and largest part of our massive lump and put the atrium there. The focus on the building's public life creates a sense of collectiveness. In this way, public life permeates all the pores of the building. That's a great quality."

Pieter— "I really find it a breath of fresh air to move through the atrium. The interior architects who designed the squares also wondered whether the walls in the atrium should be clad. They found it bare, too empty. But I find it a very pleasant experience moving through the space on the escalators. The neutrality of the vertical space with the escalators makes you more aware of your surroundings, both inside the building and outside."

This spatial structure has different consequences for the urban context. If you push all the closed spaces against the façade, you get a very closed building.

Pieter— "Only at the ends."

Indeed, because you created the big keyhole in the side walls. How did the keyhole and the tapered façades come about?

Kamiel— "The keyhole is the outcome of the interlocking open and closed functional clusters. At the beginning of the design process, we looked at various options. One of the models was more like a tree, the opposite of the current building. That was a promising scheme but at a certain point we turned it inside out and found that that worked even better. We then went through several iterations to determine the final volume. We began with the specific shape of the site and extruded it to the maximum height. Then it turned out that we had far too much space, so we decided to taper the volume."

So the tapered form was simply the result of having too much space?

Pieter— "Yes, a surplus of volume that we had created ourselves. We reduced the rather large footprint at the bottom to a smaller shape at the top. Of course, we hoped that the inclined planes would make the building less massive. That hypothesis proved to work well in practice. It provides a huge perspectival foreshortening if you stand close to the building that makes the building appear surprisingly modest, like a gentle giant."

Kamiel— "The basic idea was for the volume to be tapered, but after that we made some more cuts to mark the entrances and to make the silhouette more slender. The 'cutting away' of the volume was literally a sculptural intervention, just like with a knife in clay. The exciting thing about that cutting away is that the atrium, an extrusion that is in principle oriented north-south, opens up to the east and the west. Suddenly, from the interior, you can also see another part of the city. Another pleasant by-product of this 'liposuction' is unexpected views through the building."

Talking of liposuction: is it true that one day during lunch you spontaneously sculpted Forum from a block of butter on a butter dish?

Kamiel— "In fact, since the competition, every piece of butter on our table has changed into a variant of Forum. Endless permutations, very contemplative, but that was not part of the form finding process."

Let's go back to the shape of the building. The other competition entries had much more clearly defined fronts and backs than your design. They followed more of a classical theatre or museum design, with a prominent main entrance and a closed volume behind it. Why did you decide to place the entrances In the two side streets?

Pieter— "We did that very consciously, even if some people were not immediately convinced by it. It was also a way of activating these narrow streets. At one point, the city's planner wondered whether the entrance would be visible from the new street leading from the Grote Markt. But I was sure it would work. Because of the orientation of the sun, the main entrance receives sunlight almost all day long. And because of the cutaway, the light falls on the small triangular plaza in front of it, which creates a visible accent, a natural highlight."

Kamiel— "A very attractive consequence of the cutaway is that the two streets next to the building are truncated and quickly open up to create a wider space."

Pieter— "The cutaway produces two extra small squares, like public urban antechambers."

I also think that the sloping façades are very important for the streets themselves. The building withdraws, as it were, and is not overpowering.

Kamiel— "Yes, and sometimes it suddenly offers a view of St Martin's Tower. Just as you cannot see Forum itself from some perspectives in the city, so the tower sometimes disappears and then suddenly reappears."

Were you aware of that during the design process?

Pieter— "I certainly wasn't. The finished building offers an even greater variety of views and surprising perspectives than I had experienced with our 3D modelling."

Kamiel— "Models don't lend themselves well to that because the eye level is missing. Fortunately, it's getting easier to simulate that in the virtual world."

Maybe that's also why I don't think aerial photos do the building justice. It appears much more colossal than from the pedestrian's perspective.

Kamiel— "Yes, because of its position behind the east wall of the Grote Markt, the building is in the second row, in the shade. Some people even have trouble finding it. In other places, further from the building, it towers over the city. But that's true only of the long sightlines of the market from the surrounding area, just as the tower and Church of St Martin rise high above the city."

The Forum had to fit in with its surroundings as much as possible in terms of materials and appearance. NL Architects therefore always made the models of the building in the colour and often also in the material of the blocks that represented the buildings in the area – in this case the Blue Foam that is typically used for design studies. Although it's an excellent material for making models, it is fragile and lacks refinement when it comes to details. Model maker Made By Mistake made a more detailed model for the Forum using a baby blue synthetic resin that blends into the rest of the model while also standing out.

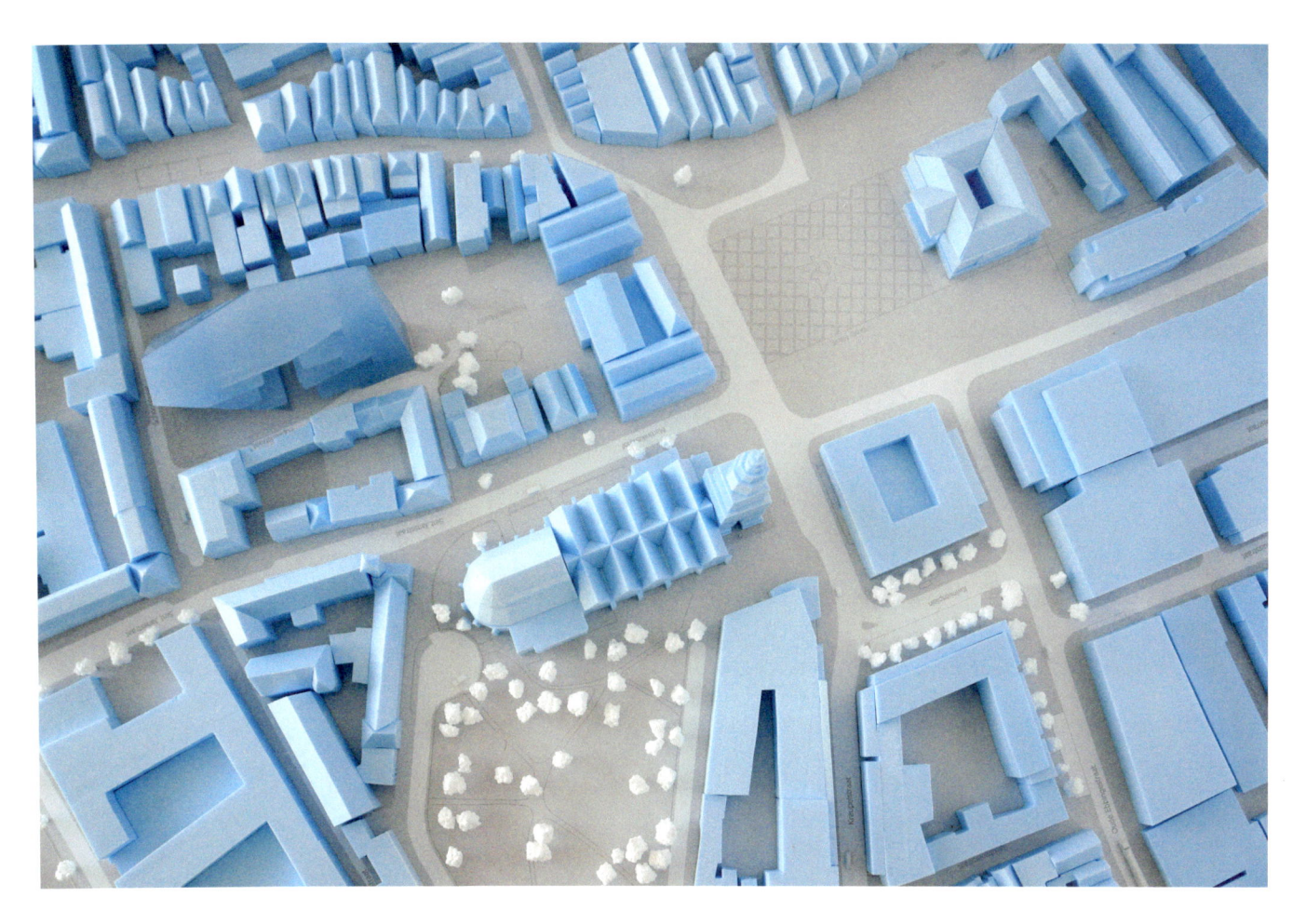

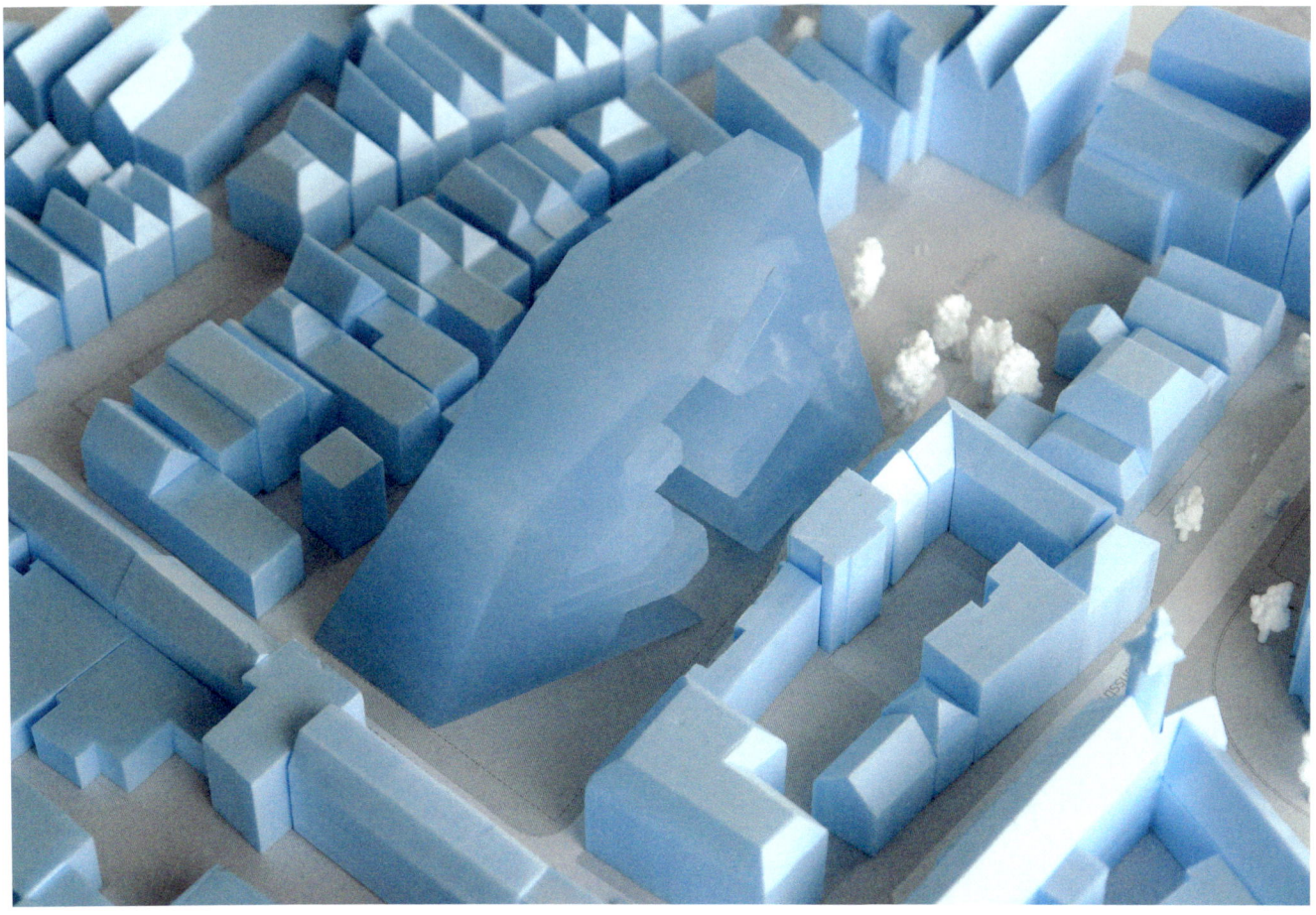

A Gentle Giant in the Shade

Design

In the competition, all the architects opted for different materials for the façades, from Delft blue tiles to glass. You ended up using Wachenzeller dolomite, a beige natural stone. Why did you make this choice?

Pieter— "In our competition design we referred to the Bentheimer sandstone of St Martin's Tower. We eventually chosen a stone that is very similar in colour and character."

Why didn't you choose sandstone?

Pieter— "That was certainly our intention, but we later discovered it's no longer allowed because it produces too many fine particles during processing. It's like a kind of natural asbestos, so we went in search of an alternative."

Kamiel— "There was a misunderstanding during the competition. Each team of architects had been given the same basic wooden model of the site and its surroundings into which their own design could be fitted. Since we wanted to connect to the context, to the town hall and the church, we also made the scale model of our Forum from wood. Some members of the public jury took this literally and were enthusiastic about the warm, natural appearance of our design. This probably got us some extra votes."

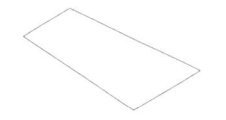

Grain

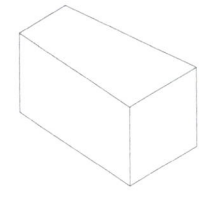

Maximum building envelope

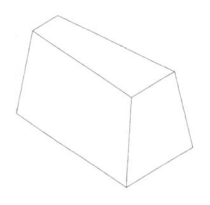

Revision to make it less massive

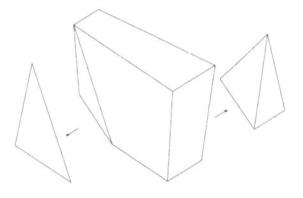

Cuts for entrances

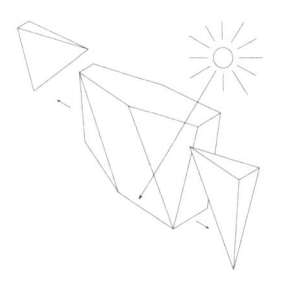

Slenderer silhouette

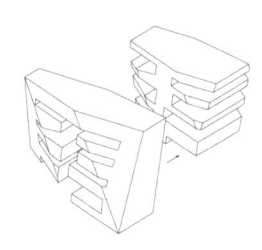

Removal of building volume for atrium

After you won the competition, it took almost thirteen years for Forum to be completed. Did the design change a lot in that time? Halfway through the process, there were new regulations for earthquake resistance, but you were able to absorb them almost invisibly. Were there any visible changes?

Kamiel— "Not many. In essence, the design remained the same."

Pieter— "There were a few changes to do with the location of specific functions. The offices were initially sited behind the natural stone façade, out of public view. When Storyworld was added to the brief, the office floor turned out to be the ideal location for it, so we moved the offices to the squares. Forum's organisation is now a visible part of the public spaces. But the building's concept and form almost completely match the competition entry."

Forum is often referred to as an icon because of its size and sculptural form. But architectural icons are rarely found on such a cramped site. They are usually highly visible as solitary entities on a silver tray. Do you see the building as an icon?

Kamiel— "Icons always have a lot to do with showing off. We prefer to see Forum as a logo, because a good logo says a lot about the content. It might seem a little strange after everything we've said, but I don't really find it that interesting what the building looks like. Due to its intelligent urban placement, in the hinterland behind the east wall, the appearance isn't an issue. That's a relief, a kind of liberation orchestrated by the municipality. I'm most pleased with how the building works. As soon as you enter, something happens. It's as if the building welcomes you and embraces you."

Atrium

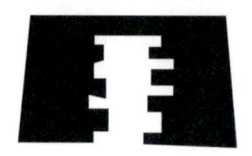

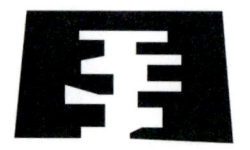

Keyhole

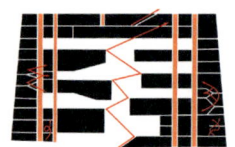

Route

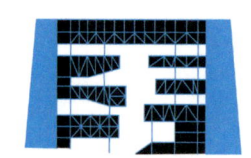

Construction

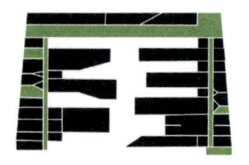

Installations

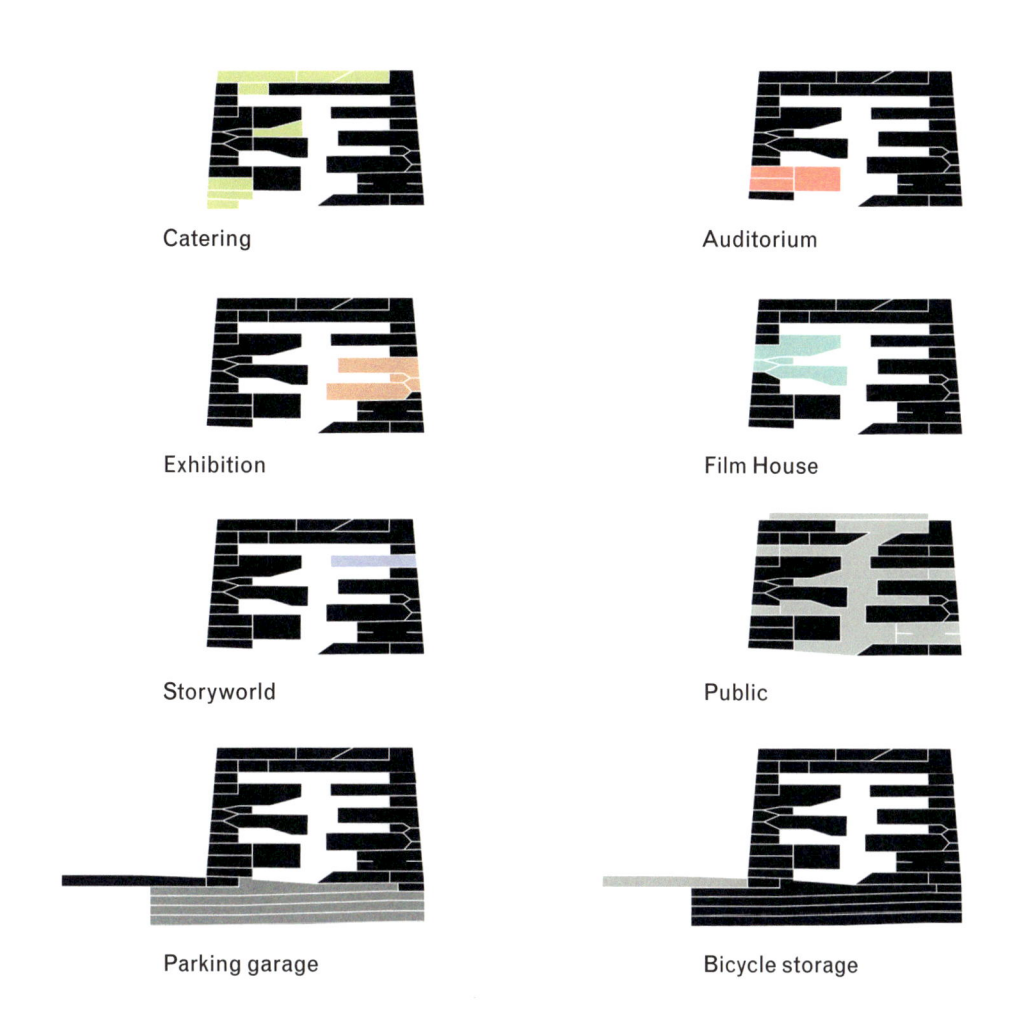

Catering

Auditorium

Exhibition

Film House

Storyworld

Public

Parking garage

Bicycle storage

Restaurant

Kitchen

Study area

Non-fiction

Film House

Film + Music

Fiction

Crime

Auditorium

Café

Entrance hall

Roof terrace

Roof patio

Installations

Offices

Storyworld

Smart Lab

Study area

Exhibition

Forum shop

Wonderland

News

Groningen Store

Logistics

Bicycle storage

Parking garage

A Gentle Giant in the Shade

West

Southwest

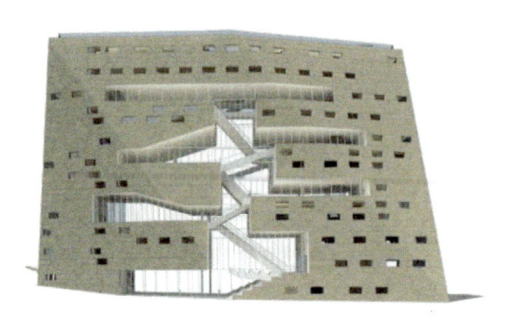

South

Southeast

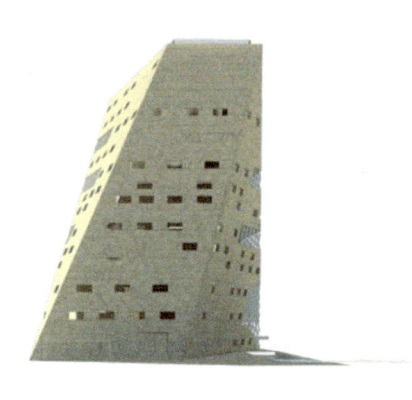

East

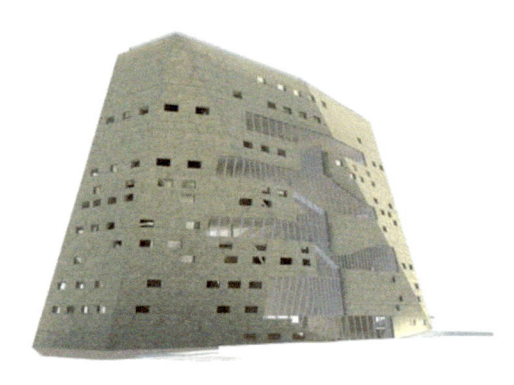

Northeast

North

Northwest

Joseph G. Gardella

The Design Explained and Illustrated

Forum[1] tells a story about a contemporary search for hybridity by nestling itself between the architectural and urban domains. It clothes and feeds itself from both worlds, but it resists its adherence to them: it merges both worlds, but seeks to become its own typology. This contradictory effect can be traced back to its name: Forum is a building that wants to be a public square.[2] Whereas the building's interior is organised as a non-hierarchical urban network, the exterior tells a story about the power of an autonomous object that can effortlessly detach itself from time and space. By finding meaning in the collision of stereotypes, Forum offers a new outlook on reality. Therefore, it is through its contradictions that its narrative will be told.

1 The term 'Forum' represents both a physical property (Forum Groningen) and a mental property (an abstract concept that goes beyond the building domain).

2 A forum was a marketplace or public square in a Roman city and is today a place where people gather to exchange ideas.

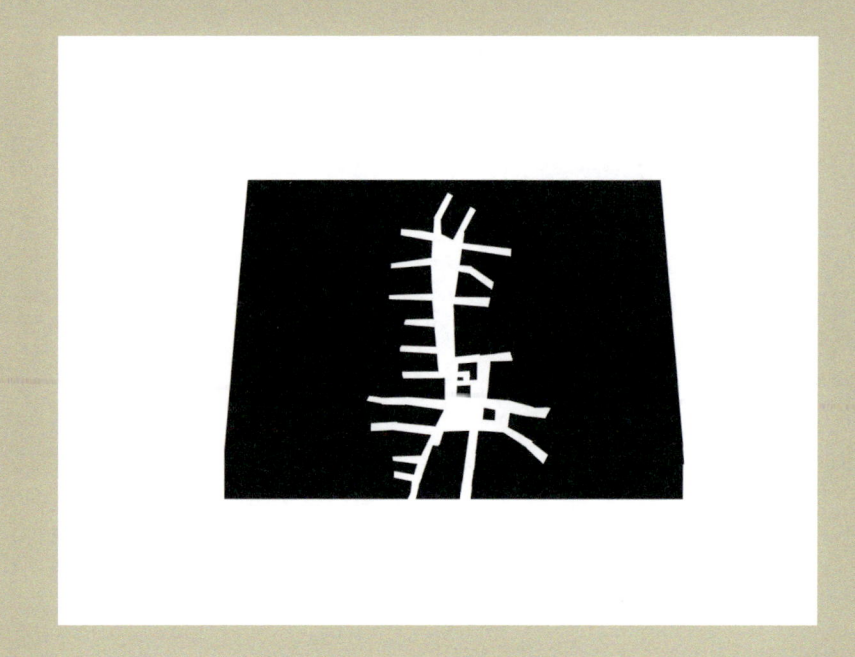

Between City and Building

In a typological sense, Forum embraces a totality of public functions that would normally be spread out over the cityscape. In doing so, it aims to create an environment in which the totality of urban public life can be embraced. Whereas a less dense environment would usually result in the need to search for a particular event, by contrast a hyperdense environment offers a wide range of potential activities and therefore allows visitors to adapt the activity to their mood. Likewise, Forum offers a highly concentrated grouping of functions in which visitors can immerse themselves. The complex comprises a library, a museum, an auditorium, cinemas, offices, study spaces and multiple cafés and is like an urban network organised around a central public space, in this case an atrium. All the functions are vertically aligned along this atrium and can be reached via a series of stacked squares.

By compressing such a wide range of urban functions within the domain of architecture, Forum brings the conventional hierarchy between city and building into question. Since the city usually determines how each building operates within the whole, architecture automatically becomes subjected to this greater mechanism of interrelations: systems which we call 'cities'. Since Forum reverses these natures, the building now becomes the authoritative domain that conditions and systemises an internalised urban network. The diagrams reveal how Forum's inherent structure emanates from the fundamental idea to reverse the order between city and building, resulting in a strictly delineated mass that envelops an empty space. Considering that cities reshape themselves over time and spread their footprint infinitely in space, they are defined by their capacity to change. Whereas the city is characterised by refinement and transmutation, architecture presents itself as a complete entity: singular in form and based on its own inherent logic. By reversing the roles of both domains, the city is now subjected to the delineation of the building: it is imprisoned within a confined system.

As an overarching spatial apparatus, Forum is like a city filled with a multitude of contents, images and references that can change over time. The building is, in this sense, a neutral framework in which urban life is allowed to unfold freely. In other words, by separating form from content, Forum aspires to become a typology in which time-bound fluctuating human need can be mastered. Time is, as it were, swallowed up: it is subjected to a higher intelligence. We can therefore interpret Forum as a *time-space compression*.[3]

Circulation Pattern

The longitudinal section of the building shows how the atrium is nestled within the enveloping mass. At both sides, each floor either closes off or opens up to this central space, resulting in a consecutive pattern of mass and non-mass that alternates vertically. The closed-off floor levels are occupied by functions that demand seclusion: a museum, an auditorium, cinemas and office spaces – venues that are either ticketed or of a private nature – while the spaces in between the volumes are directly accessible and occupied by non-ticketed functions such as a library, cafés and study zones. Although both sides of the atrium are vertical sequences of positive and negative spaces, they are not horizontally aligned. Since visitors enter the building through its western section, this side of the atrium starts off with an entrance hall, while the opposite side is tilted to form an adjacent tribune that spans to the first floor. The result is a system of interconnected split-levels that constantly shifts the visitor's position between both sides of the atrium and directs him into the depth of the building.

The building's internal organisation can be divided into three levels of public movement. The first and most public level follows the vertical sequence of escalators through the atrium. Since they are oriented in such a manner that the visitor is obliged to cross each individual square when proceeding to the top, the latter might be tempted to wander around and interact with the amenities offered on a particular square. The second level of movement occurs if the visitor disconnects from this chain of circulation and makes use of these amenities. We could therefore say that the first and second domain are almost inseparable as they are merged within the same territory, an overlap that is further strengthened by stripping each square almost entirely of supporting structures. The third level of movement occurs if the visitor continues into the depth of the square and enters the ticketed venues that are nestled within the enclosed volumes. Since these are primarily accessed via specially designed stairwells at both ends of the building, visitors are encouraged to experience the full depth of the interior. The vertical line of movement thus gradually transitions into a horizontal dimension, and so guides the visitor into the enveloping mass.

3   *Time-space compression* is originally a Marxist concept that indicates a changing relationship between time and space, further elaborated upon by the geographer David Harvey (1935) in: *The Condition of Postmodernity: An Enquiry into the Origins of Cultural Change* (1990). It is an effect of advanced communication and transportation media that render time and space almost completely valueless. Since Forum seeks to compress both dimensions, it can be interpreted as an architectural equivalent to these media.

In order to create a renewed sense of curiosity in the visitor, each square is characterised by a particular thematic intervention. From an intimate world where children play in and among the wooden bookshelves, or a step back in time where a fiction library becomes a novel in its own right, to a future-oriented museum with a disorienting sculptural staircase, or a glamourous art-house cinema fitted with pink carpets and velvet curtains. These theme-bound spaces are nestled in the depth of the building and contrast with the atrium's neutral appearance, allowing visitors to orient between both territories and adapt their position to a particular mood.

Aside from this kaleidoscope of themes, each square has a different shape, resulting in a constantly shifting spatial relationship between square and atrium. The diagram shows that each of the seven closed-off volumes has a different distance to the atrium's centre point. The volume on the ground floor (1), which is covered by a tribune, recedes from the atrium, while the overhanging volume (3) protrudes into the space. This gives the entrance hall a sense of spatial enclosure. From here, the visitor is guided into the library on the third floor. In contrast to the vast entrance hall, this function occupies a more intimate domain. The overhanging volume (4) protrudes into the atrium, thus blocking any visual connection with the upper floors. The downward sloping soffit created by the stepped seating in the cinema above (4) gives the library a necessary degree of introversion. The seats in the cinema above the grand foyer on the fifth floor face the opposite direction so that the soffit below tilts upwards (6). As a result, the foyer opens up to the atrium and has a more extroverted appearance, further enhanced by having the opposite volume (5) recede from the centre of the atrium. The library and study area on the eighth floor are given a sense of enclosure by the fact that the volume below (6) protrudes slightly into the space. The atrium's *promenade architecturale* is thus based on an alternation of restraint and release: a constantly shifting density between openness and closure where each configuration affects the other.

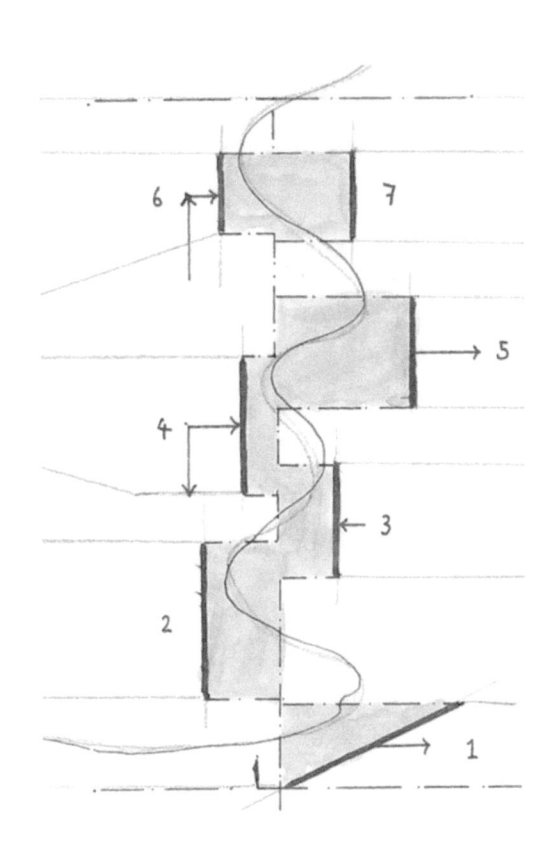

Joseph Gardella, schematic section (2021) showing the position of the building volumes in relation to the heart of the atrium.

The diagram shows how the atrium is vertically divided into a succession of open and closed spaces. The entrance hall, grand foyer (film square), and roof terrace become the public zones that are divided at two intervals. In the words of the designers, this system of stacked public spaces together forms the 'High Market'. The distribution of functions is also based on the patterning of restraint and release. Since the base, the middle section, and the top each has its own café, these levels offer opportunities for relaxation. The library, museum and study spaces, by contrast, require greater concentration. As they circulate through the building, visitors sequentially come into contact with activities that demand varying levels of mental absorption. Forum can thus be interpreted as an organism whose functioning relies on a breath-like circulation pattern, manifested through both space and function. The irregular stacking of escalators also gives a physical expression to this flow of energy, gradually structuring lines of sight into new areas and so luring the visitor through the building. By creating a variety of places that are ordered in accordance with different moods, Forum aims to be an environment in

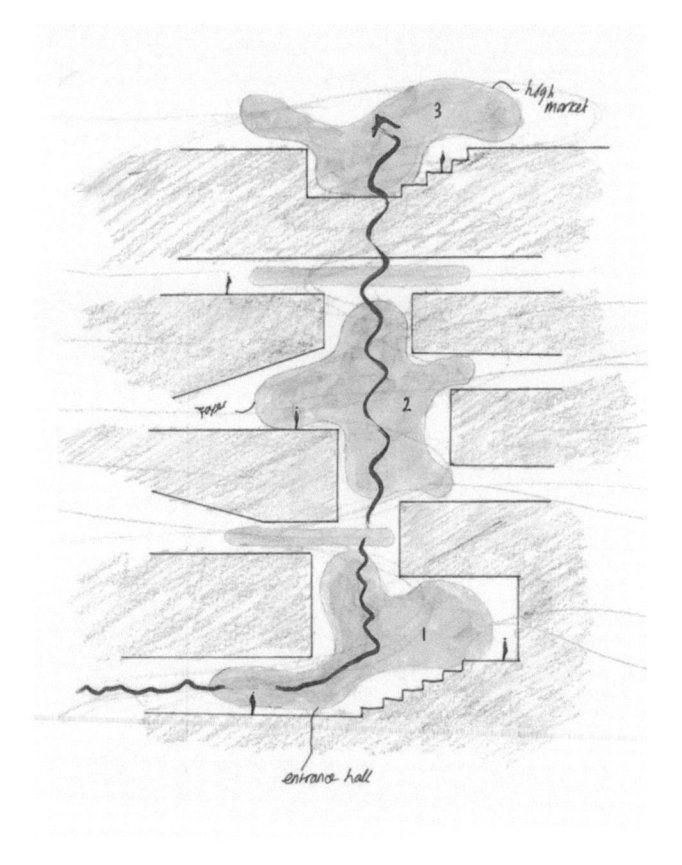

Joseph Gardella, schematic representation of the Forum (2021) showing the series of open and closed spaces that together form a spatial system of public zones.

which the entirety of public life can be embraced, since visitors are now enabled to insert their daily lives into a concentrated routine of entertainment, information and culture consumption.

In order to be an all-inclusive type of public space that can adapt itself to changing human needs, Forum makes a distinction between form and content. In other words, its shape is able to house a multitude of venues and events. Interestingly, it is this distinction that allowed the brief to adapt throughout the design process, while conforming to the principle that mass and non-mass are respectively coupled with ticketed and non-ticketed spaces. For example, the museum and offices eventually switched locations and thus support this idea. The former is now placed in a ticketed area, while the latter merges with the public domain, being partly located on a square and thus more transparent to the public.

One could say that the brief adapted, almost naturally, to the building's formal layout. Connecting this observation to the earlier statement that cities are defined by their ability to reshape themselves over time, one could interpret this transmutative character as a parallel that exists between the city and Forum. Its desire to change was thus already a constructive part of its own genesis.

Mirror Realities

"Forum Groningen is a new-style public amenity. It is neither a library, nor a museum. Nor is it a cinema. Here in this space the traditional boundaries between these institutions are simply eliminated."[4]

In Forum, the elimination of the typological boundary is achieved by distributing its contents among different branches of the building. In the case of the library, this typology is distributed throughout the entire organisation and merges with social activities. For example, the children's library on the first floor takes the form a playground, while the neighbouring tribune has a small kiosk where people can read newspapers. Similarly, the fiction library on the third floor is moulded around a social zone where people can interact and play a game of pool, and the study area on the eighth floor surrounds a non-fiction library whose primary purpose is study. Since young people are reading less because of the rise of new electronic media, Forum aims to embed the library within its social zones, thus bringing information closer to the public. The squares thus become platforms where the typologies merge with public life. To the same end, short clips of featured movies are projected on the white-plastered protruding volumes, allowing the opposite square to become an informal cinema auditorium. The content of some of the museum exhibitions will also spread across the squares, attracting visitors to buy a ticket. The individual venues and their programmes thus extend beyond their enclosed volumes and merge with the public realm.

The need to break down the typological boundary thus emerges from an ambition to bring information closer to the public, highlighting a drastic shift in contemporary data consumption. Ordinarily, the museum, library and cinema are isolated repositories of information, accessed only by those who decide to participate in a particular activity. For example, generally speaking, people go to libraries in order to read. Data is, in this sense, retrieved actively. In Forum, this relationship is turned on its head. The library is now brought to the visitor, allowing him to be less active in acquiring information. This reversal of roles is a consequence of a rapidly

4   Quote NL Architects retrieved from: Press kit Forum Groningen (p. 3). Date of Publication: November 25 (English version on the 26th), 2019.

evolving digital means of data consumption. Digital media can communicate data in such vast quantities within such a contracted timespan that active participation is no longer required. This convenience in retrieving data thus increases our risk of becoming addicted to this passive form of consumption, and we may ask ourselves: does Forum contribute to this passivity? It functions simultaneously as a hyper-dense database through which the user can browse effortlessly to access a wide range of information, while it also provides a physical environment that digital media are incapable of. Instead of a virtual world that attempts to represent a real-world structure in digital form, Forum, paradoxically, becomes a mirror reality of a process that is already taking place on the digital plane. It is a physical world infused by a digital reality. Forum thus thrives on its contradictions: it is a hybrid of two realities.

Oddly, the overall shape of the building can similarly be compared to a kind of digital flux, for it appears as a non-static and ever-changing entity. It orients itself within the cityscape as a sculptural mould that constantly changes in form and size, depending on one's perspective within the surrounding city. Because each of its façades is different and because it is nestled in a dense urban fabric, the building cannot be experienced in its entirety, but reveals itself in a fragmentary fashion. Also, the building's exterior does not provide a single indication of scale, since its proportions are autonomous and based on an internal logic. It is through this immeasurability that its form might evoke a sense of the sublime. Since this quality operates most powerfully in nature, one might associate the building with a gigantic rock formation. Forum thus lives between associations: it is impossible to pin down exactly what kind of entity it is. One could be tempted to think that an alchemist had turned a small three-dimensional fragment of an infinitely large, digital flux into actual matter.

0

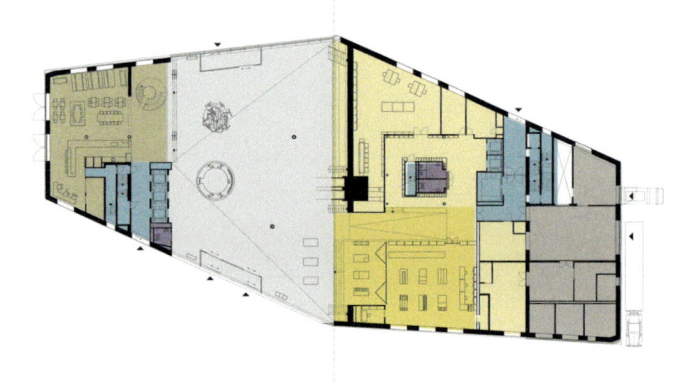

1

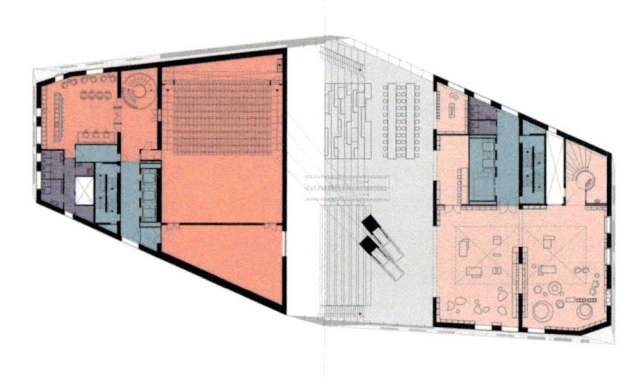

2

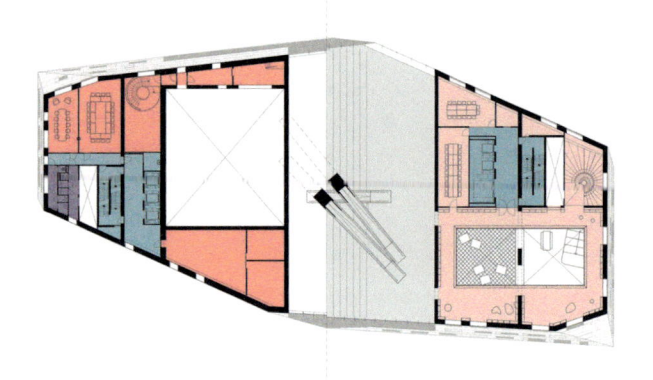

3

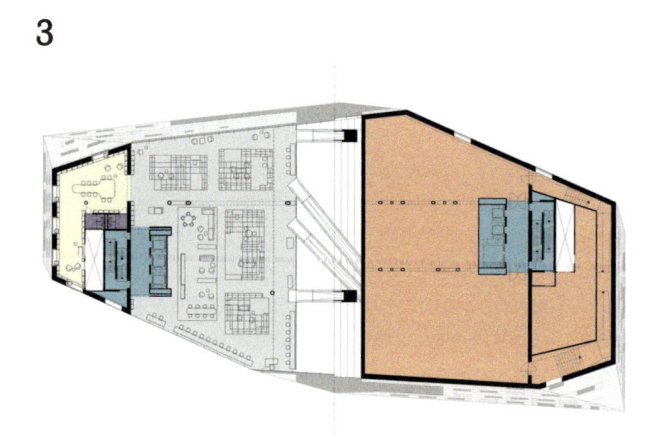

4

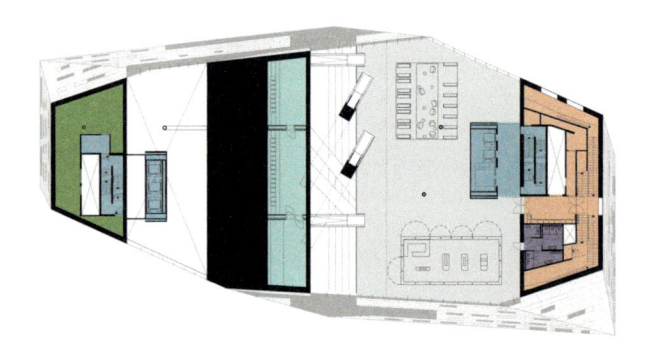

4.5

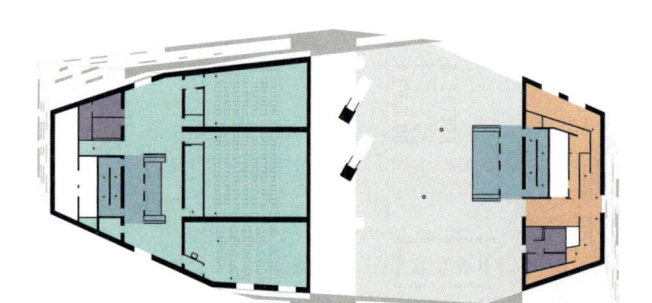

5

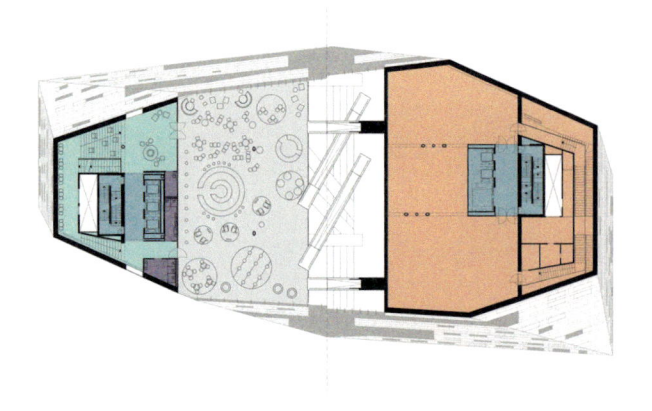

6

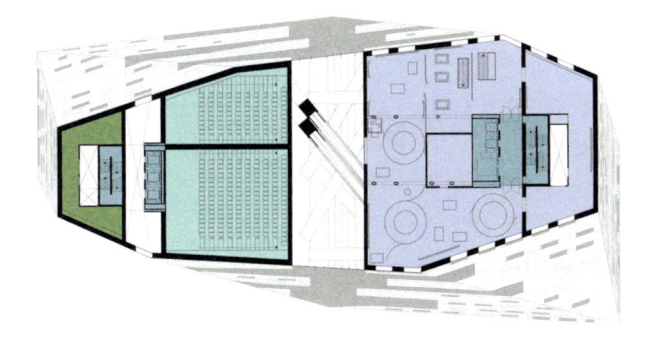

7

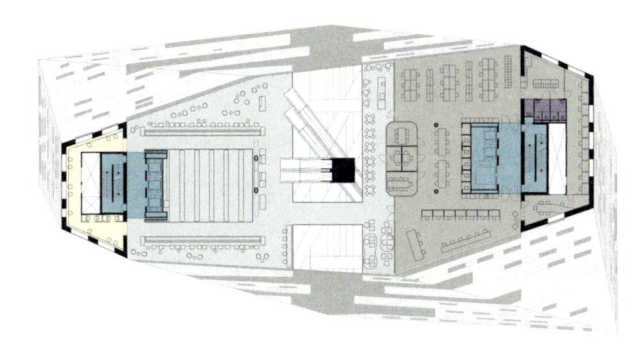

8

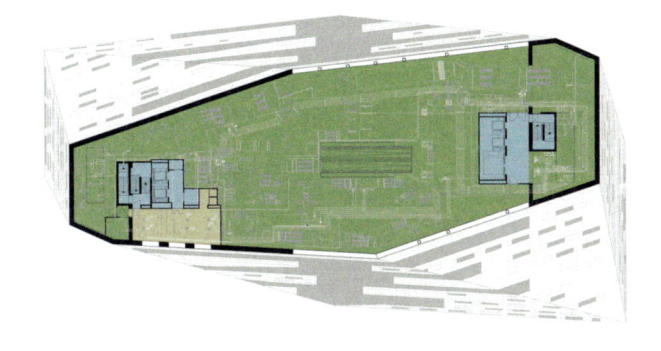

9

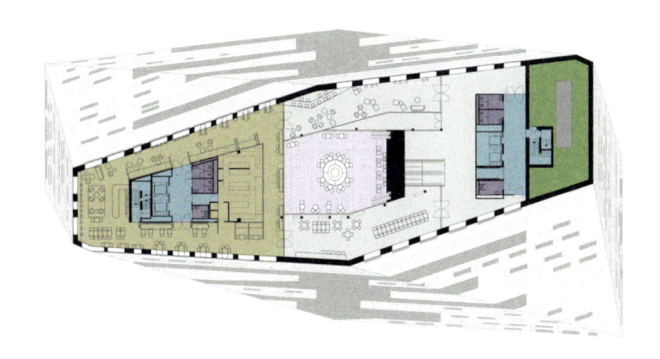

10

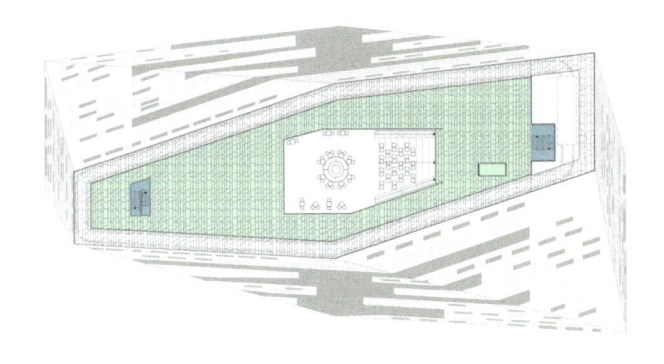

11

■ Parking garage	■ Public	■ Wonderland	■ Study area	■ Roof terrace
■ Bicycle storage	■ Groningen Store	■ Crime	■ Storyworld	■ Stairs and elevators
■ Catering	■ Logistics	■ Exhibition	■ Offices	■ Toilets
■ Installations	■ Auditorium	■ Film House	■ Roof patio	

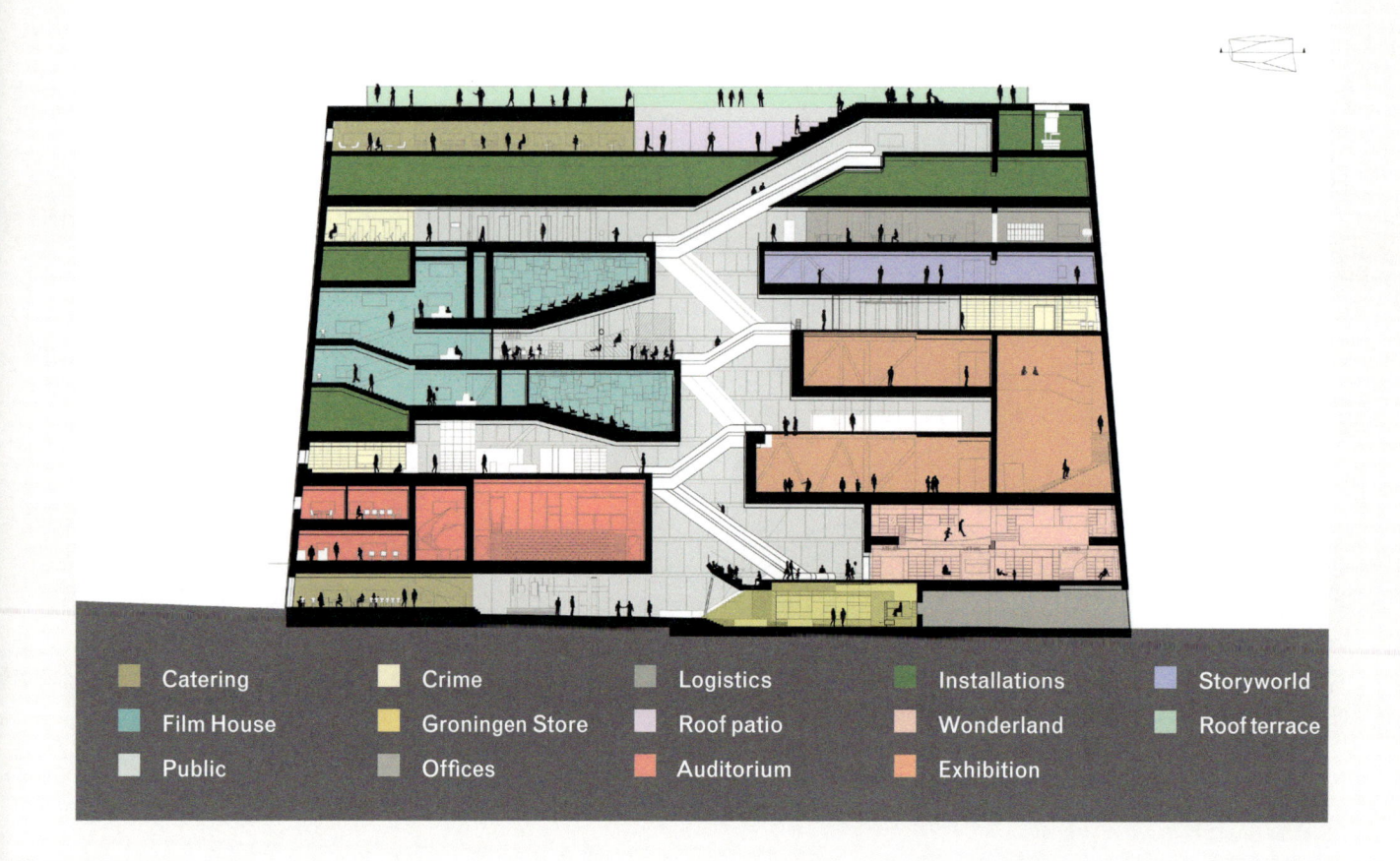

Catering
Film House
Public

Crime
Groningen Store
Offices

Logistics
Roof patio
Auditorium

Installations
Wonderland
Exhibition

Storyworld
Roof terrace

Section CC

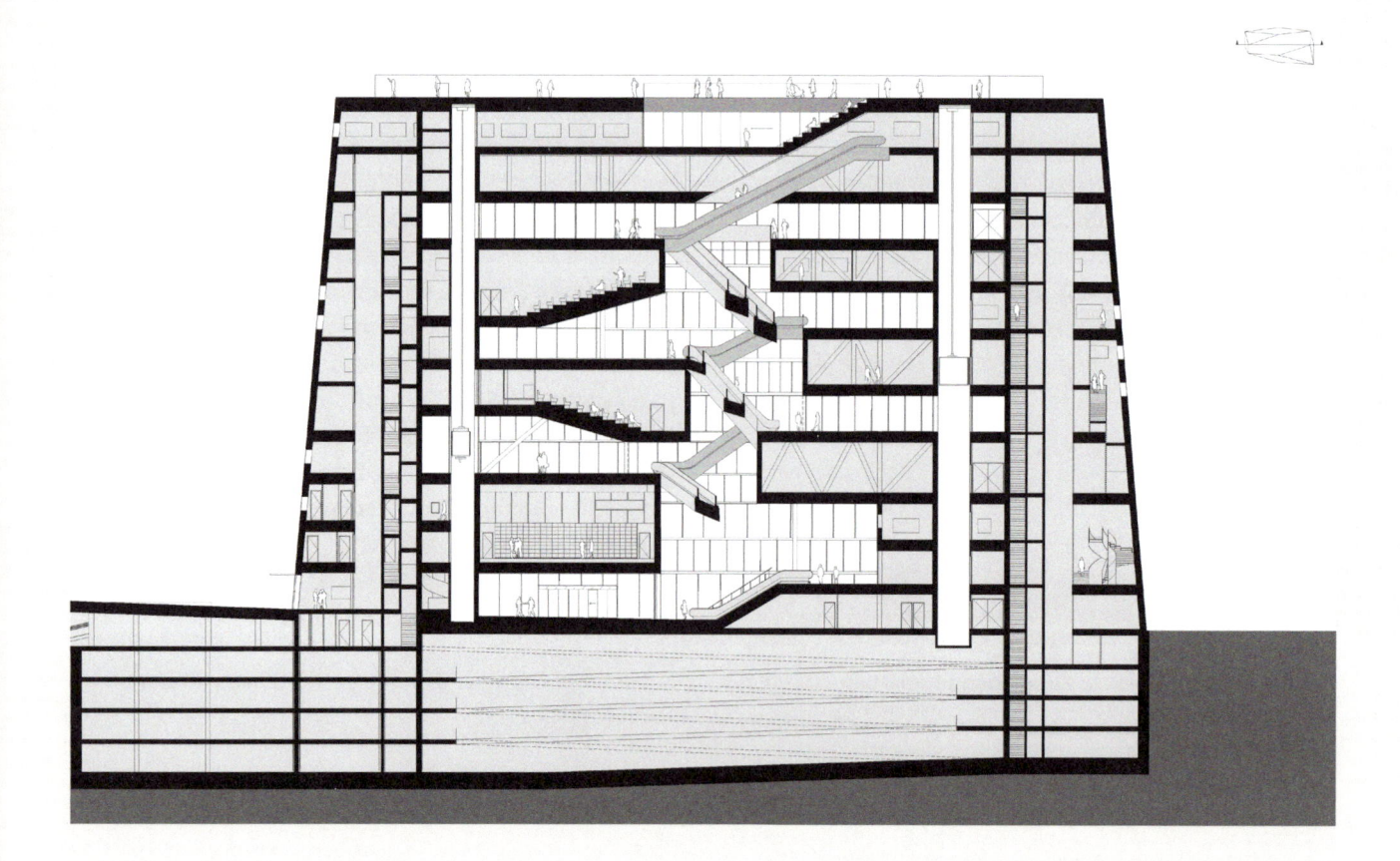

South façade

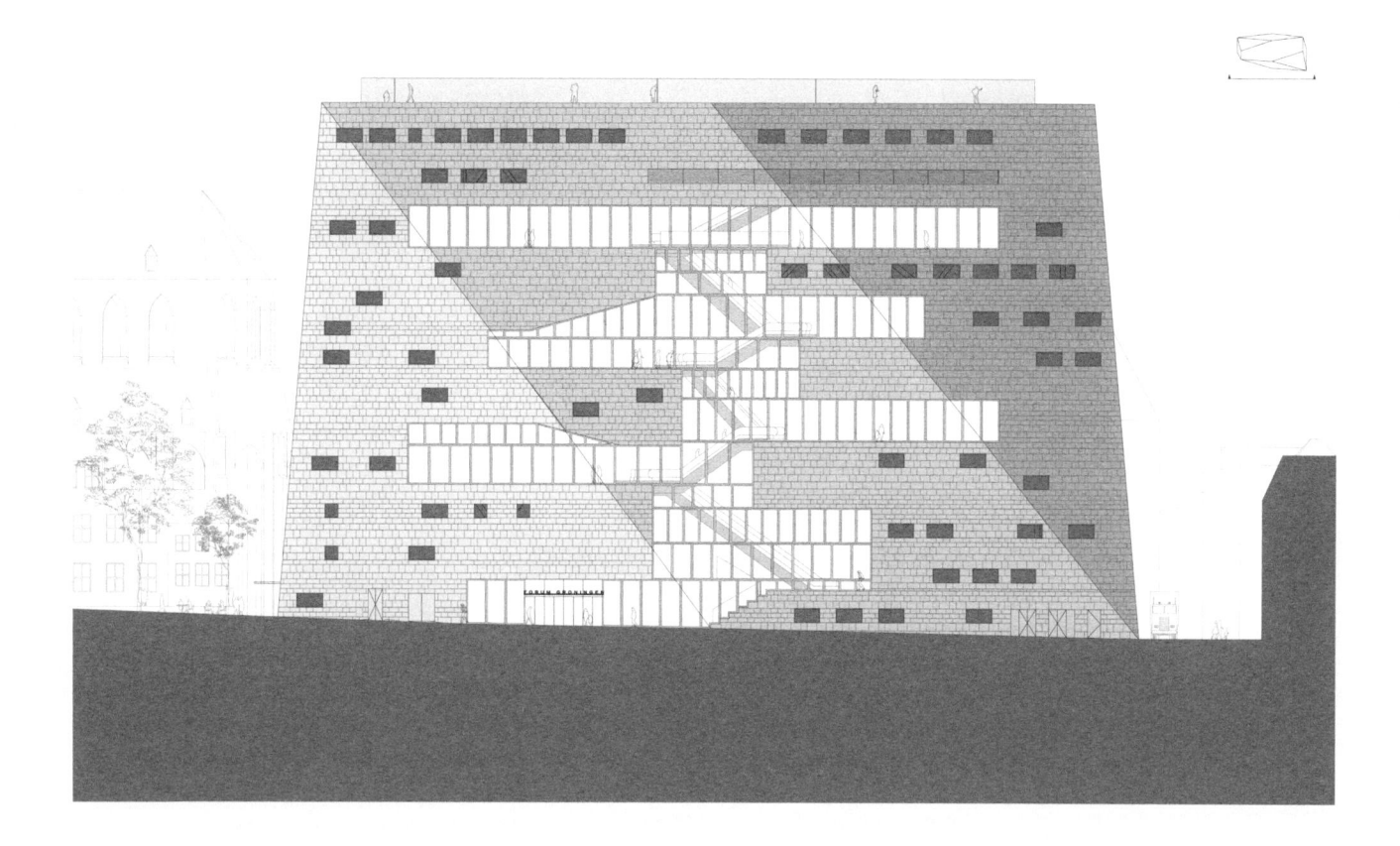

North façade

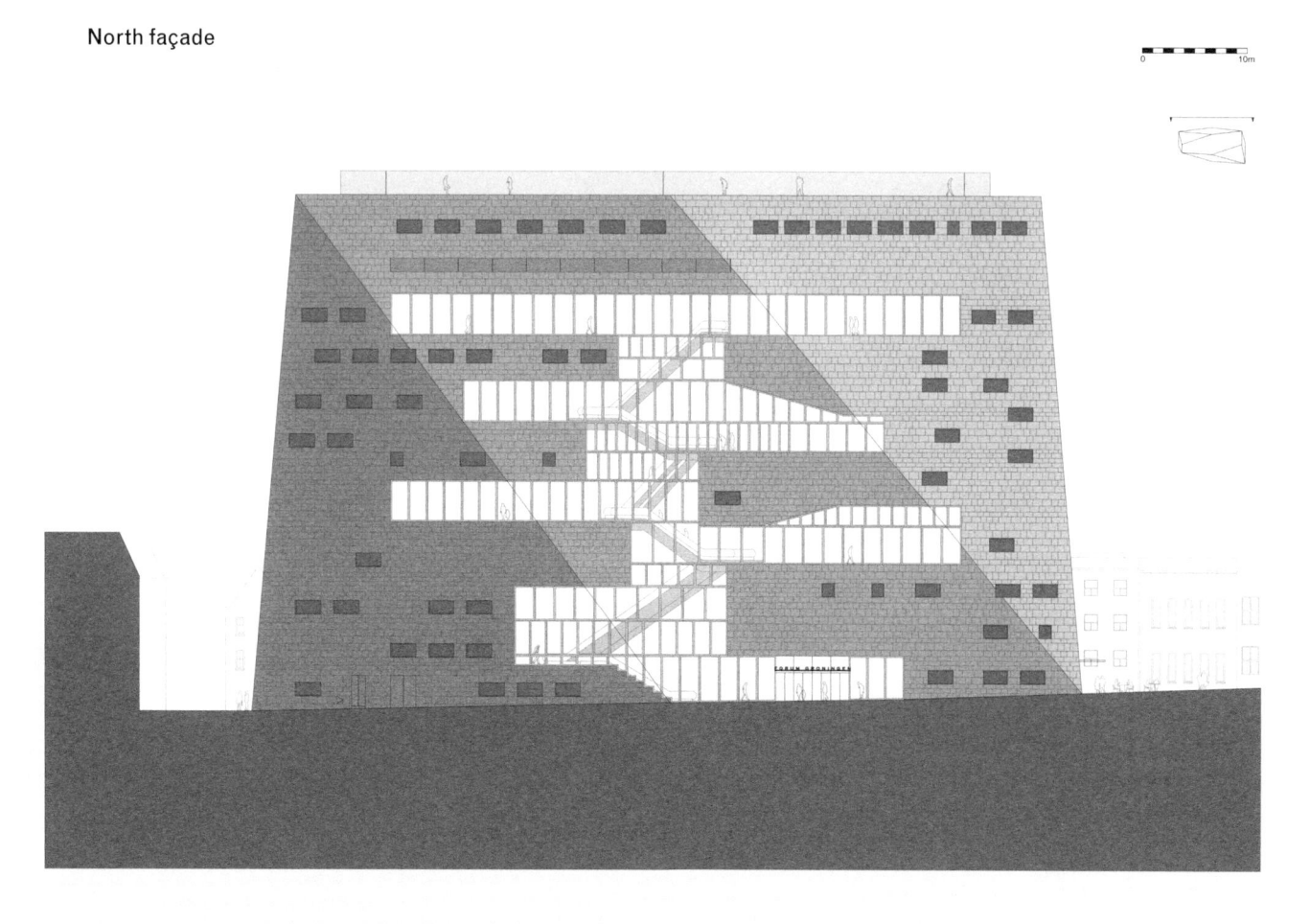

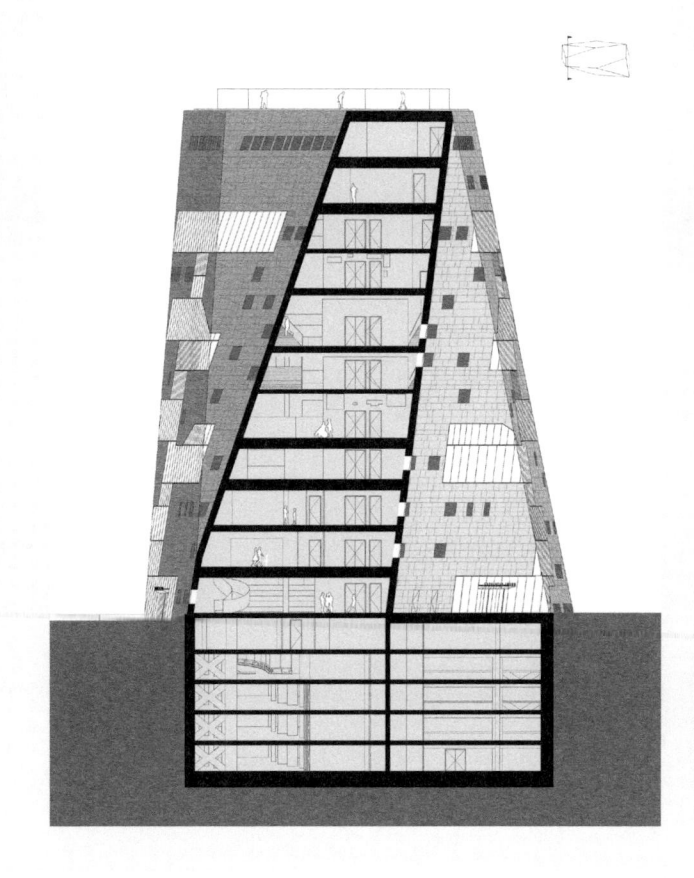

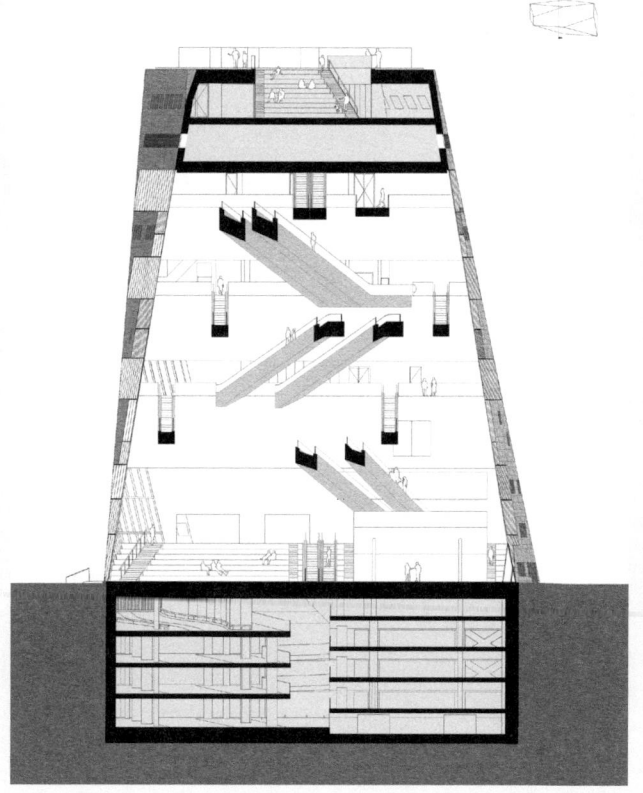

Section FF

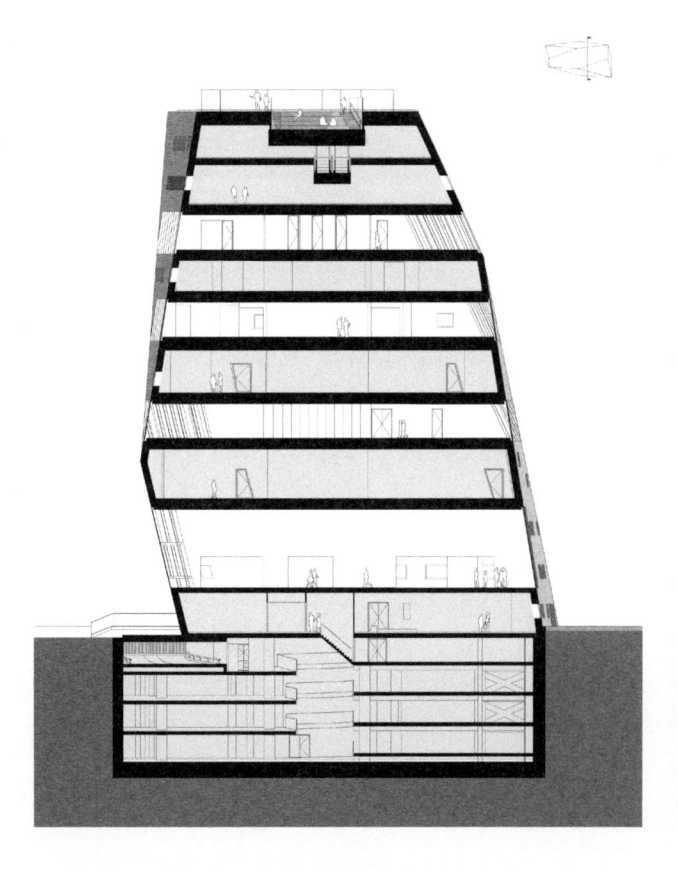

Section GG

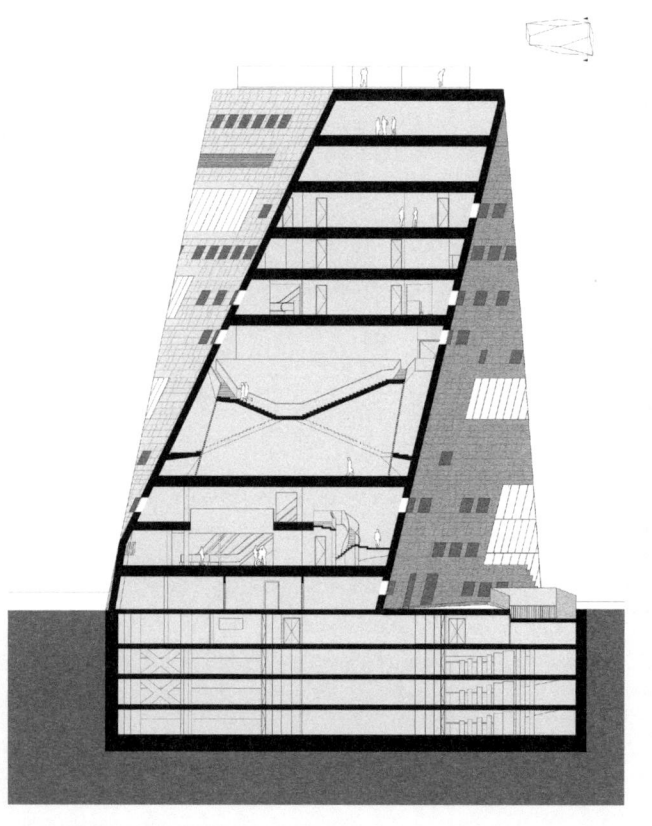

West façade  East façade

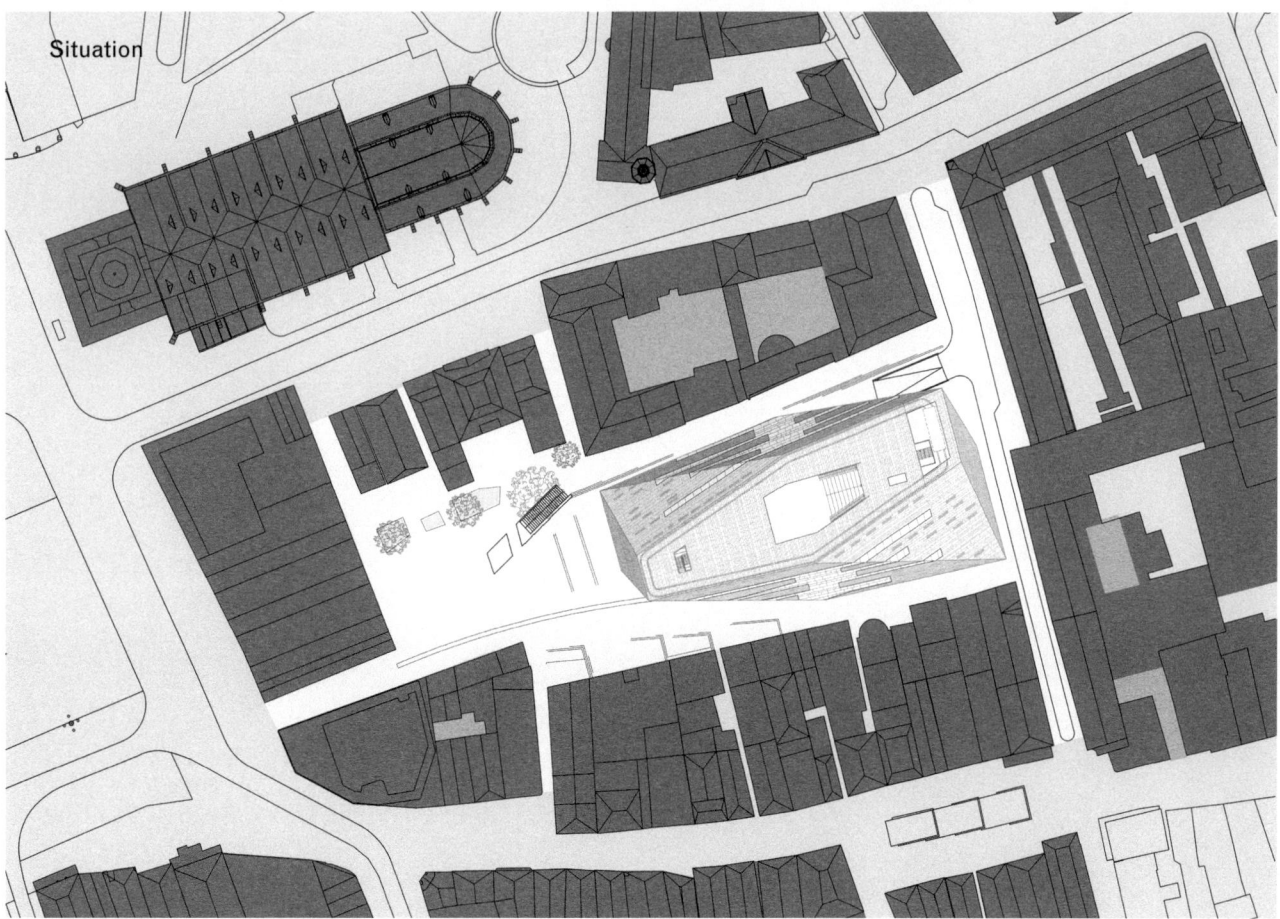

Situation

The Design Explained and Illustrated

BRANDMELDPA

BOUWLAAG 6.5
etage 5west ↓

BOUWLAAG 6

BOUWLAAG 5.5
etage 4west ↓

BOUWLAAG -3 / -2.5

BOUWLAAG 0

U BEVINDT
ZICH HIER

BOUWLAAG 3

BOUWLAAG -4 / -3.5

BOUWLAAG -1

BOUWLAAG 2

BOUWLAAG 5

BOUWLAAG -5 / -4.5

BOUWLAAG -2 / -1.5

BOUWLAAG 1

BOUWLAAG 4

Dräger

Designed with Integrity and Respect

Forum Groningen's striking form derives in part from the building's highly sophisticated structure. In essence, the building consists of two sloping cores connected to each other by the top two floors. The atrium in between is punctuated by enormous building volumes that protrude from the cores, surmounted by open squares interconnected by escalators. On the exterior, the building masses and open spaces are expressed as alternately closed and transparent areas so that the whole resembles a glass keyhole in a natural stone volume. It is an ingenious piece of engineering art. And all the more ingenious because the original spatial concept has been preserved despite the structural adjustments required to meet stricter codes following earthquakes in the province.

The engineering firm ABT was involved in the design of the Forum from the very start. It was the structural and geotechnical consultant for the competition design that NL Architects drew up in collaboration with Bureau Bouwkunde in 2006. When Bureau Bouwkunde went bankrupt in 2009, ABT also took on the technical design, the calculation of the construction costs and the coordination of the design.

ABT structural engineer Erwin ten Brincke has worked on the project since the earliest stages and explains the implications of the spatial concept for the construction: "As an analogy with the urban squares in Groningen's city centre, NL Architects wanted to create a series of squares inside the Forum, but on several different levels, culminating in a roof terrace. The idea was that this vertical structure should not be a rigid stack but a looser composition of more and less extremely cantilevered volumes. The squares had to be attractive places, without heavy, conspicuous supporting structures. As a structural engineer you want to design as invisibly and as intelligently as possible. In this case, we did that by constructing the cantilevered building volumes as light floors that can be made stampfree, in the form of composite slabs and steel girders, supported by steel trusses."

In addition, steel columns were added in a few places. The trusses can protrude a maximum of eleven metres from the columns. "The design principle for the squares within the atrium was that there should never be more than three columns in a row. Otherwise it would read optically as a wall and that went against the desire to preserve the openness. The structural design has contributed to the spatial experience of each square by allowing arbitrary column positions within a manageable and safe construction system. The columns are not in a row horizontally and are not positioned vertically above each other but are staggered. The vertical forces meander from top to bottom, via the columns and the diagonals in the trusses. Each box rests on two columns so they can stand individually on their own, separate from the concrete cores on the outside."

Transition Between Lower and Upper Structure

The Forum has fifteen storeys, five of which are below ground. The subterranean structure with parking for cars and bicycles is conceived as a traditional concrete table construction. Hybrid concrete has been used in the basement construction, with both traditional reinforcement and steel fibre reinforcement. Like the underwater concrete, the cantilevered floors of the parking garage are reinforced with steel fibres. Marco van der Ploeg, project coordinator at ABT, explains why: "With the basement structure, we also considered very carefully how we could give the space the optimum quality. Using steel-fibre-reinforced concrete made it possible to have smaller supports and thinner floors. As a result, each floor has approximately 5 cm more height than if we used traditional concrete. That extra height gives a greater sense of spaciousness." At the centre of the parking garage is a void from levels 1 to -5. Suspended from the void is an illuminated artwork, *Turmoil*, which gives the space the cachet of an urban plaza and acts as an important point of orientation. This 50-metre-long void presented an extra challenge for the construction, after all without it, the floors would balance the lateral earth pressure on both sides of the basement. The transverse forces and moments created by the void in the floors have been solved with extra reinforcement in the hybrid floors.

Erwin ten Brincke: "The next challenge was to resolve the imbalance between the substructure and the varied construction above. Here too, this was achieved not with heavy structures but by making smart use of the available space. Level -1 is a 'transitional' floor, with steel transitions between the relatively regular pattern of the parking garage and the irregular pattern of the upper structure. These transitions take the form of trusses, V-shaped columns and HD beams in the floors." The steel transitional structure is very robust but has also been designed so that the entrance, the pedestrian areas and the parking spaces look and feel spacious.

Steel Bridge Between Concrete Cores

The idea of the two stabilising cores thus emerged logically from the concept of the large central atrium with the series of stacked plazas. Ten Brincke initially worked out the cores in both steel and concrete, but it turned out that steel would deform too much to guarantee a safe construction. The two concrete cores are connected only at the ninth and tenth floors. The ninth floor has an almost completely closed façade and is used for technical

Part of the south façade of the eastern core slopes by no less than 24.4 degrees, making it the world's most inclined load-bearing concrete wall.

Designed with Integrity and Respect

The same 24.4 degree sloping wall from the outside.

installations. This layer is constructed like a bridge from steel Vierendeel girders and trusses and spans the 26 metres between the cores. The floor above contains the restaurant, and above that is the roof terrace. Erwin: "You could design the bridge so that it is attached to the core on one side and has about 20 cm of tolerance at the other. In the event of an earthquake, the two cores would be able to move independently of each other. However, we opted for a construction that is as stiff as possible, because otherwise we would also have had to make a 20 cm sliding connection in the façade. This would have been clearly visible from the ground, which would have disrupted the desired monolithic façade and made waterproofing more complicated."

Integrated Design Approach

Every aspect of the Forum's design is interrelated. The movements in the cantilevered parts of up to eleven metres obviously also affect the design of the cores and the construction of the façades. For this reason, it was crucial that ABT's architects and engineers worked together as a project team in the same room. For Ten Brincke, the integrated design approach was a new and very positive experience: "In the preliminary design phase, my architectural design colleagues told me that they were designing a façade with a maximum tolerance of 25 mm. At that time, I was working on the design of the cantilevered boxes myself; 25 mm tolerance is nothing when you're working with cantilevers of eleven metres! At first, I wondered what I was supposed to do with such information at that stage of the design. But afterwards it turned out to be very valuable for the project and for the client. I therefore made the steel trusses very robust and rigid in order to facilitate that low tolerance in the façade. Because the dimensions of the main supporting structure were carefully calculated, the amount of steel remained the same in the later design phases, and the construction costs didn't increase as they normally do during the design process with projects of this kind."

Marco van der Ploeg: "We were goal-oriented not task-oriented. That required a different mentality. We brainstormed together more and looked for the best solution together. At ABT we previously worked in business units, but at the Forum we worked with a project team in which the structural and civil engineers and cost experts worked together integrally. This allowed us to approach and discuss complex bottlenecks very directly in an interdisciplinary manner."

Designing with BIM and Revit

Due to the Forum's complexity, it was necessary for the designers and engineers to make a 3D model. The building's final design was rendered in Revit software and processed into a Building Information Model (BIM). While this is standard practice today, that was not yet the case in 2009. NL Architects and ABT worked together closely on the model. Was BIM the linchpin in the integrated collaboration between the architect and engineer? Erwin: "Integrated design depends primarily upon the people who are working together and how well they communicate with each other. Revit and BIM are tools for this. The interaction between the architect and the structural engineer was very transparent. We explained very clearly to each other what we wanted to achieve, why we thought something was important and what the limits were. This way you can come up with new solutions together."

Architect Pieter Bannenberg of NL Architects adds: "There were two sides to working with BIM. On the one hand, it was exciting and clearly had great advantages that benefitted the design. On the other hand, because Revit was still so new and not fully developed, we spent a lot of time trying to figure out how to model the design properly. We also worked closely together on this." Marco agrees: "BIM is especially important for project coordination. The collaboration was so good because we had clear goals and ambitions. That made the design process very open. Because of the integrated approach, it sometimes took a long time to come to a decision: we looked at every part from all sides, from the construction, the installations, building physics, aesthetics and functionality. So, we made very deliberate decisions, which we then stuck to because they had been made so carefully."

For the tender, the team used the 3D model rather than the usual 2D drawings. That was actually unavoidable, given the complexity of the design. Marco: "The 3D model had a higher legal status than the resulting drawings. That was new. In any case, we were at the forefront when making the model. We had to invent all sorts of things ourselves, for example how to insert sloping façades or columns that incline in two directions. That wasn't yet in the software at the time. We came up with it ourselves. Fortunately, the architectural design was very structured, so we were able to set rules and import them into the model. All the dimensions and forms were then derived from the model. Once that worked, we concentrated on the content. We no longer had to check whether the different drawings fitted together correctly. After integrating the architect's and

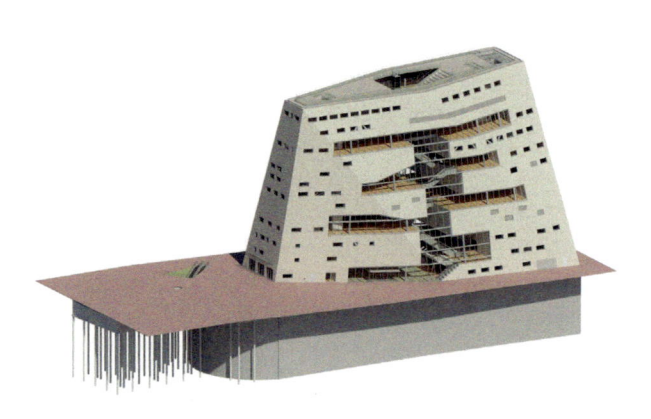

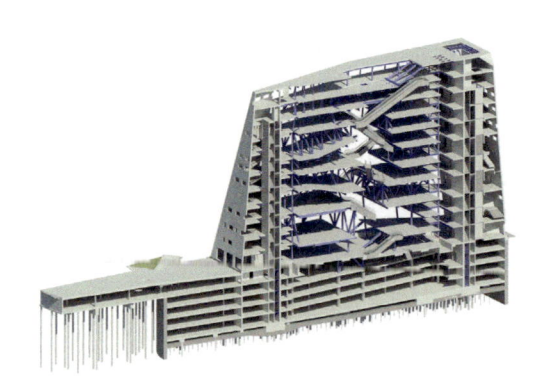

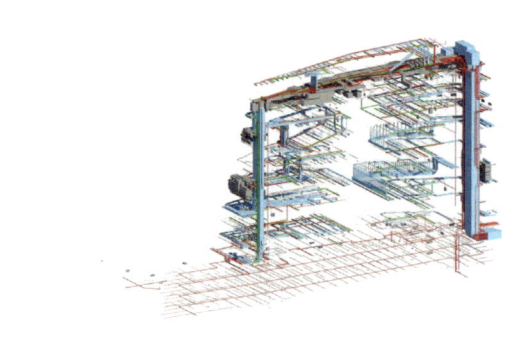

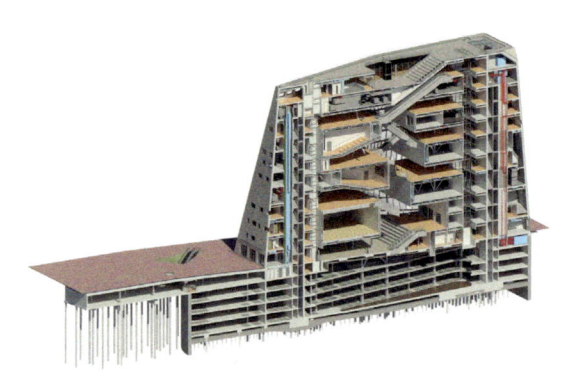

Four BIM images. In addition to the complete Forum, the cutaways highlight the steel construction, the installations and the technology shafts.

engineer's workflows, we were able to focus on more essential matters in the design, such as the correct locations of doors and windows."

Erwin: "The 3D model made it possible to match all the parts in the building very precisely. This allowed us to share data quickly with the architect and other parties, but it also helped enormously to visualise the spaces clearly for the municipality and future users."

Everyone in BIM

NL Architects and ABT were convinced from the outset of the need to use Revit for the complex building design. The municipality also quickly realised that the 3D model would reduce the risks in the design and construction process. The next step was to get the installation technicians on board, so that they were willing to integrate their design into the model. Marco: "To ensure the same high quality of all parties involved in this project, we worked hard to convince them to go along with the 3D approach." One of the consequences of this was that ABT took on a different role in the project: the municipality commissioned the engineering firm to coordinate the design.

Marco: "We wanted to be sure that all installation components would fit into the building design. At our office, we trained the installation technicians to work in Revit. They all went along with it. The benefits of a model in BIM increase exponentially as more information is entered. When the installation technicians put their components into the model, we ran into things that didn't fit. We had to adjust the architectural and structural design to make everything fit. That was a lot of work, but of course it's far easier to make adjustments in the model than during the construction. By creating a 3D environment, the building has gained in quality – and it gave us the certainty that everything would fit."

The Forum went to tender in 2012, at a time when almost all contractors were still working with 2D drawings. The 3D model functioned excellently in terms of technology and content, also for the engineers of the main contractor, BAM. But at a strategic level, the contractor was not yet completely BIM-minded, which sometimes made discussions more difficult.

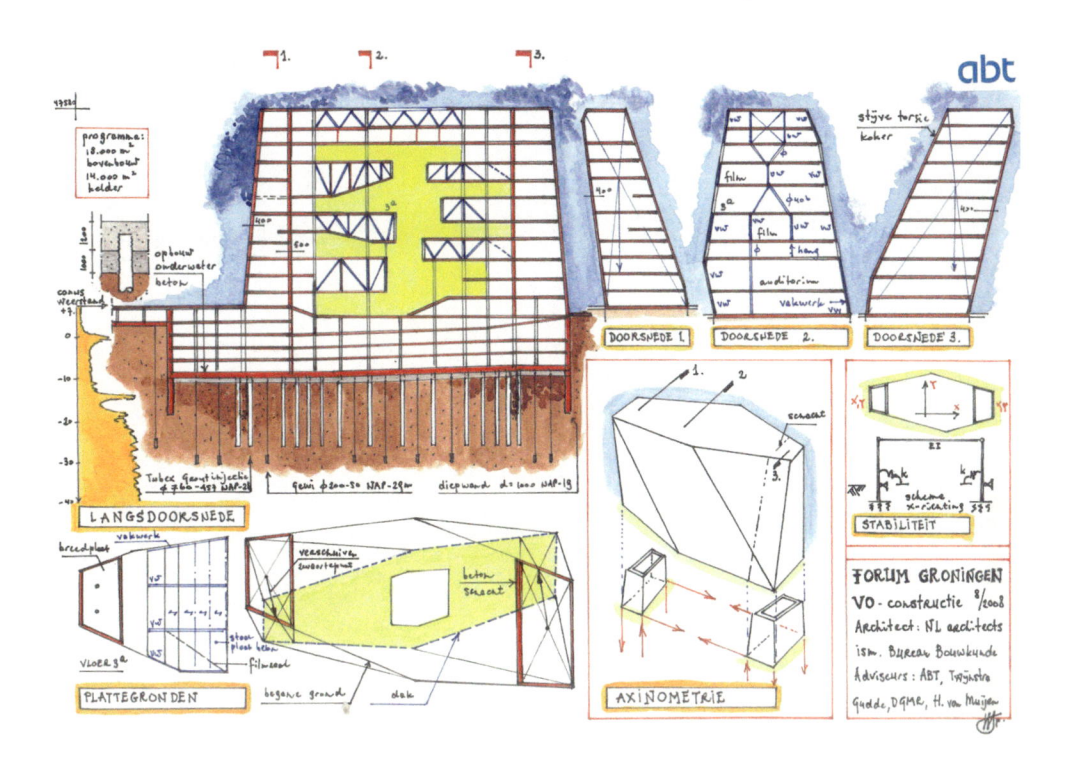

Drawing of the main structural principles in the preliminary design phase (2008).

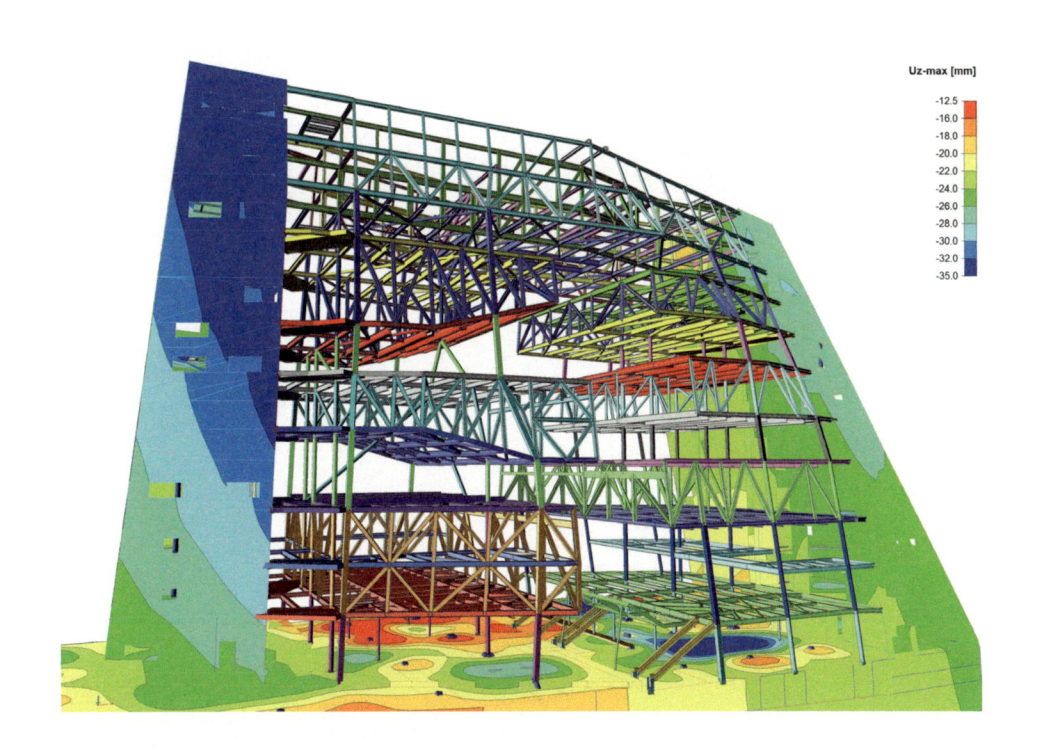

3D analysis of the extent to which the concrete cores sink and the ground floor bends. The steel girders of the cantilevered volumes are supported by steel trusses that cantilever a maximum of eleven metres from the columns.

Designed with Integrity and Respect

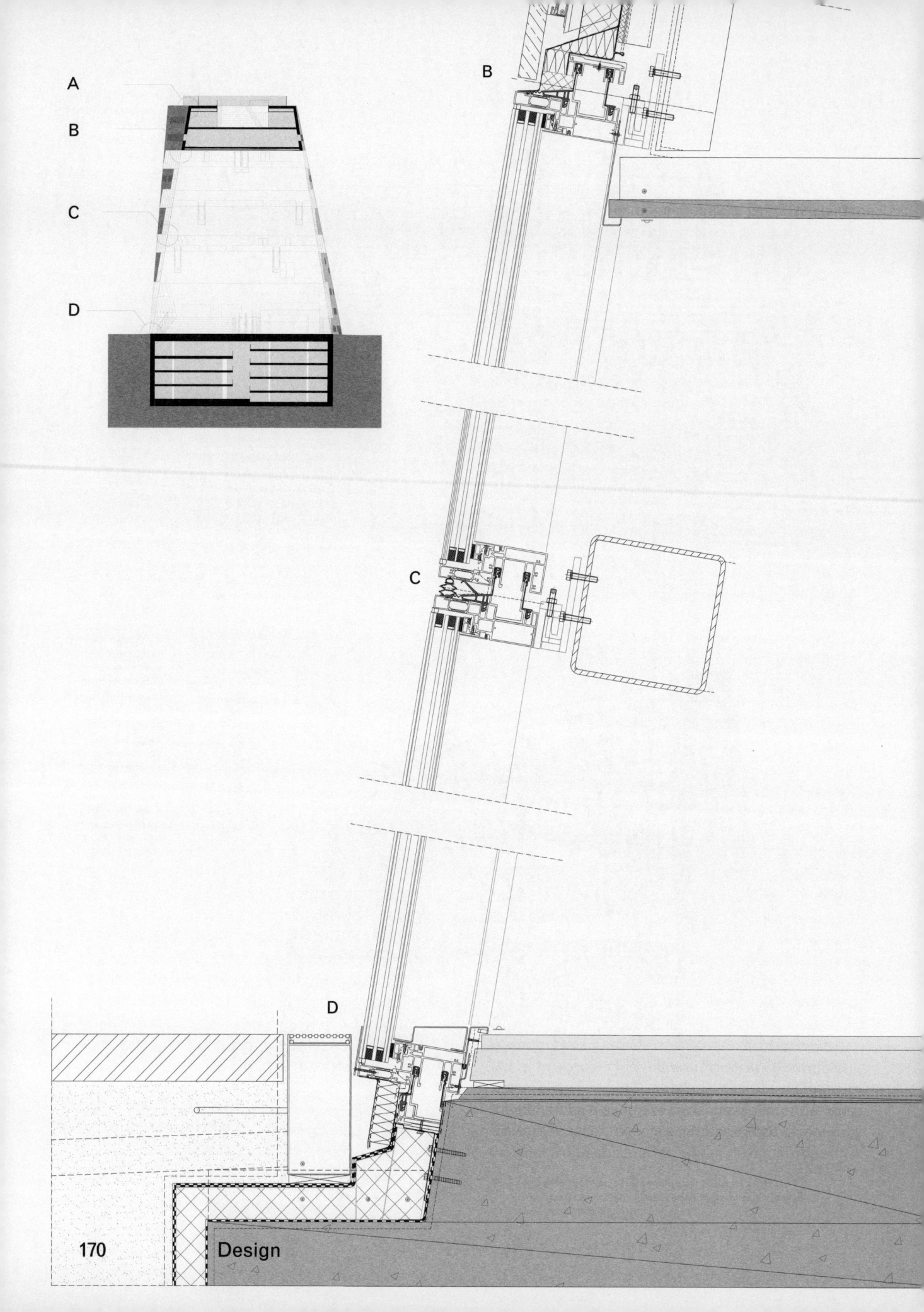

A

B

C

D

B

C

D

170 Design

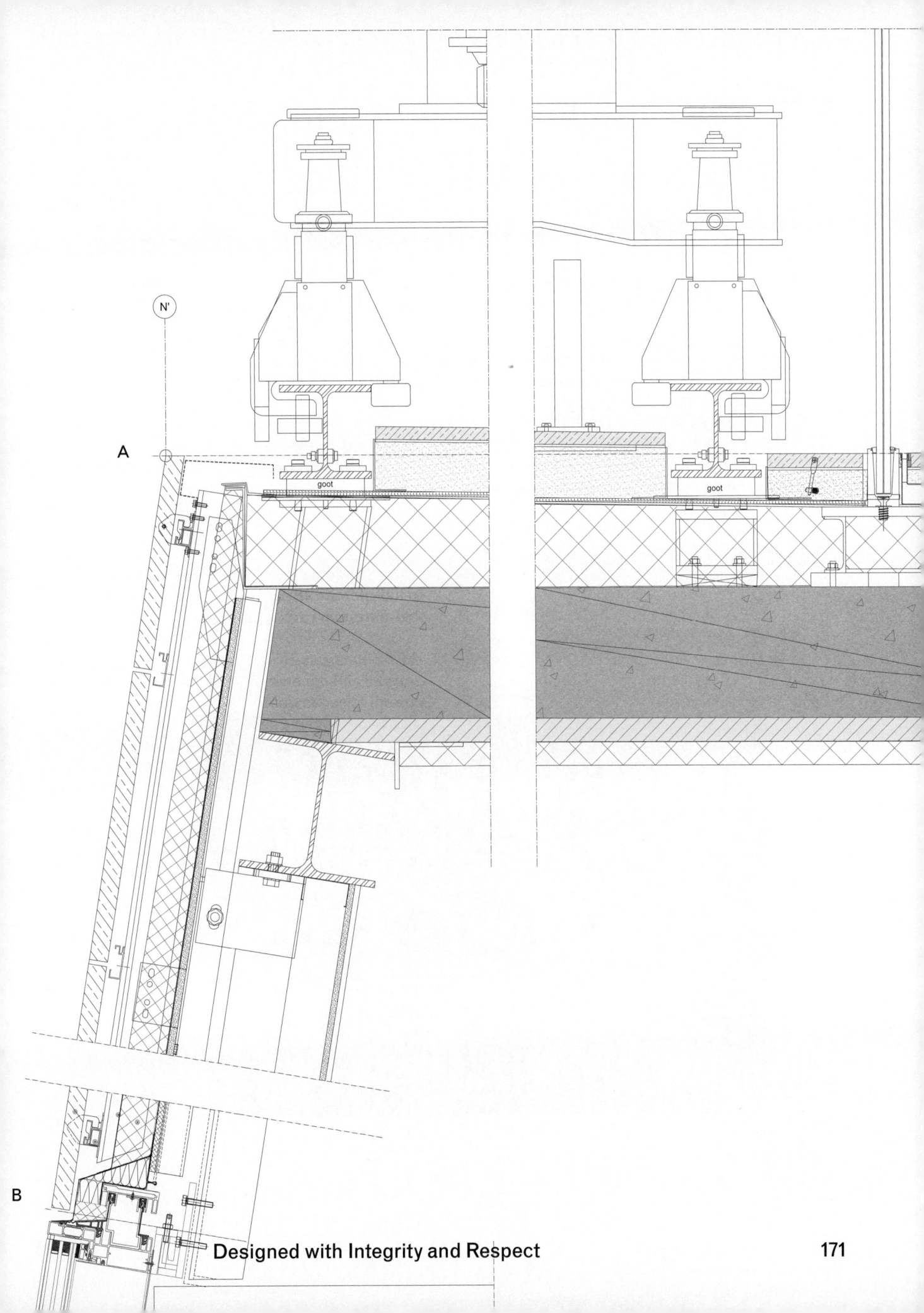

N'

A

goot

goot

B

Designed with Integrity and Respect

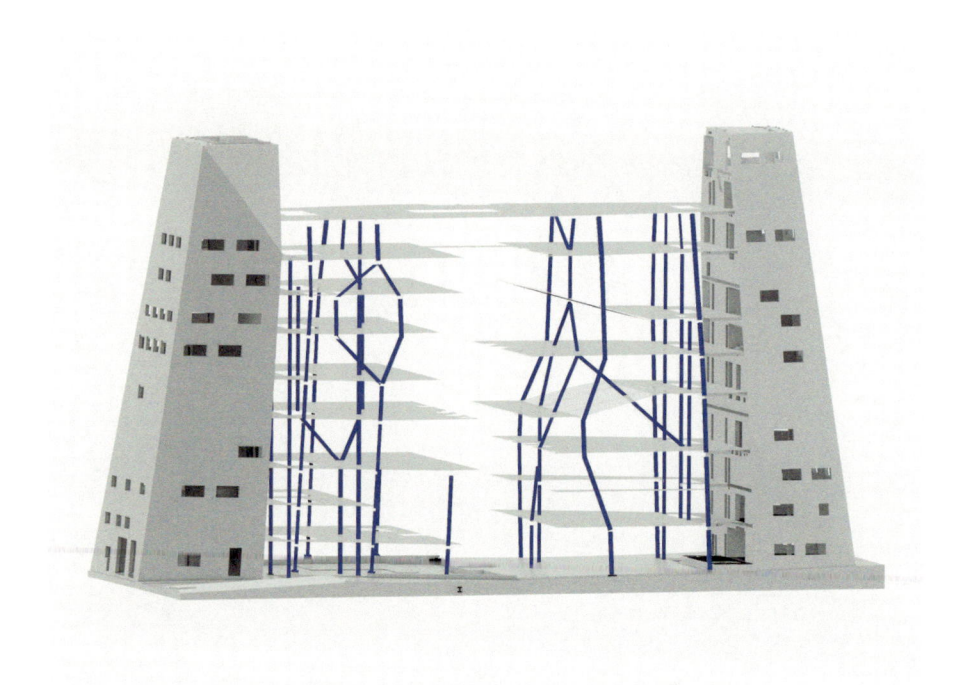

In addition to the steel trusses, steel columns have been added in some places. The vertical forces meander from top to bottom, via the columns and the diagonals in the trusses.

May 2017: the construction of the auditorium with trusses and meandering columns.

Monolithic Façade

Ten Brincke believes that an engineer's job is to make all the architect's and client's wishes possible. With the Forum, one of those wishes was to combine a spacious and welcoming building with a high-performance façade. "The architect wanted a monolithic building with smooth façades and razor-sharp edges. We achieved this with natural stone panels and glass. We opted for concrete cores because the façade also benefited from this. Steel cores move and would lead to significant dilations. By using an integrated design approach we were able to solve all interfaces immediately. Although steel in a façade can be an architect's wet dream, we looked for the best for project solution. For example, the façades of the cantilevered building volumes are fitted with a sliding steel sub-frame structure."

Van der Ploeg adds: "We had an internal discussion at ABT about the problems, looking at them from the perspective of the main load-bearing structure and the façade structure. We looked at the tolerances of every building component in an attempt to find an integral solution to all the problems, but it proved difficult to compensate fully for certain movements in the building within the main load-bearing structure. We therefore looked for a way to accommodate them partially in the façade and came up with the idea of dividing the façade into smaller parts. Each window and each natural stone slab is one such component, and small deformations are possible in the connections between all those parts. This way you can have the façade absorb movements in a very controlled manner. When the earthquake issue came into play later in the process, it turned out our façade design had anticipated the new requirements with regards to earthquake-resistant construction."

Wachenzeller Rhombuses

The closed parts of the Forum façade are clad with a natural stone called Wachenzeller dolomite. From a distance, all the panels appear to be rectangular, but are actually rhombuses of varying angles. To make them appear rectangular, each panel has its own specific shape, calculated in Revit. ABT designed aluminium sliding brackets for attaching the natural stone panels and the glazed façade elements. The panels are able to move slightly horizontally, allowing movement to be absorbed across the entire façade. Originally, each panel was to be fixed with four anchors, but with the tightening of the requirements following earthquakes in the region, they are now fixed with six or more anchors to horizontal aluminium profiles. In the event of an earthquake the panels cannot fall out of the façade.

An integrated design approach was also essential in achieving the desired smoothness of the façade. Marco: "Normally in a façade design you have to deal with all kinds of functional elements, such as water drainage. With the Forum, the façade had to be as smooth as possible, so we couldn't apply those kinds of standard solutions. Not only because of the desired aesthetic but also because of the façade's varied angles of inclination. We had detailed discussions about the exact functions of the standard components with the suppliers of the façade elements. We undertook an extensive analysis of façade systems and integrated the functional requirements in a new form within the façade design." Facilities for water drainage, other installations and fixings were eventually concealed invisibly in the Forum's façade. The flush alignment of the glass and natural stone panels created the monolithic façade the architects had envisaged.

Earthquakes Halt Construction

When the Forum was in its design stage, no seismic building regulations were in place in the Netherlands, but as construction was about to start in 2012 an earthquake was felt in Groningen's city centre. The tremors in the province resulted in guidelines for earthquake-resistant construction in 2014 and the National Practice Guideline (NPR) 9998 (the so-called 'green version') came into effect in early 2015. Erwin: "Our client, the municipality of Groningen, asked us to check the Forum against that guideline. We concluded that the building would not be sufficiently resistant to earthquakes. It was also immediately clear that making the building safe would involve more than merely minor adjustments." Construction was therefore halted on 10 February 2015.

Marco: "As far as the regulations were concerned, the construction could have gone ahead, but the municipality wanted to adhere to the principle of due care. They didn't want to risk having a completed building that might not be safe. It took considerable guts to stop construction and have the design adjusted." When construction was halted, the basement layers up to and including the ground floor had already been built, the concrete for the first two layers of the cores had been poured and part of the steel construction had already been prefabricated and was ready for assembly. But everyone had to take a step back: the future of the Forum was uncertain for several months.

Searching for Solutions

Together with the main contractor, BAM, ABT explored various options for making the Forum earthquake-resistant. Advice was also sought from two construction firms in New Zealand, Aurecon and Holmes, who specialise in earthquake-resistant design. Erwin: "We recalculated the Forum using their advanced calculation programs. Reinforcing the building with an external construction was out of the question, of course. We could also disconnect the superstructure from the substructure and put it on 'rubbers' – this is known as base isolation – but then we wouldn't have been able to use the basement as a parking garage. Another option was to make the ground floor a weak link, allowing the floors above to move, which would have given the façade a completely different look. We opted for the fourth option: strengthening the overall construction. As a result, the building now stands firmly on the ground, even if it trembles."

From December 2014 to May 2015, the architects, engineers and contractors worked together on a new design with a structural surplus intended to prevent parts from breaking or warping too much. This resulted in a building with a 'near collapse' rating in NPR 9998: it can withstand earthquakes to the extent that users have more than enough time to evacuate safely.

Revisions to the Design

The Forum's concrete cores and ground floor were demolished and rebuilt with additional reinforcements, as were the walls on level -1 below the cores. By closing up or reducing the size of several apertures, the structural engineers reinforced load-bearing lines in the corners of the concrete cores. In the café on the ground floor, for example, there are now two instead of three openings, both placed slightly further from the corners. The concrete in the cores and façades is of higher quality and more heavily reinforced. In the basement, some columns have been strengthened by adding metalwork on the outside and pouring extra concrete, creating columns with oval rather than circular sections in order to keep as many parking spaces as possible.

Steel truss bars, beams and columns are now of a heavier construction or have been reinforced with extra supports by linking the steel-frame concrete floor to the steel structure using dowels and lateral torsional buckling supports. Joints in the steel construction have also been reinforced, especially at the points where the steel boxes connect with the concrete cores. The ceilings have also been seismically reinforced. Heavy parts have been secured more firmly to prevent them from falling. All these reinforcements have been designed so that the structure is almost invisible: the atrium is light and transparent, surrounded by the squares, enveloped by a smooth shell in glass and natural stone. This would never have been possible without the integrated design approach and respectful cooperation. "We solved all the problems without really having to compromise on the architectural and structural concept," concludes Erwin ten Brincke. "That's what I'm most proud of."

Sliding details for fixing the glazed façade elements to the steel girders.

December 2017: on the far right a glass element has just been suspended from the steel beam. On the left the concrete façade with sliding details for hanging the natural stone cladding panels.

Kink in the north façade, completely flush on the outside, with the necessary tolerance between the glass surfaces in connection with earthquake resistance.

Kink in the south façade: the glazed façade construction also has slender detailing on the inside. Because the façade construction connects seamlessly on the outside, it is staggered on the inside.

Designed with Integrity and Respect

The north façade:
the kinks in the
glass façade have
an especially
minimal design.

The large cinema
on levels 6 and 7 is
supported by two
slanting columns on
the film square and
in both the north
and south façades
by one of the two
façade columns.

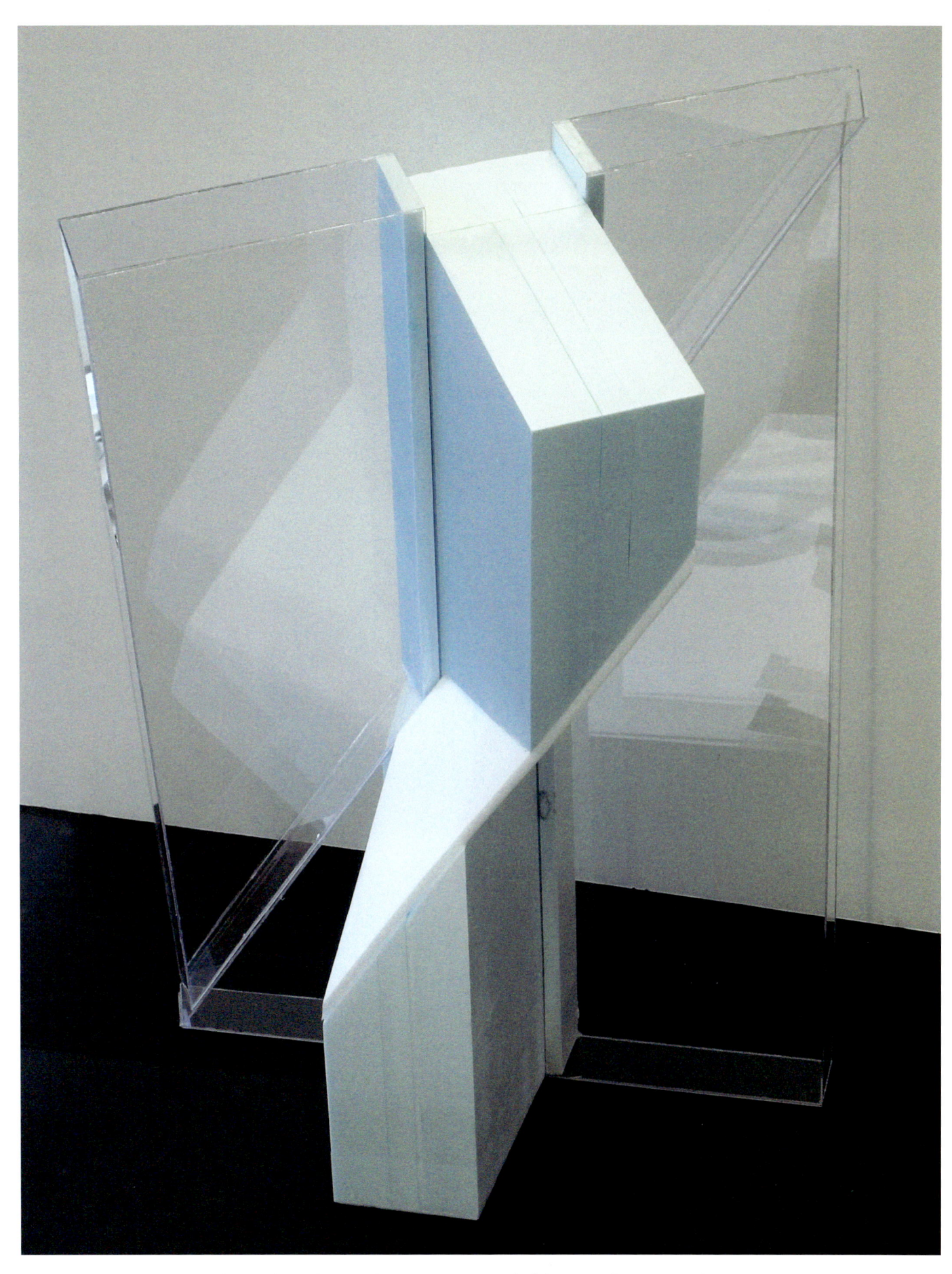

Triple glazing has an excellent insulation value, making it a relatively new weapon in the fight against climate change. Indeed, its insulation value is so high that virtually no heat loss occurs. Surprisingly, under particular circumstances, when the outer shell is sufficiently cold, condensation on the outside occurs, making the glass façade temporarily opaque.

ign

Simon Henley

The Architectural Promenade of the Parking Garage

Reflections on car parks rarely begin with the geology. But mine does, because here it has had such a huge impact on how the landscape was settled, and how the city of Groningen, the Forum and the parking structure beneath it came to be. Groningen is close to the Wadden Sea, the mouth of the River Ems and trading routes in Northern Europe. This is no accident. A ridge of sand called the Hondsrug stretches diagonally across the Netherlands to this remote northeast corner of the country, once forming a land bridge through marshland. The Hondsrug quite literally provided a causeway to, and foundation for, a city that was once a strategic outpost and member of the medieval Hanseatic League.

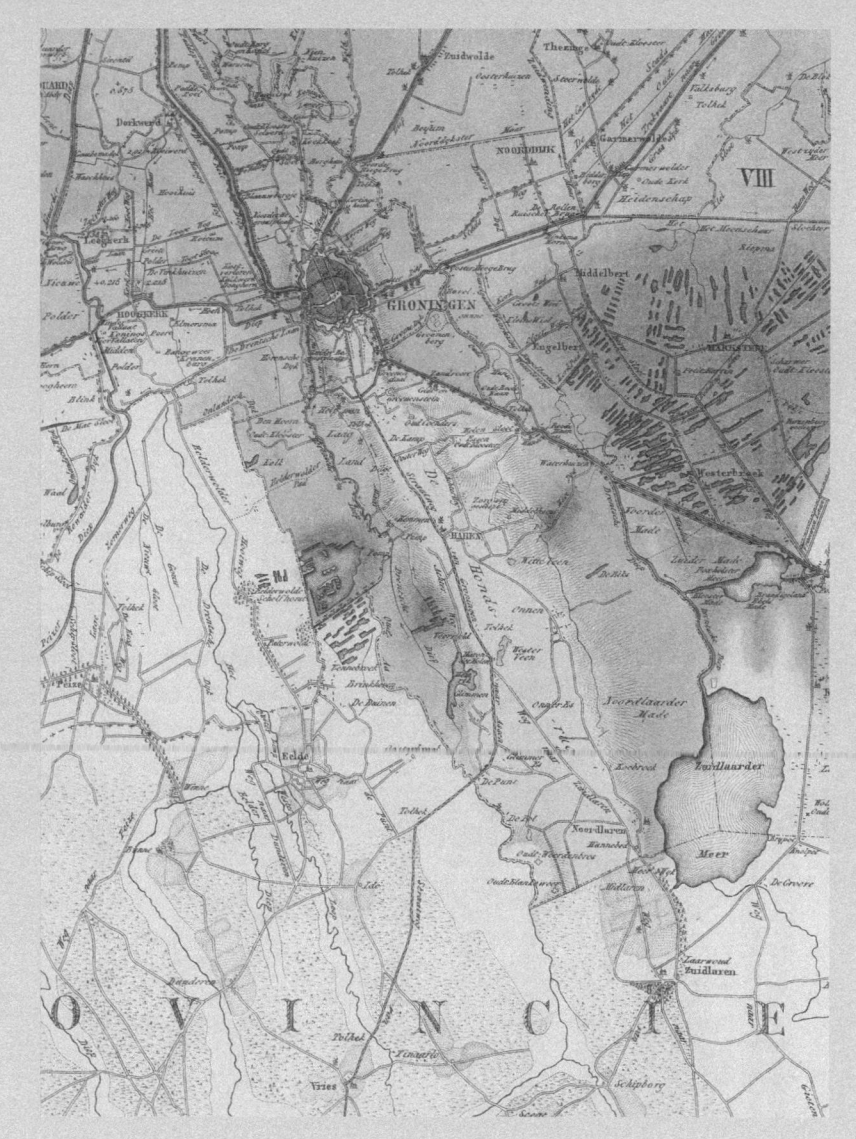

Map of Groningen by G. Acker Stratingh, 1837, with soil conditions and water management. The map clearly shows that Groningen lies on the border of different soil types: sand (yellow), clay (blue) and peat (grey).

Not surprisingly, the car park beneath the Forum is very definitely a parking *structure*. To be more precise, it is a nexus of structures. Here, engineering and architecture are inseparable, as indeed are the design and construction. The car park must deal with the immense hydrostatic pressure from the water-saturated earth that surrounds it, the shear mass of the nearby buildings that bears down on that earth, and the forces descending from the eleven-storey structure of the Forum itself above. The convivial street life of Groningen belies the fact that, below ground, this parking structure has been built in a geologically hostile and challenging landscape.

The Herculean task of construction began with the excavation of a 17-metre-deep trench that was to form the car park's perimeter. The trench was cut in sections and, as the earth was removed, the cavity was pumped full with a material called bentonite slurry. This mix of clay and water, which formed a thick, sticky, yogurt-like liquid, stabilised the walls of the trench, and in doing so, stabilised the ground and buildings that surrounded it. A permanent metre-thick diaphragm wall was then cast by pumping concrete into the cavity, displacing the slurry. The wall is thicker on the south side to protect the neighbouring historical buildings.

Once the diaphragm wall was complete, the excavation of the hole could begin. The walls were braced with a line of huge, tubular-steel struts – the so-called 'shoring layer' – that was moved to a second, lower level during excavation. Then, the 17-metre-deep space was flooded, and a tank of water was created to further stabilise this temporary structure. Floating barges, tethered to the walls by cables, were then used to sink the pile foundations for the building above to a depth of thirty metres beneath street level. Then a metre-thick blanket of concrete was laid by divers at the base of the tank.

Walking around the streets of Groningen today, it's easy to forget what lies beneath the ground. That is until you need to excavate a vast hole for an underground car park. The Forum's position to the east of the Grote Markt places it just on the edge of the Hondsrug ridge, on boulder clay – a mixture of sand and clay – and it is this that drove the design, at least of the car park, and has left an unmistakable mark on its interior. Above it, the Forum – a chiselled monolith of stone – slots into a void in the city fabric, surrounded by streets and several historical monuments.

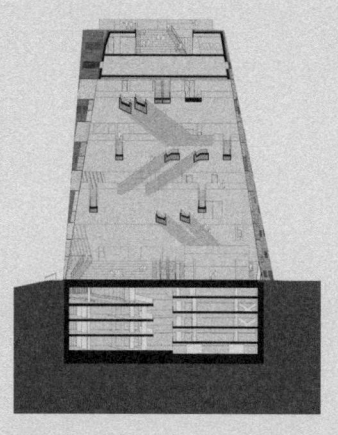

The Architectural Promenade 187

The technical drawing for this concrete slab is a curious thing. The top and bottom faces of the slab are illustrated with sinusoidal lines representing the dimensional variance of its surfaces – 25 cm below and 7.5 cm above – due to its being cast under water. Finally, the slab is anchored down with 7 cm-diameter steel cables tethered by balls of grout embedded in the earth.

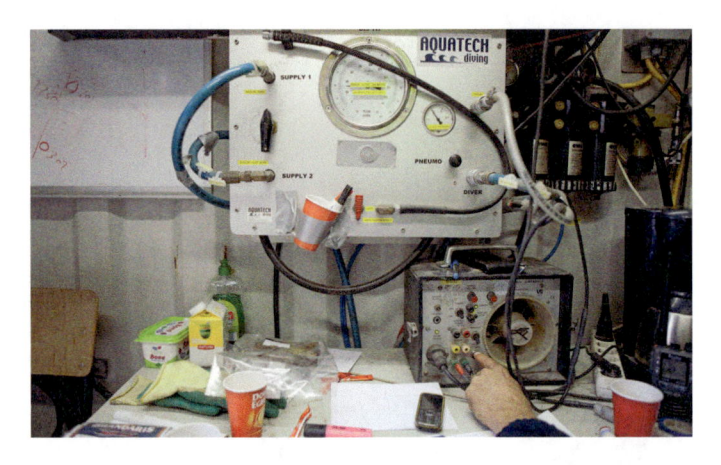

The water was then drained from the tank and the pouring of the decks could begin. Together the slab and diaphragm walls make a watertight compartment for the car park. Its first deck was cast fifteen metres below ground level, (two metres above the 'underwater slab'), followed by the remaining decks that form a continuous surface that spirals up five floors to street level. These oblique planes of concrete are stacked three metres apart, one above the other. Because the decks were slowly curling up from the construction pit, the shoring layer was brought back to the first level halfway during the pouring process. Just before the last underground layer was poured, the steel struts were completely removed.

Sadly, the construction covers up much of the engineering and yields few clues about its extraordinary process. Except for the walls, which immediately attracted my attention. I had descended by lift from inside the Forum to the car park's lowest level, where the spiral that starts some fifteen metres above at street level comes to an abrupt halt beneath the inclined soffit of the penultimate deck above, the space beneath closed up by a wall painted in bold red and white arrowheads. Here I stood next to a rugged, uneven surface that appears more like something found than made. What I was actually looking at was the interior face of the perimeter diaphragm wall, which had been created by pumping concrete into the earth-lined trench at the beginning of the process. Everywhere I walked, my view was enclosed by this rock face – the structure and composition of

The Architectural Promenade

compounded earth layers as a natural counter-mould of the parking garage, the literal imprint of clay cavities and erratic boulders as an artificial rock formation petrified in the wall.

The geometries are subtle. The car park is almost rectangular but for a semi-circular end to the west – like the apse of a cathedral – and a splay in the plan that finds expression in a narrow chasm with a tight radius to the west and larger one to the east. At each end, where the decks span the full width of the plan, they work as permanent struts transferring the ground pressure from one side of the volume to the other, the roadway wrapping around the outside of the two circulation cores, as if they act like the reels of a tape.

What I was standing in was a huge 15-metre-high, 102-metre-long and 46-metre-wide cavern formed by water. Into this huge space the delightfully thin concrete parking decks – there are no downstand beams – had been seemingly lowered onto variously shaped and positioned columns. These provided a second clue to the complexity of the building as a nexus of structures. Above street level, huge steel trusses and hangars span the volumes of the Forum. These are carried by a heterogenous array of columns. And beneath, the pile foundations descended thirty metres into the earth. Here, these two systems meet, in the 15-metre-high volume of the car park.

The engineering in part resolves these two systems with some explicitly interstitial structures in the car park's soffit (the floor of the Forum) but, in effect, all the columns within the space are transfer structures of one sort or another, positioned and dimensioned to resolve the complex vectors of force from above with the substructure below. This generates a family of variously dimensioned circular and stadium, 'sausage-shaped' columns (45 cm diameter, 45 x 75 cm and 60 x 100 cm). All are positioned between

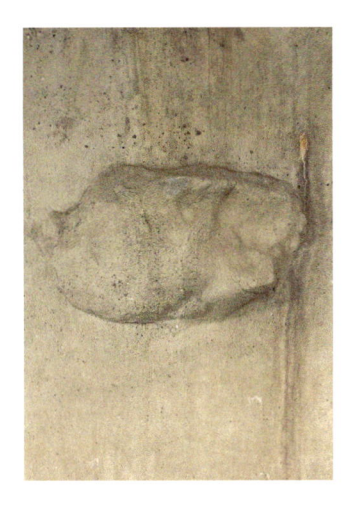

the parking bays, but their location varies in relation to the carriageway, and their frequency – every three or four parking bays – betrays the fact that much more complex forces are at work than one might expect wandering around a more conventional parking structure. Further clues to the forces at play are revealed by a pair of concrete cross braces in the northwest and southeast corner.

The columns, like the soffits of the parking decks and walls of the cores, are all fine fair-faced concrete. This careful precision intensifies the contrast between the elements and exaggerates the texture of the perimeter wall, where in several instances large lumps, like boulders, project from the wall into the space. These contrasts in the architecture are continued and heightened in the monochrome painted surfaces of the parking decks. Predominantly light grey, the parking bays, pedestrian crossings and dashed lines in the centre of the carriageway are marked by differently dimensioned and proportioned rectangles and directional arrows, all of which are black. There is a delightful synchronicity in the coincidence of the linear white lights on the grey soffits and black dashes on the light floors.

At the centre of the space, the elongated five-storey void is lined by a spiralling balustrade made from sheets of unframed glass cantilevered from the edge of the parking deck. Into this canyon, an artwork – a ribbon-shaped, double-sided screen with ever-changing, colourful digital imagery – has been suspended. The combination recalls the Art Nouveau, stained-glass cupola of Galeries Lafayette, the department store in Paris. Ultimately the architecture establishes a spectrum of surface textures, with its rough monochrome perimeter and colourful, highly reflective centre. I might not have really appreciated the glamour of it all had I not witnessed a fashion shoot in the canyon fifteen metres below the street.

The Architectural Promenade

The Forum car park does not share the precise circular geometry of the Q-Park Ossenmarkt on the north bank of the Spilsluizen in Groningen, or other underground car parks further afield such as Parc des Célestins in Lyon by architects Michael Targe and Jean-Michel Wilmotte and visual artist Daniel Buren, but instead has more in common with UN Studio's four-storey, continuous-surface car park beneath their Arnhem Central Bus Terminal. Where Q-Park Ossenmarkt and Parc des Célestins are idealised by their pure concentricity, the drive, maintaining the same lock behind the wheel for the duration of the descent or ascent is not so fun. Whereas the same journey in the Forum car park is more akin to an alpine road, memorable for the long, straight stretches, occasionally interrupted by the sweeping curve of a corner: an altogether more lyrical drive.

Of course, most twentieth-century car parks were built above ground. It is only in the last thirty years that city-planning policies and city-centre land values have led to the development of underground parking structures. Together with the greater attention given to the driver-as-pedestrian in these spaces, this has brought with it a new humanism, and a variety of poetic explorations, including the dramatic use of artificial light in Eduardo Souto de Moura's car park beneath the Marginal de Matosinhos in Portugal, the refinement of finishes in two of OMA's projects – Souterrain in The Hague and another under Euralille – and the introduction of vivid colour and graphics in Teresa Sapey + Partners' car park beneath the Hotel Puerta America in Madrid.

More than any other characteristic, though, it is the obliquity of the continuous-surface parking structure that clearly appeals to NL Architects, demonstrated in the design of their unbuilt Parkhouse/Carstadt in Amsterdam, which dates back to 1994. Indeed, their

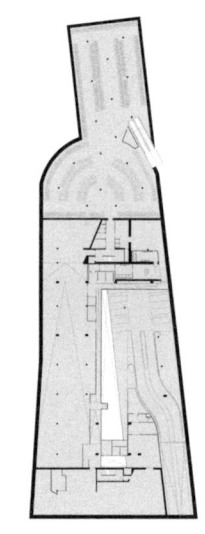

Level -1

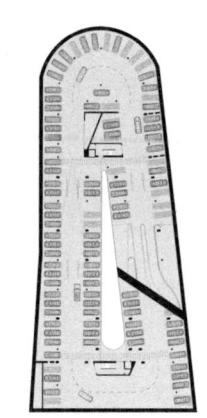

Level -2

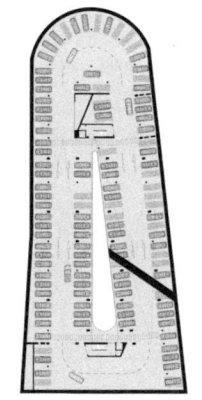

Level -3, -4

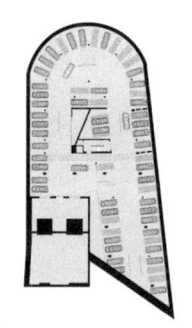

Level -5

preoccupation with obliquity, evident in this early work and their Roof Road NT project from 2001, which envisaged a road and parking on the roof of a row of terraced houses, has become an enduring characteristic of their language and mature works, including the interiors of the Forum building itself. One might argue that the architecture of the Forum above owes much to the car park below.

Finally, it is important to pause to imagine this parking structure (as one might any building) in its native landscape prior to civilisation. Its position below ground affords an abstraction from the contemporary city above, inviting a more direct reading of landscape, not as topography and vegetation, but instead as the geological ground – which we rarely consider, let alone understand – that generates the landscape we encounter.

The Architectural Promenade

The Architectural Promenade

Spectacular Challenges and Smart Solutions

To bring a complex project such as the Forum to a successful conclusion required not only an enthusiastic client, architect and engineer, but also skilled, knowledgeable and energetic people to implement the design. The most important party in this respect was the main contractor, BAM, who worked on the project for seven years. The sloping cores and angled façades presented significant challenges in themselves, but the contractor also had to deal with the construction being halted. Remarkably enough, this also brought new insights, which benefited the implementation.

8 October 2013

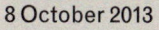

2 February 2014

As BAM's structural engineer, Arnold de Jong was closely involved in the construction of the Forum. The logistics of such a large project on a postage-stamp-sized site in Groningen's busy city centre was one of the major challenges that he and his colleagues faced. "You want to limit the nuisance to the environment as much as possible. There's a lot of traffic in the immediate vicinity of the construction site. A large quantity of materials had to be delivered and we had limited storage space. That was a huge logistical puzzle," explains De Jong. "So, we rented a site on the outskirts of the city that we used as a hub, where construction elements were collected and prepared. One of our small trucks shuttled between the satellite and the construction site on the Nieuwe Markt, so instead of numerous trucks delivering one type of material, we were able to bring a variety of materials to the construction site in a single truck. The driver was familiar with the city and so knew the best routes and took into account the delivery times of the shops in the area."

The hub was used for the bulk materials, while the concrete and floor slabs went straight from the supplier to the construction site. "We organised those deliveries using logistics software. For example, we reserved space under a construction crane for the supply trucks. In the beginning we had two tower cranes and there were two entrances to the construction site. Gradually, the boom of one crane was extended to eighty metres so that it could cover the entire construction site, which meant we could remove the other crane."

7 April 2014

27 May 2014

Underwater Construction

The construction of the five-storey underground car park was also no mean feat. The building site is located right in the heart of the city centre and there were concerns that historic icons such as St Martin's Tower could subside. That did not happen thanks, in part, to a carefully monitored construction procedure. Arnold: "First we constructed the diaphragm walls that make up the boundary of the parking garage. The bottom of the trenches served as natural formwork for the metre-thick walls. From ground level, a large excavator then dug deep trenches into which concrete was poured. Then we partially dug the tank and installed crossbeams to stabilise the lateral pressure. We dug to a depth where the buoyancy had to be compensated with water in the tank, and then continued to dig under water to the required depth. A team of divers cleaned the bottom of the tank, especially in those places the excavators could barely reach because the crossbeams were in the way of the boom. The divers couldn't see a thing and had to clean by touch."

13 August 2014

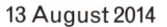

22 October 2014

Logistical Puzzle

The excavation was followed by an even more complicated operation: the pouring of the concrete that forms the garage floor. Arnold: "We interwove the reinforcing metalwork for the floor on pontoons. The divers attached them to GEWI anchor piles in the ground using cranes. We had calculated the amount of underwater concrete in advance and planned its supply exactly. The concrete was fed to the bottom from a pump on land via a second pump on the pontoon. The divers also assisted with this process: the floor had to be approximately one metre thick, and the divers monitored its thickness with the help of a float with GPS."

Henk Broekmans, the main technical supervisor at BAM for the Forum from tender to commissioning, adds: "For one and a half to two days, the concrete was supplied from the concrete plant through the city centre in a continuous flow. We couldn't have any interruptions in the pouring so there were extra mixers on standby at the concrete plant in case one of them should fail. An entire BAM team coordinated this logistical operation, with road closures and exemptions for access to the city centre. About 360 trucks were involved."

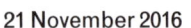

21 November 2016

3 February 2017

While the concrete was poured, water had to be gradually pumped out of the tank. Ultimately, Arnold admits, the floor was not perfectly flat – there is a difference in height of a few centimetres – but it is not noticeable. The lowest level of the parking garage was poured next, followed by the next four parking levels, one per week. Then construction above ground could begin, starting with the two concrete cores.

2 May 2017

Complex Concrete Cores

The next challenge for BAM was to build the two concrete cores with sloping and angled walls. Arnold: "We had never done anything like that before. There is only one straight wall in each core; all the other walls are angled. Before concrete hardens, it has a tendency to sag and can fall off. We looked at a range of scenarios and decided to pour the walls first for each level and then the floors. Each core has twelve floors and was constructed in fourteen pours. The formwork had to be adjusted with every pour, which is why we drew it in BIM. Because the corners of the cores slant in two directions, we had corner pieces made based on the 3D model."

When fabricating and positioning the formwork, you have to calculate with coordinates in a three-dimensional system, explains De Jong. "We worked with a geometry team who plotted the formwork in three dimensions. Based on the points that we clicked on in the model on the underlying floor, the formwork was virtually projected and placed in the correct position. We then built it up in straight lines from the corners. These lines run straight until the point where the angle of the slant changes. We then had to repeat the process from a new angle. We split the corner formwork into two parts, so that we could use some of the formwork elements several times."

26 July 2017

15 August 2017

A slipform platform was hoisted up from the walls that had already been poured in order to pour the walls above them, allowing the construction workers to ascend after each pour. "The geometry of the cores posed a challenge, but so did ensuring the workers' safety during construction," emphasises Broekmans. "But we came up with great solutions for that too. There was scaffolding not only at the height we were working at but also at the bottom, creating a doubly safe workplace. In addition, there were extra escape routes on the inside of the cores."

17 August 2017

BIM and BAM

For the construction of the cores, Building Information Modelling (BIM) proved invaluable. BAM played an important role in the development of the 3D model. Henk: "At the tender stage, there was a bare BIM model that incorporated the steel structure and the installations. We had a good guideline, and the measurements were correct, but many details had not yet been worked out. As a contractor, at the tender stage you have to be able to fill in the gaps in the model. In fact, as with the specification drawings, it is important to prepare the model from the point of view of implementation." Working closely with the consultant engineer, ABT, BAM developed the model to a high level, including all the connections and details, and converted it into working drawings for implementation. The contractor then added the formwork and scaffolding to the model.

10 October 2017

16 Oct

The Council Pulls the Emergency Break

The concrete cores were already at level +2 when the city council decided that the design had to be adapted to meet the new earthquake guidelines. Construction was halted on 10 February 2015. Arnold: "That was a bizarre situation, as if someone pulled the emergency brake and the train suddenly came to a stop. We had never experienced anything like it. We had to call all the suppliers to tell them to stop. Halting construction had a huge impact, not only in Groningen, but on companies nationwide and the quarry in Bavaria. The steel production was in full swing, and from one day to the next, production in two steel factories was shut down for a year."

After announcing the construction freeze, the design team spent two months looking for a new, earthquake-resistant solution, which then had to be fully worked out. Henk: "After that, the suppliers were able to start production again. In October 2015, we began the controlled demolition of the cores and the ground floor. From the beginning of 2016, we made reinforcements at level -1 and construction was resumed. The total delay was almost eighteen months. That wasn't too bad because all the parties remained on board and continued with the project. And we were able to involve them immediately in the design solutions, which worked really well."

7 November 2017

Arnold de Jong worked with ABT on the modified design for the Forum. "It was a great experience tackling the earthquake problem together. We pooled our expertise and together worked out how best to implement the chosen plan. ABT gave us space and contributed to the new ideas and the improvement of the implementation technique."

The building was reinforced by, among other things, inserting additional steel rods of a greater diameter in the concrete. Arnold: "We delineated certain wall and floor nodes in 3D specially for the metalworkers, to indicate exactly where which rod should go. That had to be done very precisely, otherwise no more concrete could be pumped in or the rods wouldn't even fit into the formwork." At a later stage in the construction, when the aluminium rails for the natural-stone cladding panels were installed, the large amount of steel in the concrete façades meant that holes could not be drilled in certain places. "We solved that by reducing the centre-to-centre distance of the holes and using more clickers or bolts, enabling us to anchor the cladding panels better in places where we were able to drill."

7 November 2017

8 March 2018

During the halt in construction, BAM not only worked on reinforcing the Forum structure, but also came up with improvements. Henk: "We developed a new strategy for the installation ducts in the concrete cores. In the Netherlands we have been 'pre-fabbing' horizontal pipe ducts for about thirty years, and I thought: why not do that vertically as well? We conceived a vertical prefab shaft cage, and our people were able to get started right away. One advantage of this invention was that we could now lower all the pipes and ducts that we would otherwise have had to install on the work floor as prefab cages, in the shafts, including floors. That was faster and safer." BAM devised this solution for the Forum and implemented it there for the first time. Since then, the construction company has used shaft cages at more locations in the Netherlands and the solution is also being adopted in England, Belgium and Germany. "You can build faster, with fewer people. And because you build the shaft cages under ideal conditions, you get a higher quality."

Arnold adds: "This prefabrication would not have been possible without BIM, because recesses had to be made in the concrete for the branching of the installations. We were about 25 metres high when the lowest 14-metre pipe shaft cage was hoisted in. And guess what? It turned out that the connections to the concrete cores fitted down to the millimetre. That's unique. It's at moments like that that you realize you're at the top of your game." Henk: "When we saw that, we had complete confidence in BIM. We then built the Forum entirely according to the model."

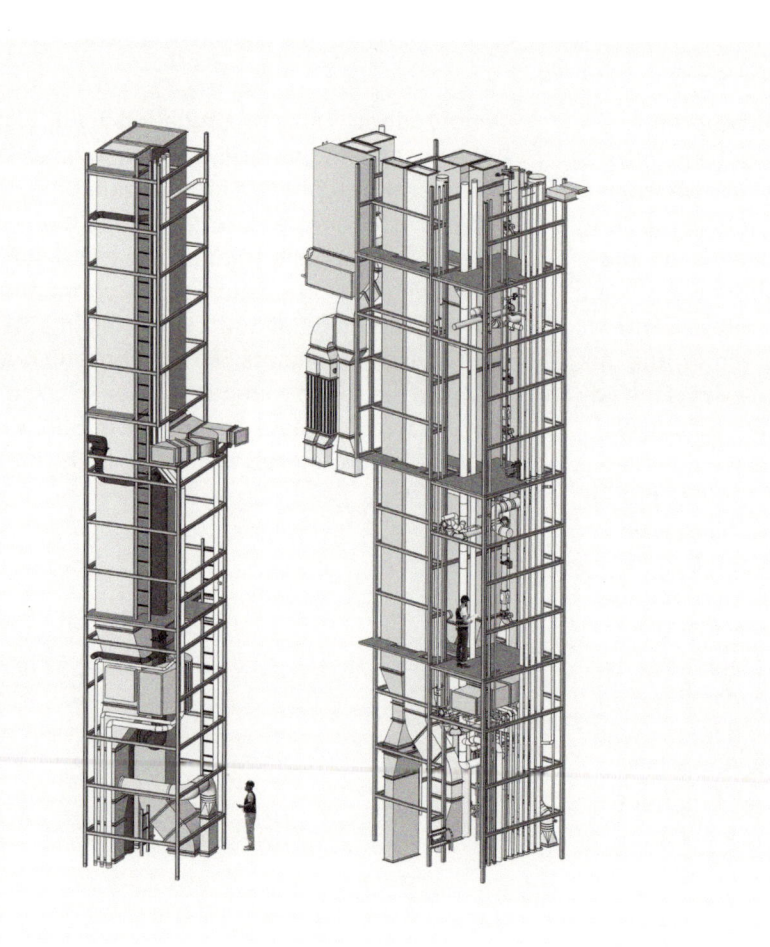

Drawing from the Building Information Model of the prefabricated,
vertical shaft cages. All the pipes and ducts were already
incorporated within the cages so that the builders could
lower them quickly and safely into the concrete shafts.

28 June 2018

17 September 2018

The architects wanted to keep the building's façades and roof as smooth as possible, so there was no place for installations at the top of the building. How did BAM solve this problem? Henk: "We were able to keep the roof empty by concentrating many of the installations on the ninth floor. We created a tech room there with all air handling units, which take in air through façade grilles. The air is then exhausted via a patio on the tenth floor, on the east side of the building, which also houses the window-cleaning installation. The position of the patio means that it is hardly visible, and it is not accessible to the public anyway. The lightning rods are also almost invisibly concealed in the glass balustrades."

The direct connection of air ducts to the façade grilles as originally devised by the installation technician was almost impossible due to the steel construction on site. "Instead, we came up with a different solution: using sandwich panels we created a large plenum, which is accessible through a door." BAM was also commissioned to carry out the technical maintenance of the installations for a period of five to ten years. "We involved our maintenance colleagues in the construction to make sure they would be able to access everything, also in other areas. Initially, the Forum was to have fixed ceilings with numerous hatches. We understood that the architects thought that was unsightly, so we made the installations accessible by positioning them above removable ceiling grilles. We also created hatches in the ceiling that look just like the grilles. This makes maintenance easy. You should always keep an eye on that accessibility, regardless of whether you have a maintenance contract yourself or not. You owe that to the client."

27 May 2019

5 November 2019

Design

220 Design

Gerard Vos

Breaking New Ground with Technology

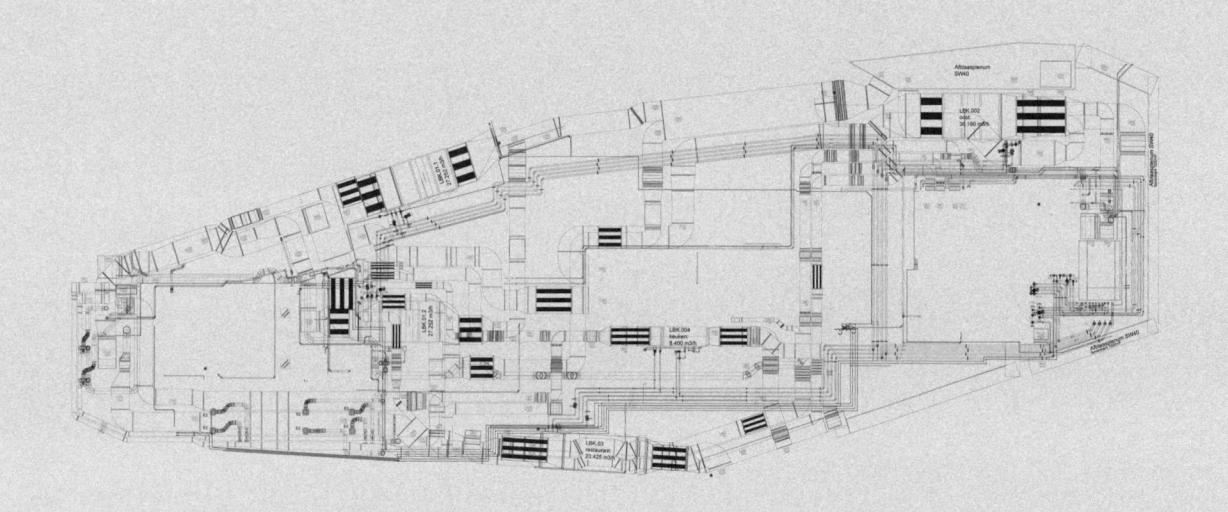

What makes Forum Groningen so comfortable? And how do
you make such a large building fireproof? Forum visitors ask
questions like these every day. Journalist Gerard Vos spoke
with Bert Vrijhof (DGMR), Will van der Weijden and Imre Janse
(both Huisman & Van Muijen) about a range of technical solutions employed in the new cultural attraction.

It is safe to say that, with the Forum, Groningen has acquired a very special building. According to *de Architect* magazine, "Everyone can discover the various places on a journey through the building and be inspired. The new connections enable the various functions to reinforce each other. The result is like a huge cultural department store, in which everyone in the city can find their own place."[1]

Intimate Character

The Forum is intended as a meeting place for residents of and visitors to the city of Groningen. The building houses, among other things, a roof terrace with an open-air cinema, an exhibition space, an auditorium, a comic book museum, a restaurant, cinemas, cafés, a library and a car park. A precondition for these functions is that the Forum must have an inviting and protective character. But how do you ensure that such a large building feels like a warm coat? How do you make each part of the building equally comfortable and ensure that activities in one part of the building do not impinge on others? And, most importantly, how do you ensure that such an open, freely accessible building meets stringent fire regulations?

The answers to these questions are to be found with the design team. Architect Pieter Bannenberg of NL Architects translated his ideas for the Forum into a technical plan together with Bert Vrijhof, building engineering physicist and acoustics expert from DGMR, and Will van der Weijden and Imre Janse, technical installation consultants from Huisman & Van Muijen. There were many new challenges, as Will explains: "Today it's perfectly normal for a building to be gas-free, but that was almost unheard of when we first sat around the table in 2007."

As a design team working on a large-scale, long-term project such as the Forum, you have to have one foot in the future. How did you deal with that?

Will van der Weijden— "We actually started out as a fairly traditional design team. We worked with 2D-drawings and models. The installation technology for the entire building has many components. We had to do a lot of research in the preliminary design phase. It soon became clear that we should convert the building into BIM."

Will— "BIM was rare at that time, certainly in the world of installation technology. Fourteen years later, it has almost become the standard for non-residential buildings. Back then, there wasn't a product library of components to draw on as there is now. We didn't have the opportunity to install parts of the technical systems digitally to see if they fitted. We had a kind of primitive version of BIM at our disposal. This was a major challenge for the three offices that modelled the Forum. To give you an idea: it took half an evening to upload the BIM model. You can't imagine that now."

To select the contractor who would build the Forum, the digital BIM model was used instead of the usual pile of drawings. The model contained both the architectural and the technical components, but it turned out that the digital file was so heavy it did not work on regular laptops. This also made it less easy to quickly extract a floor plan or cross section from the model. Working with BIM was a learning process for all parties, but ultimately it was an indispensable element and one that enriched the experience of all involved.

1   https://www.dearchitect.nl/architectuur/artikel/2019/11/
select-architectuur-van-gestapelde-pleinen-forum-gronin-
gen-door-nl-architects-en-dmdjs-101233162

What is BIM?

Building Information Modelling (BIM) is a digital representation of a building. It is used by all parties involved in the design and construction of a building and enables the client, the architects, consultants, contractors and installation technicians to exchange information. The data is input once and is then available to all involved.

In 2007 there wasn't so much discussion about CO_2 emissions and global warming. How did the choice for a gas-free building come about?

Will— "There was a lot of talk about gas extraction. After all, the Netherlands' natural gas reserves are just a stone's throw away from Groningen. We thought it was an important subject and as a design team we made a rather bold decision: we're going for gas-free. But that certainly wasn't common at that time. There were lots of raised eyebrows. People asked: how can you make such a huge building gas-free? Of course, we weren't a hundred per cent sure that it was realistic, but after various calculations we were confident that it was feasible."

The Forum has freely accessible areas and ticketed venues. The free parts are linked to the atrium with the glass façade and are housed in a clustered series of squares with different functions connected by escalators. Opting for an atrium means that you have to think carefully about the indoor climate, taking into consideration aspects such as overheating and drafts. How did you manage to achieve a comfortable temperature everywhere?

Will— "The atrium was an interesting challenge. A lot of heat is admitted from the external environment and heat is also produced by the visitors, the lighting and equipment. We have used the atrium as a return channel for the air, which converges there from almost all the spaces in the Forum. The warm air rises and is extracted on the eighth floor and conveyed to the central air-treatment room on the ninth floor, after which it is transported to the various spaces via air-purification cabinets and shafts in the cores. This makes it possible to create different environments on different floors."

The Forum's shape is such that it's as if two buildings converge on the ninth floor. Because one of the architectural starting points was that the roof should be a public space with a variety of activities, it was out of the question to have technical installations on the roof.

Will— "It therefore made sense to house the technical heart of the air treatment system on the ninth floor. This also made it easy to vent on the tenth floor, where the restaurant is located. From the ninth floor, a technical 'aorta' for each core transports heating and cooling, electricity and sanitary facilities to the various squares."

Bert Vrijhof— "As a building engineering physicist, you want to keep as much heat as possible out of the building in summer. The original idea was to create a climate façade for the atrium, consisting of an outer double-glazed layer, an inner single-glazed layer and a cavity in between. By ventilating the cavity, you dissipate the heat so that it doesn't enter the building. But we abandoned that idea when we began developing the climate ceilings for the squares."

Specially for the Forum, we worked with a supplier to develop a slatted ceiling with water-carrying elements. Bert: "This gives you a much higher cooling capacity, allowing you to cool or heat the squares individually. It ensures that you have sufficient capacity for cooling in the atrium and can remove the heat, which you can then use in the winter. So, you actually 'harvest' heat. With this system, a climate façade was no longer necessary. We then opted for a façade with solar-control glazing."

Thermal Energy Storage (TES)

By opting for a thermal energy storage system, the Forum does not require a gas connection. A TES installation is an open soil energy system. The system has two groundwater sources with a capacity of 110 cubic metres per hour. In the winter, warm groundwater of about fifteen degrees Celsius is obtained from the heat source. Heat pumps in the Forum heat this water to the temperature required to heat the building. In the summer, groundwater from the cold source is used to cool the building. Two heat pumps are connected to the TES. The warm and cool water finds its way into the building via a central transport system to the reheaters in the air handling units and to the floor systems. The floor systems in the entrance area are able to both heat and cool the space.

Comfort is not only a matter of temperature; acoustics are also an important factor. How did you take this into account in the Forum?

Bert— "It was a complicated puzzle. On the left and right you have fairly massive blocks with stairwells and lifts. These are the building's backbone. Between them, in the atrium, you have the squares, staggered in relation to each other and connected by the escalators. For the squares, we used the 'open ceilings' to absorb the sound, by placing black polyester wool between the ceiling and the underside of the floor above. This creates a good acoustic climate. When it comes to sound, the heart of the atrium is really buzzing. There is more peace and quiet towards the squares and the closed venues. Because the squares are at different heights, the noise from one square doesn't impinge upon the others. I think we struck a good balance. The advantage of polyester wool is that, unlike traditional insulation materials, it doesn't contain additives or chemical binding agents and it's made from recycled plastic bottles."

Acoustically speaking, the cinemas and the auditorium are the troublemakers. Bert: "For these, we devised a light box-in-box construction because the volumes hang in the atrium and mustn't be too heavy. The Technostar walls and the 'vibration-isolating ceilings' in and below the volumes muffle the sound sufficiently. To absorb the noise to the outside, we opted for a light-weight sub-structure as the basis for the natural stone. The heavy façade's mass helps to absorb the low frequencies. Little was known about the construction principles within such a spatial set-up, so without recourse to professional literature and without a 'measurable' situation we were breaking new ground in terms of the influence this would have on the sound. We had to rely partly on feeling and experience. We also had to research and calculate, calculate and calculate again. We had used the box-in-box principle before, but not in combination with this light structure and floor."

How did you make the Forum fireproof? Did the open construction pose a big problem?

Bert— "To keep a fire under control, you normally 'cut' a building up into fire compartments. Because of the open design, we had to take a different approach. For the squares and the enclosed spaces, we ultimately opted for a standard sprinkler system: a ceiling-mounted, fire-extinguishing system with spray heads that can detect, control and extinguish a fire. In the atrium, we used a so-called 'deluge system'. These are sprinkler heads controlled by an infrared detector and a flame detector that can release large volumes of water."

Imre Janse— "The sprinklers for the parking garage are embedded in the concrete. That was a requirement of the municipality. However, in an unheated parking garage, sprinklers close to the entrance run the risk of freezing. Here the sprinkler system is filled with a kind of antifreeze, a glycol mixture that protects the sprinkler system against frost. Deeper within the garage, where there is no danger of frost, we used the traditional water pipes."

In addition to the sprinkler and fire alarm systems, the escape routes play an important role, another area in which the design team broke new ground. Bert: "At both ends of the building you have two independent escape routes housed within a double stairwell. The space in front of the lifts is used as a smoke lock: in the event of a fire alarm, two sliding walls containing a wicket door close automatically so that the stairwells can still be used safely. The fire locks go unnoticed in everyday use. We came up with this design in 2009 with knowledge of the European standard for smoke resistance, which eventually came into effect in July 2021." In short, the building already met *future* requirements.

Deluge System

The deluge system used in the Forum is a dry sprinkler system in which all sprinkler heads are open. In the event of a fire, all sprinkler heads simultaneously release a large amount of water, which provides a reliable extinguishing system in high spaces and on the staggered squares. Because the system must be activated at the right time, infrared detectors and flame detectors are used.

Harvesting Heat

At the heart of the Forum is the atrium. The open design creates a series of split-level squares. The atrium's glazed, south-facing façade lets in plenty of daylight and some solar gain. The solar-control triple glazing ensures that not too much heat enters the building in summer and that as little heat as possible escapes in winter. The glass keeps out seventy percent of the heat. The thirty percent of heat that enters the building is extracted at the top of the atrium. Air from the various venues is also transferred to the atrium. The harvested heat finds its way to the air treatment room, which is located on the ninth floor, directly adjacent to the atrium.

The evacuation is done in phases. Bert: "If you have to evacuate the building in one go, you don't have enough capacity in the stairwell. If there is a fire alarm in the cinema, then that area is evacuated first and then the rest of the building. We have calculated many different scenarios to determine the capacity of the stairwell. In 2009, there were no clear guidelines for this but the solutions we chose now meet the regulations because they incorporate much of the knowledge gained from our design process."

Looking back on the entire design process, what is the most remarkable aspect of the Forum?

Imre— "For me it's the integrity of the design. Everyone has put their own knowledge, skills and professionalism entirely at the service of the integral design. The great thing is that the design originally conceived by NL Architects has been preserved as a result."

Bert— "I agree. We have always given each other time and space, listened to one another and brought out the best in each other. And as a result, we have a building to be proud of."

LEDs in the Forum

In terms of colour temperature and adjustment, in 2008 LED lighting was still in its infancy, but one thing was already clear: energy-efficient LEDs would quickly gain ground over traditional lighting. Will van der Weijden: "The technology had not yet been refined, but we kept an eye on it. In the end, we were even overtaken by the rapid development. In 2016, the lamps we had specified were no longer on the market."

"In 2011, we issued a tender for traditional LED lights. The specific lamps and fixtures are usually chosen at a later stage so that the user can specify their needs. Construction came to a standstill in 2014 due to the earthquake problem, and it wasn't until 2016 that we made the final choice of lamps and fixtures. In the five years since the tender, so much had happened in the development of LED lighting that the switch to LEDs was ultimately an obvious choice."

Bert Vrijhof: "The user was also actively involved in the design. There was a wish to project imagery onto the volumes in the atrium. At first, we considered video projectors, but then large LED screens came onto the market. They were still quite primitive at the time and all those lights gave off a lot of heat, which would be released into the atrium, and you'd rather avoid that. But LEDs suddenly developed very quickly. When the building opened in 2019, it had a state-of-the-art LED screen, at that time the largest in the Netherlands. Whereas heat emissions from LEDs used to be a problem, it's now negligible. It's not an issue anymore."

Teething Problems

Every building has teething problems, and the Forum was no exception. Soon after opening, a problem was identified with drafts, mainly due to the unforeseen huge influx of visitors. More than a million people visited the building in the first three months and many of them visited the roof on the tenth floor. As a result, the sliding door to the roof remained open all the time, as did the draft locks on the ground floor. This created an open channel, with the atrium acting as a 'thermal chimney'. The eventual solution was to install revolving doors.

Breaking New Ground

The art of engineering: during the development of a façade-cleaning mechanism for the Groninger Forum, Manntech (Alimak Group Benelux) built a 1:40 steel model to test the system on the building's complex, slanting form in three dimensions.

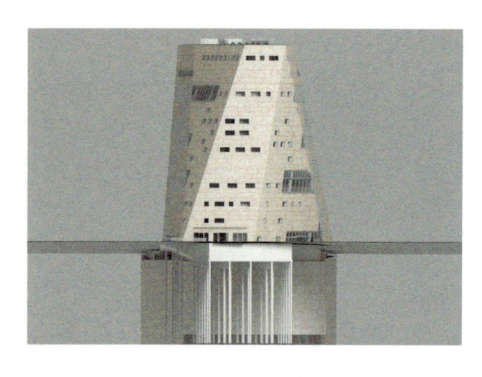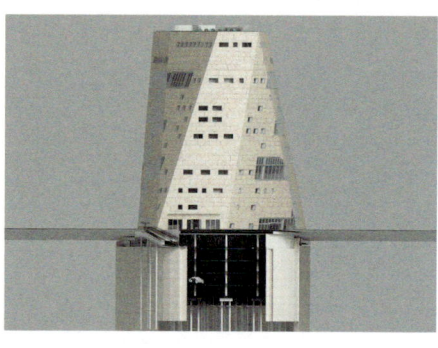
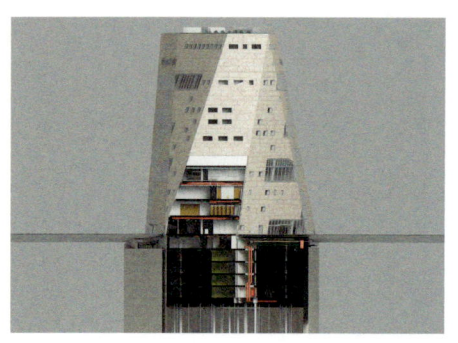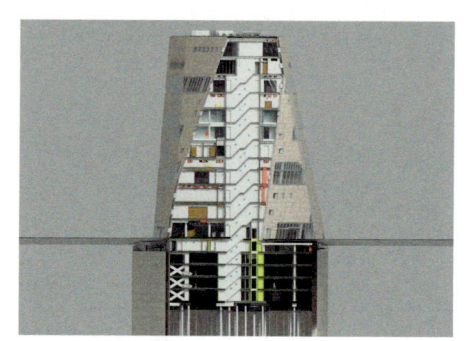
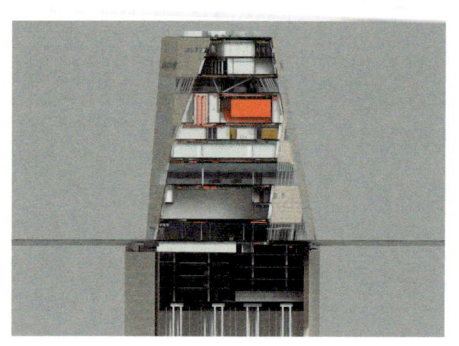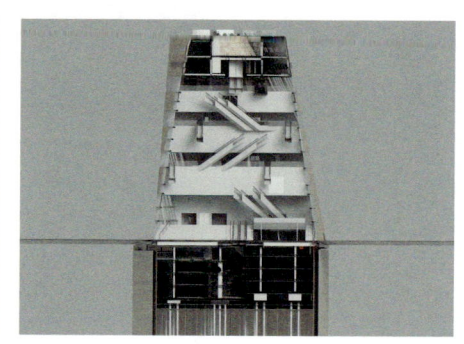

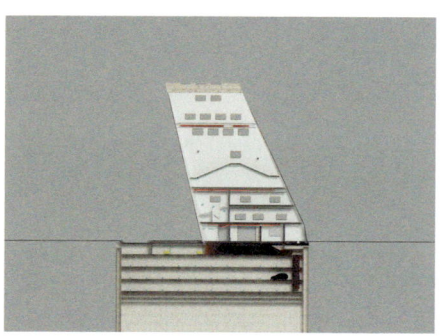

236   Design

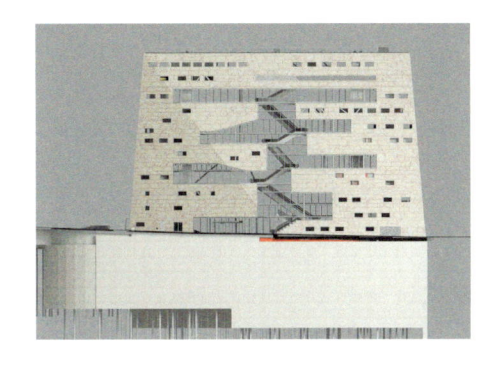
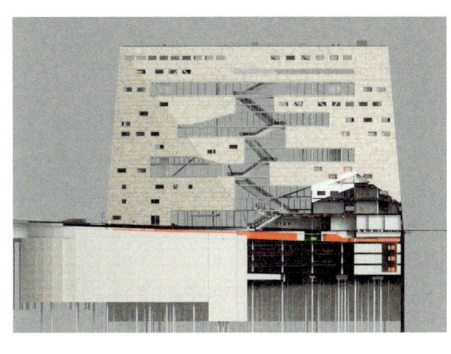
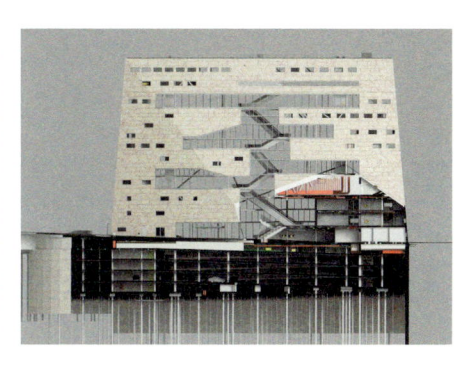

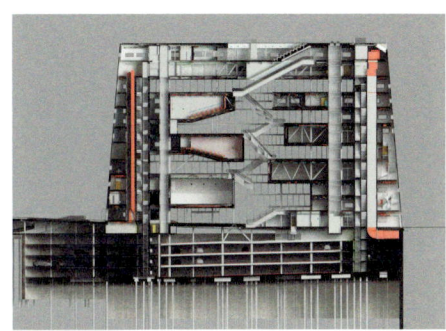

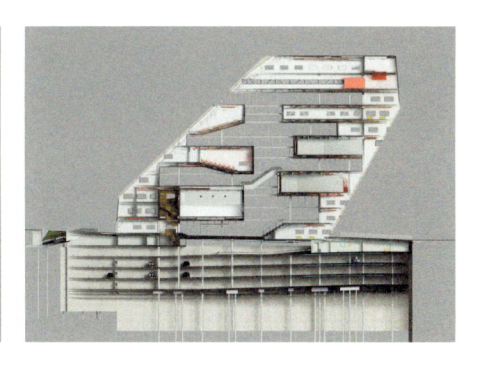
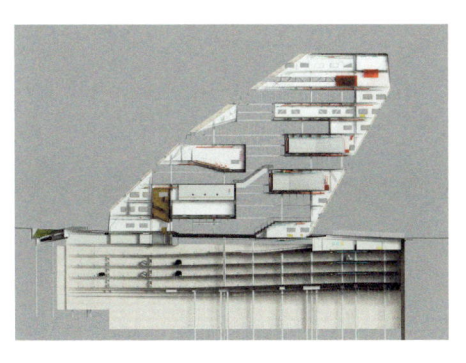

Dirk van Weelden

Looking Beyond the Boundaries of the Existing Paradigm

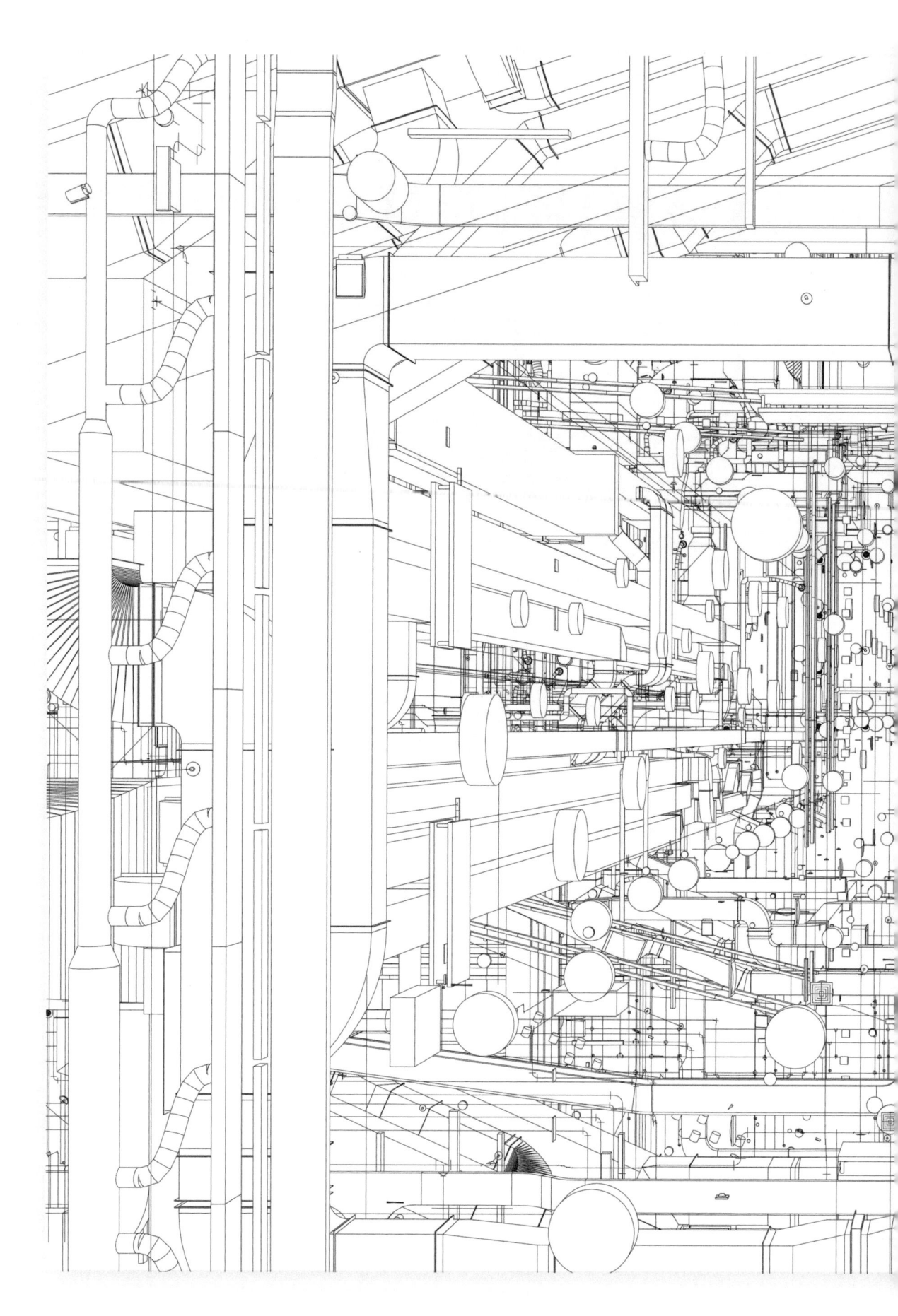

At an exhibition at the Cityscapes Foundation in Amsterdam's Marine Terrain, NL Architects showed images that were part of the final design phase of Forum Groningen. The visualisations showed no floors, façades, or walls but only the building's technical plant, those elements that are usually invisible to users and visitors and which perform their job silently and efficiently: the heating, cooling and ventilation systems, the electricity and water supply, sanitation, and waste extraction and rainwater drainage.

The way these drawings were displayed clearly had nothing to do with what an architect, builder, technician, or contractor would consider useful information. They were either magnified details or overview images containing such an insane number of lines and quantity of information that it was impossible not to view them simply as pure images, as forms from a strange world. They elicited associations with a kind of spectral, twenty-first-century Piranesi. Like everyone else, I stood in front of the framed drawings and looked and looked. But what did I see? And why did I keep looking?

Building Information Modelling (BIM) can best be described as a design model made up of digital data. A model not only of the objects and spatial relationships but also of the materials (their quality), how they are connected to other objects, in which phase of the building process they belong, and what they cost. Such models are intended less for visual contemplation than for digitally posing functional questions. You can link the building's structural drawings and plant diagrams, and quickly discover that air shafts have been accidentally routed through the toilet bowls, or water pipes through the stairs. BIM has become an indispensable tool that enables architects, builders, technicians, and contractors to collaborate more effectively.

BIM is a no-nonsense product whose aim is to minimise embarrassing mistakes, but it also has a whiff of hubris about it: the twenty-first-century delusion that we can have a firm grip on reality by translating everything into a gigantic cloud of dimensions and coded data. NL Architects' BIM prints seemed like a playful gesture to question and test that hubris.

241

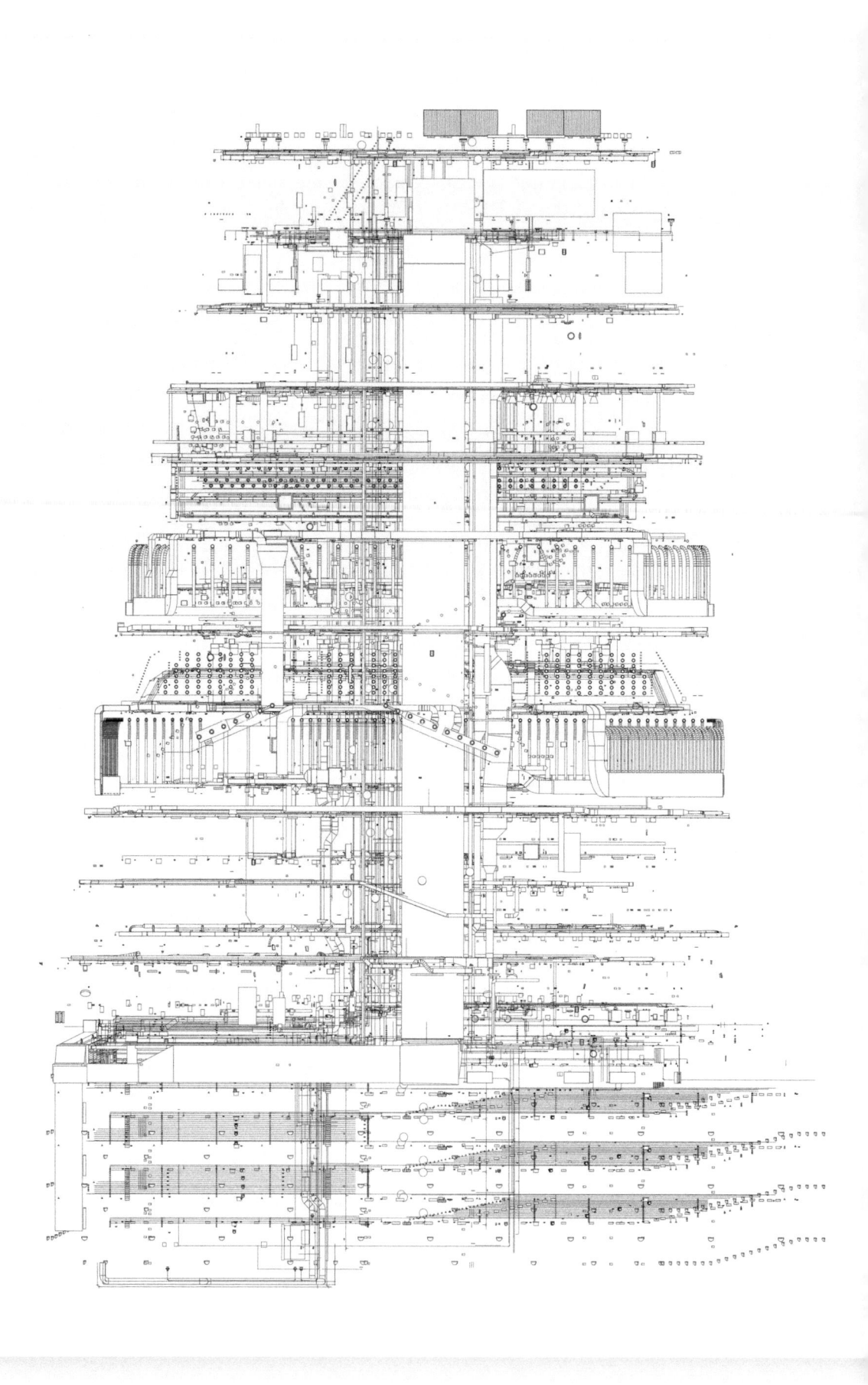

The images also called to mind the anatomical drawings of Leonardo da Vinci, who, together with medics, dissected and examined some thirty corpses of men, women, and children. He described and drew what he saw in an attempt to understand how the human body works and how it is put together. Such research encountered considerable resistance in his day as the Catholic Church and the universities considered it degrading and unchristian. All that God wanted men to know about the body and nature was contained in the writings of classical antiquity and of Christian scholars and theologians. Further investigation was dangerous, vain, and sinful. Leonardo kept the notebooks with hundreds of sheets of anatomical drawings and texts to himself during his life. Sometimes he showed them to colleagues, such as the German artist Albrecht Dürer, but he did not publish them.

Why did the framed BIM prints make me think of these five-hundred-year-old drawings? It has something to do with Leonardo's manner of perception, his way of looking when focusing on, for example, the cardiac muscle. His motto was *ostinato rigore* (relentless rigor). Unlike the university doctors with their theological biases, Leonardo did not see what is invisible in the human heart: a soul or divine purpose. He looked at it as he looked at the reflection of sunlight on a beech leaf. He did his best to look from a non-knowing point of view in order to have the most direct contact with nature. He wanted to acquire knowledge of matter and living beings that he could use as an artist, architect, and designer. That was a new relationship with nature.

Leonardo's gaze was that of an artist, but one who sought knowledge, not just beauty. He wanted to free his perception from magical thinking, from moral, ideological or social norms. That suited him well as an illegitimate child, an autodidact and a craftsman. He was guided by his senses. He was also constantly looking for a preliminary synthesis. Even when working on the basis of conjecture and hypothesis, he wanted to understand how a heart works, why it is the way it is. He always said that he wanted to understand everything in order to become a better artist and to pass on that knowledge, to capture the poetry of nature. That is why he not only weighed and measured, but also used his intuition and imagination. He felt his way and asked

243

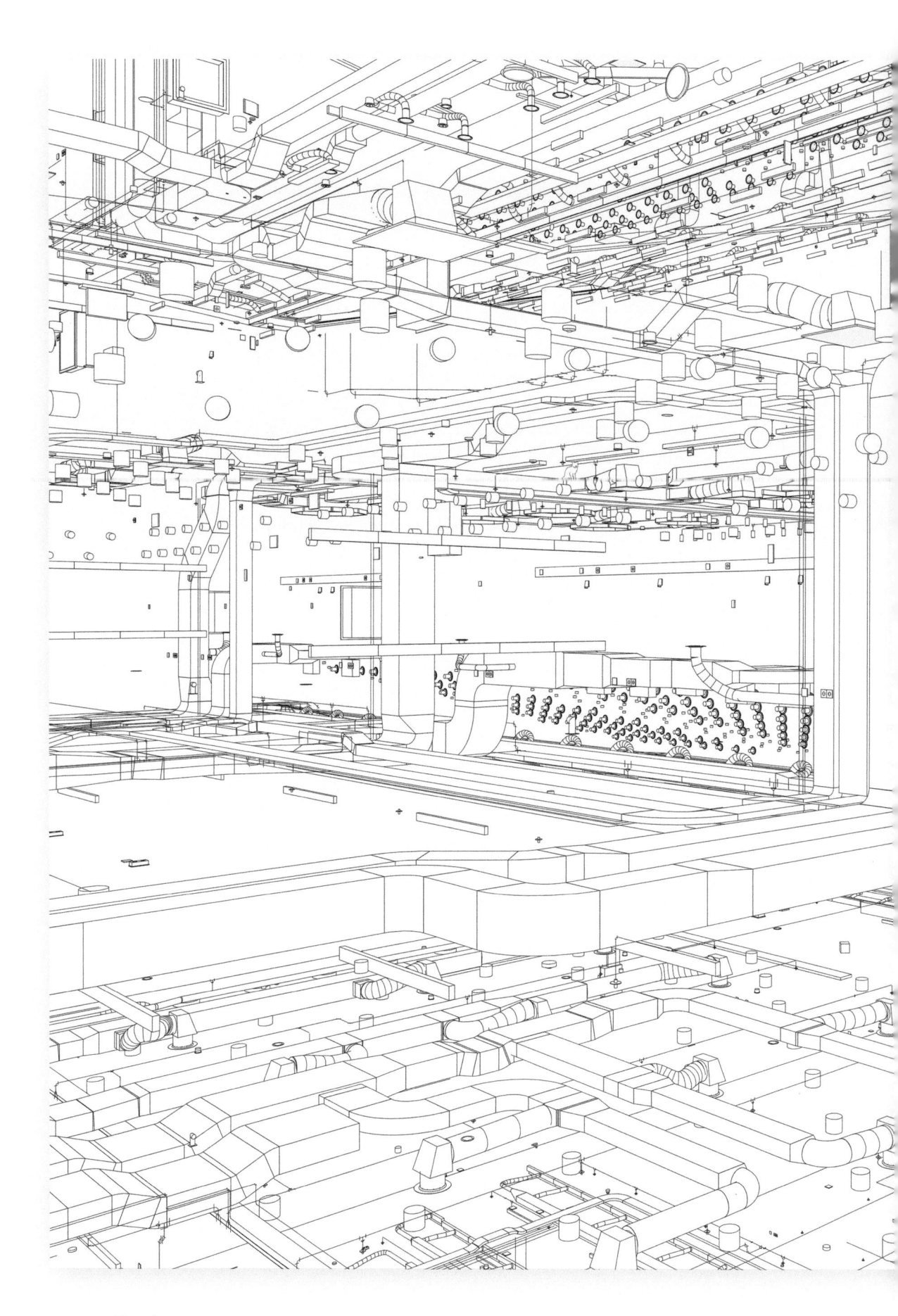

Looking Beyond the Boundaries

questions. His drawings depict the same organ or body part from multiple angles, varying his drawing style to capture different textures, relationships, and workings. He injected molten wax into a bull's heart and veins in order to make a cast in transparent glass that enabled him to observe the vortex movement of grass seeds in water as the heart pumps and the valves open and close, accurately describing the fluid dynamics within the heart that were confirmed scientifically by cardiologists only in the 1960s. What was so special about his manner of perception was that it was precise, questioning and open: by definition incomplete, unstable and ambiguous, without stating his primary and subsidiary aims in advance. It was meticulous but undirected, intuitive and without a goal.

NL Architects' jarring BIM prints are an invitation to look at such digital data clouds as Leonardo looked at a gallbladder or a calf muscle. Of course, a BIM drawing represents a completely artificial universe, exclusively comprising conscious human choices and decisions, but such a digital model also has a natural dimension: as a complex and heterogeneous whole, it is not merely the sum of all the conscious choices and intentions it describes. In addition to the construction errors it highlights, it is also a vast swarm of emergent properties, possibilities, comic absurdities, dangers perhaps, which no one designed or wanted.

    If you cast off the hubristic and quasi-omniscient gaze of an architect, builder, technician or contractor, you will be amazed: we can install virtual cameras in the data cloud and see faces in the tangle of pipes and shafts hidden behind a wall. But do we exploit this potential? Between Forum's floors I see a huge bar with high ceilings and spherical lamps floating at varying heights above long tables. Are there spaces that might serve as indoor vegetable gardens? Why is this not the ideal place to allow the rainwater to drain as a waterfall in the atrium?

    If BIM is so good at detecting internal contradictions and errors of a technical and practical nature, it is also the ideal environment to track down the enormous wealth of 'unsought finds'. Surely it would be a shame to spend years working on something without sensing and using that potential.

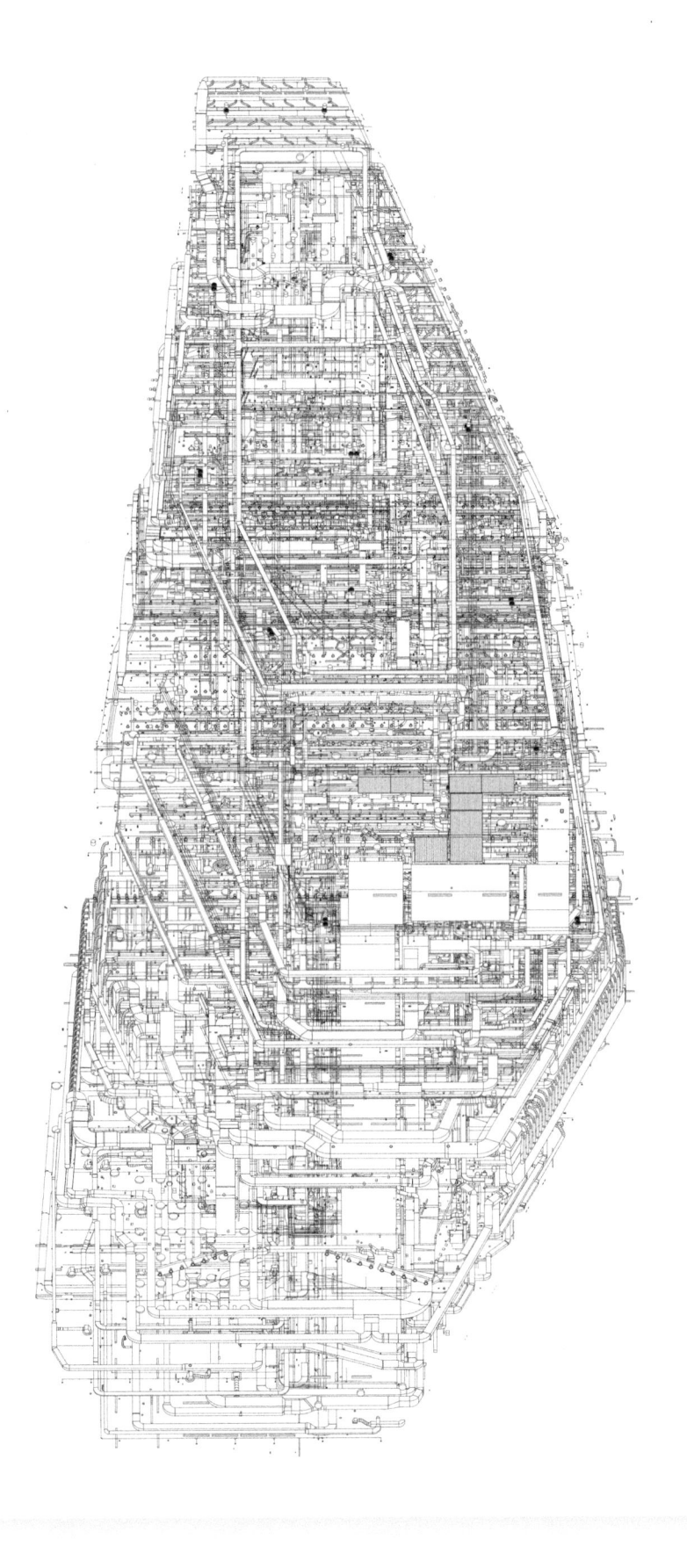

Looking Beyond the Boundaries

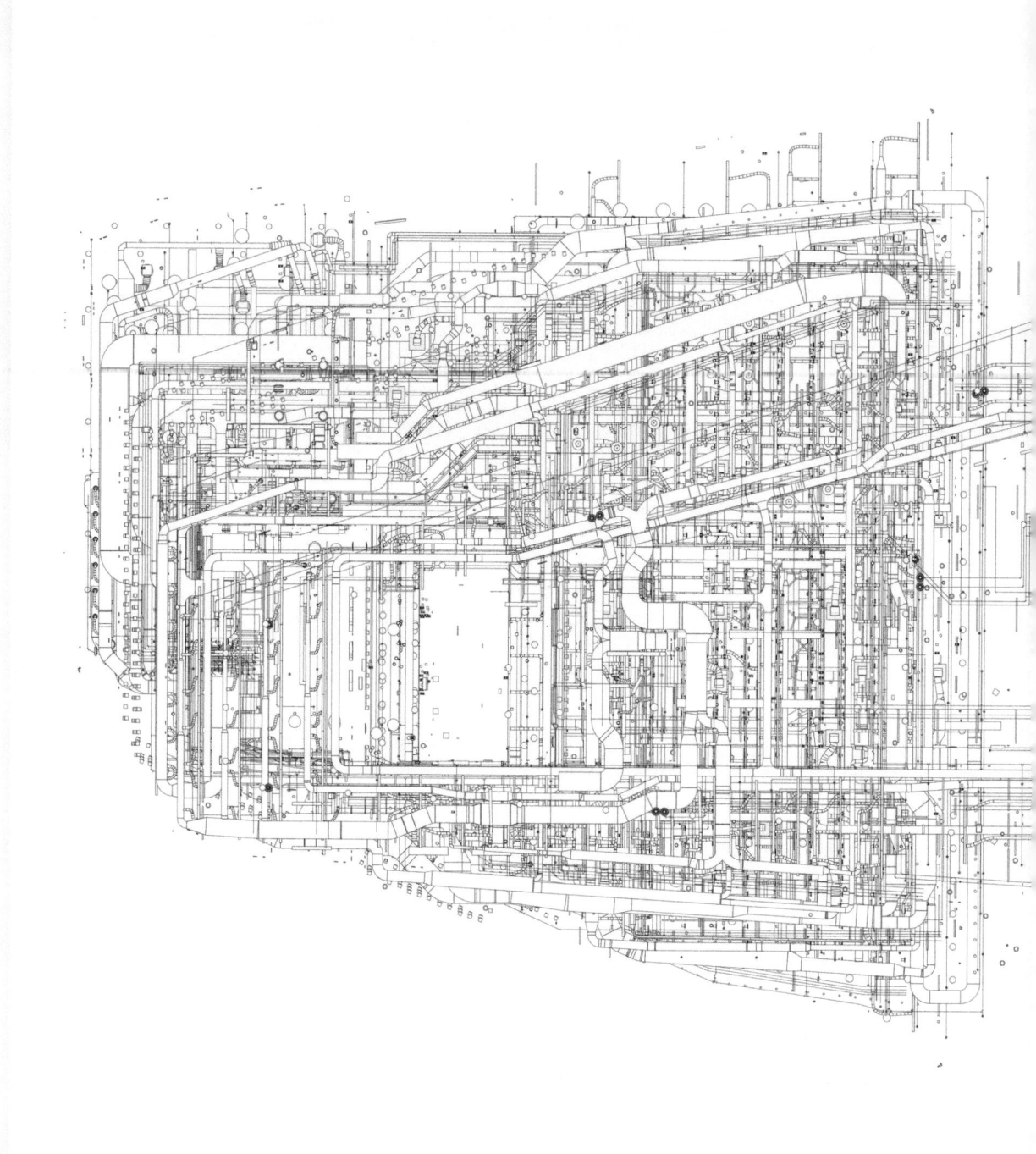

248

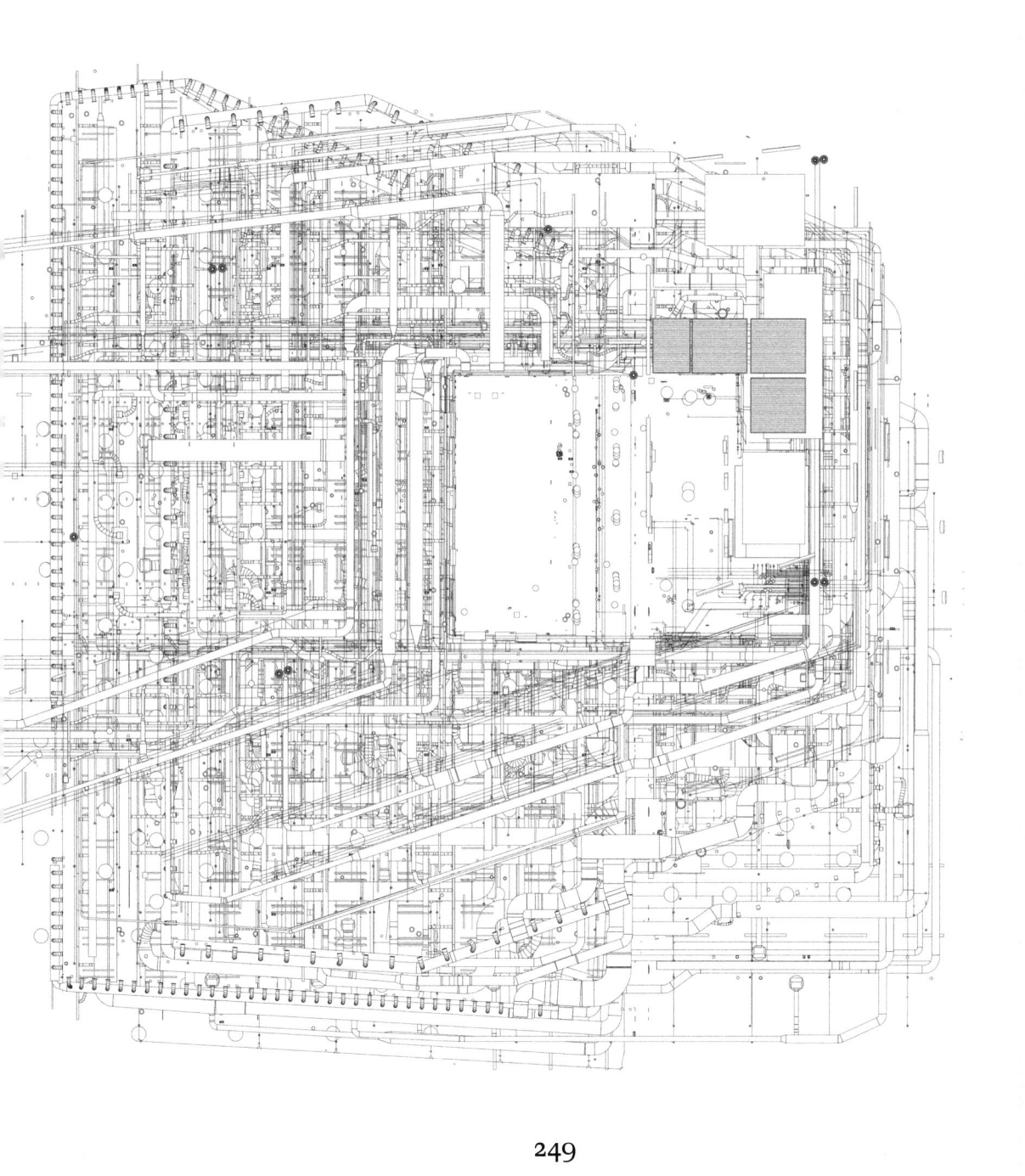

249

Inspired by Leonardo, I advocate freeing up hours in the design process in which artists, dancers, musicians, poets, diviners and pathological liars are invited to embark on an expedition through the BIM data cloud, recording their perceptions, thoughts and associations as a unique form of knowledge of the unintended but valuable potential of the design. Their contribution would not be fantasy but knowledge that lies just beyond the paradigm of building logic, as Leonardo was working on the boundaries of the medieval intellectual paradigm and saw a new world thanks to a free and relentlessly rigorous perspective.

250

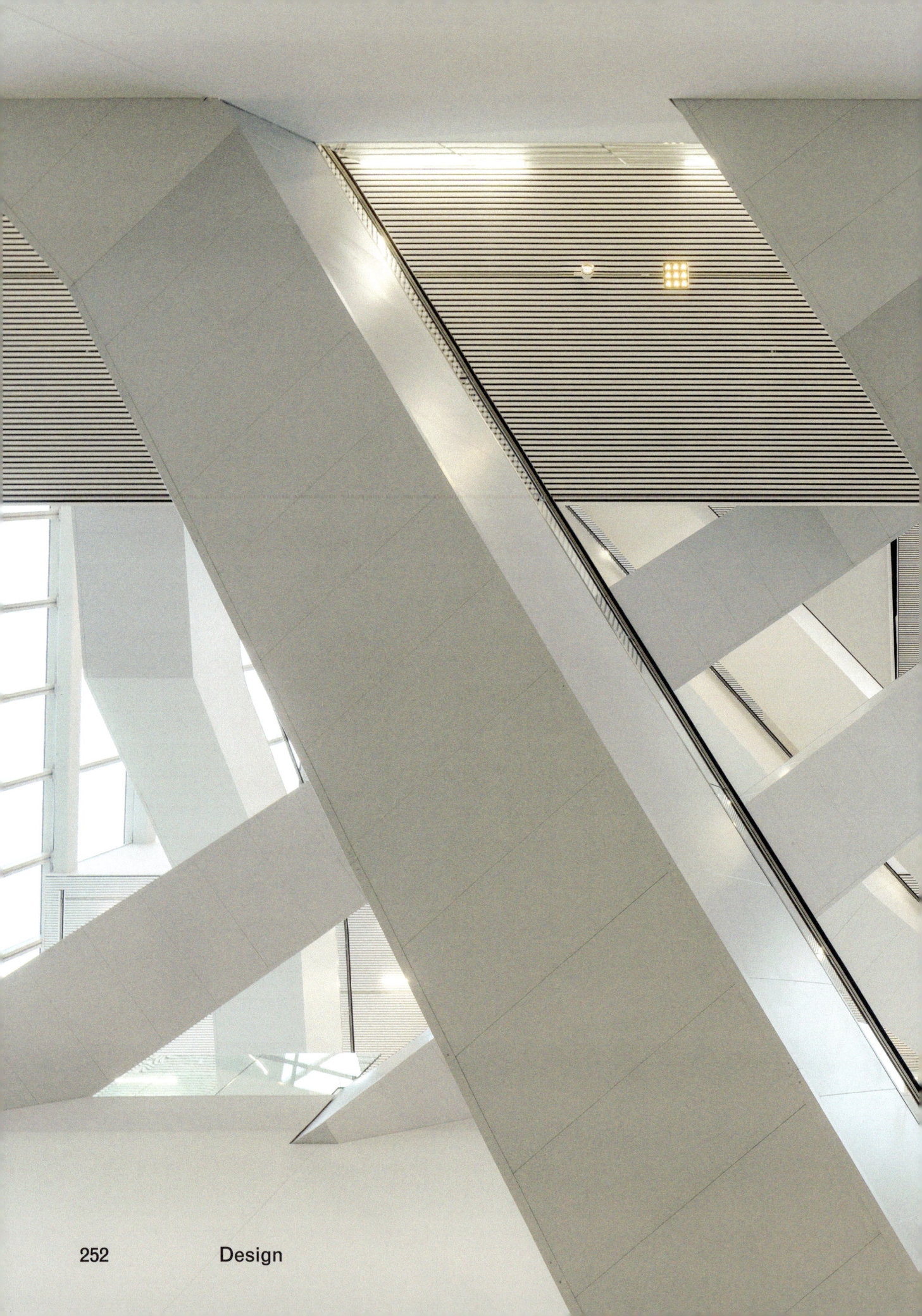

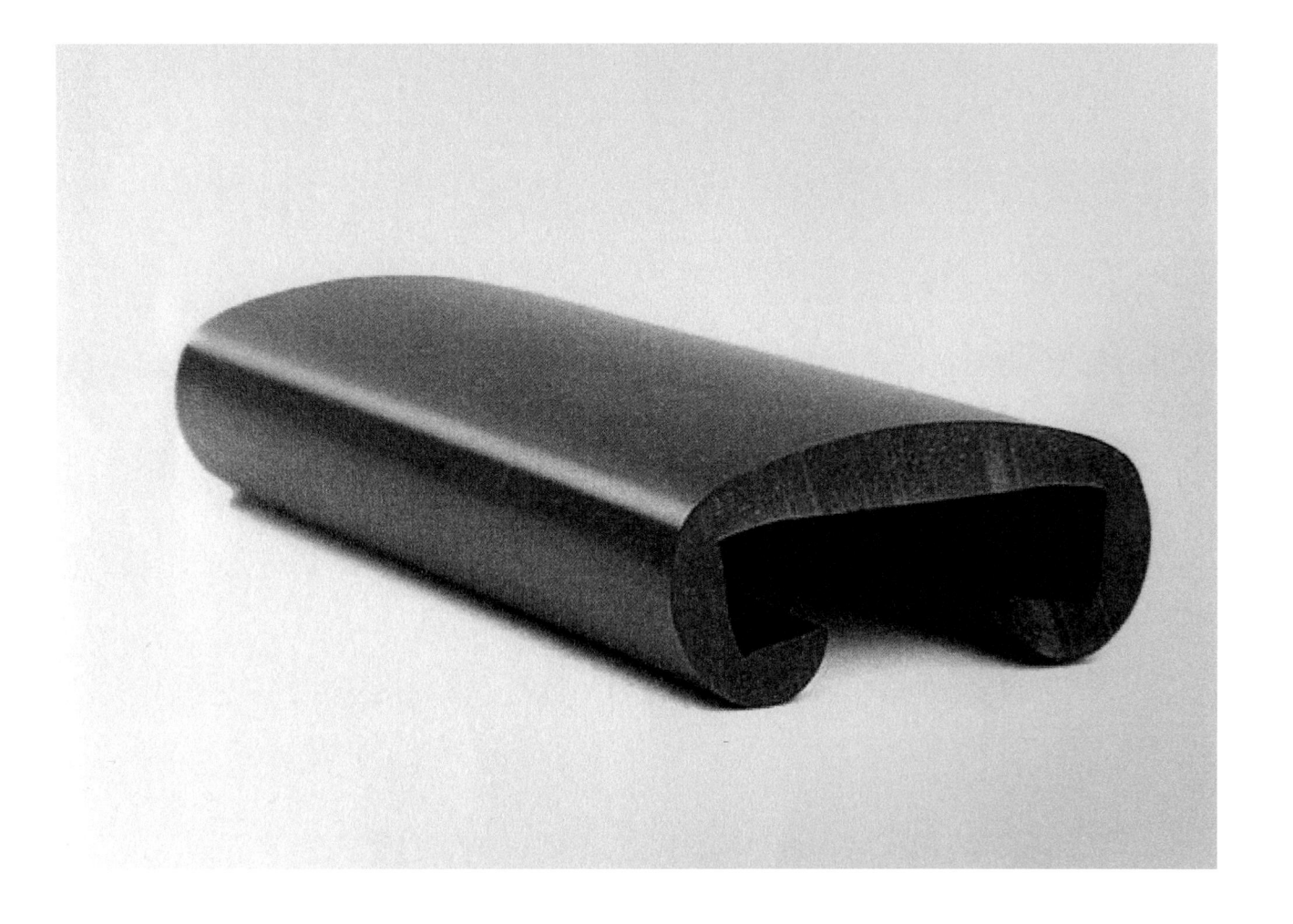

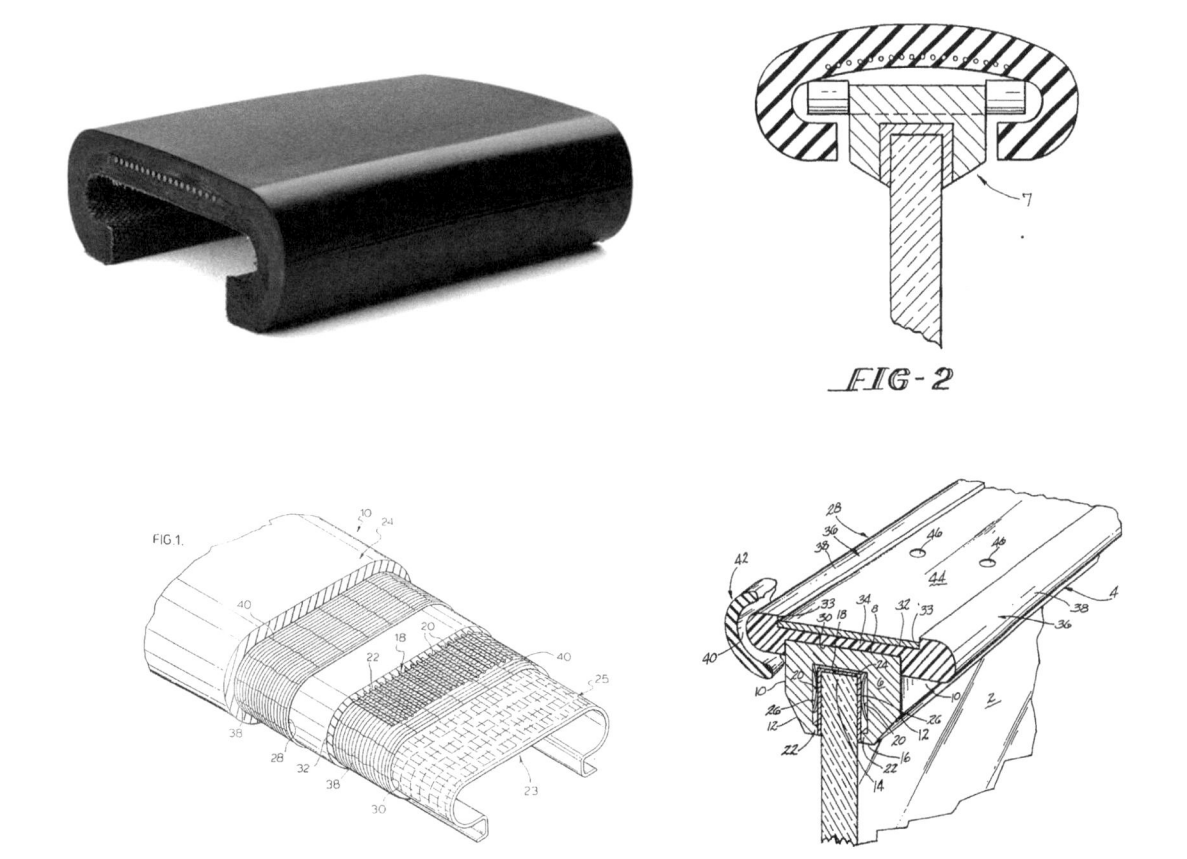

FIG-2

FIG.1.

USE

Use

Pieter Hoexum

A Public Library, a People's Palace... or a Big Friendly Butler?

The invitation to attend a friend's doctoral graduation in Groningen in January 2020 came at just the right moment. It had been a while since I had been in the city where I studied, and I wanted to visit it again. And it would afford me the opportunity to see the recently opened Forum building, of which I had read very enthusiastic reviews in several newspapers.

To be honest, that enthusiasm surprised me. During visits to Groningen over the years, I had watched the construction on the east side of the Grote Markt with growing concern. And now that the building was complete, I could see it standing head and shoulders above the city in several photographs accompanying those newspaper articles. Not a pleasant sight. My suspicions were sparked by an angry column (on the website of the National Renovation Platform) by architecture historian Vincent van Rossum, who called it a "pompous party venue." He notes that, "the first visitors responded with: *Wow*. That tells you everything you need to know: 'Wow' means spectacular foolishness."

Is the Forum part of that worrying trend in which architecture is reduced to sensational spectacle? A few years ago, I heard an architect complain that his role seems to be limited to that of 'aesthetic consultant': the architect as stylist. That must indeed be frustrating: like a heart or brain surgeon being mistaken for a plastic surgeon. Architecture is, after all, not image building. But that, unfortunately, is increasingly what architects are called upon to do: to design an eye-catching landmark, an icon... a logo. Architecture has fallen into the hands of city marketeers and has become a billboard, a trend that started with Gehry's Guggenheim Museum in Bilbao. This alarming development is the subject of the book *The Age of Spectacle* (2018) by the British architecture critic Tom Dyckhoff, even if he offers some hope in the subtitle: *The Rise and Fall of Iconic Architecture*. Surely, they should be aware in Groningen that the iconic building trend is already a thing of the past?

And then there was another, more important reason to visit Groningen and the Forum. In my recently published book *Thuis – Filosofische verkenningen van het alledaagse* (Home: Philosophical Explorations of the Everyday, 2019), I had expressed surprise that the Forum was supposed to become a kind of living room for the city. That sounds very cosy and therefore attractive, but I wondered whether it was possible to reconcile that with the fact that the building had to be publicly accessible. Everywhere nowadays, not only in Groningen, we hear that libraries should become the city's living room. And it's not only libraries: it's impossible to redevelop a square without someone expressing the ambition to turn it into a living room for the

neighbourhood. How can this domesticity be reconciled with the pursuit of public space? Is it even possible to reconcile the two? Had the Forum indeed become a private living room, I wondered, or had they succeeded in turning it into an open, public building?

Filled with a mixture of fear and hope (who knows, perhaps it wasn't so bad after all), I took the train to Groningen in January 2020, still ignorant of the emerging coronavirus pandemic. From the station I walked towards Grote Markt, keeping a look-out for the Forum... But where was it? I walked the entire length of Oosterstraat until I arrived at the Grote Markt. St Martin's Tower had been beckoning me all the while, but I saw no sign of the Forum. Surprised, I retraced my steps to Poelestraat. I knew for certain that this giant building had to be somewhere... But where? I turned into Schoolstraat and then ended up on a square I didn't know at all. Nieuwe Markt, where suddenly the sand-coloured, wondrous monolith rose up like a Big Friendly Giant.

It immediately became clear to me that you cannot call this building a 'showpiece'. Its only truly spectacular aspect is the view you have from the roof terrace. For me, the enjoyment of a view from a high-rise building is usually tinged with guilt: as beautiful as it may be, to enjoy that view you are by necessity standing on a building that obstructs the view for those living around it. But at the top of this 'invisible' building, I could enjoy the view without a care.

Reaching that roof turned out to be quite a journey. The countless, endless stairs in the huge void at the heart of the building made me dizzy. Although predominantly white, this 'stairwell' reminded me of Piranesi's *Carceri d'invenzione*, etchings of imaginary dungeons: huge shadowy, vaulted spaces with puzzling staircases. I also felt sorry in advance for the staff of the library, which is spread over several floors, though this may be an advantage for the library's users, who can curl up in a corner with a book.

A Big Friendly Butler

All in all, my first encounter with Forum Groningen was certainly not a disappointment. Seen from the street, the building turned out to be anything but a loudmouth and was instead pleasantly retiring. In any case, it is neither a logo nor a trademark, but a real building – and moreover a public building. During my visit it was already quite busy, attracting a mixed group of visitors, who didn't really get in each other's way. A Groningen-style compliment is in order: it could have been much worse.

A little later, as I walked towards the Academy building on Broerstraat, where the doctoral graduation was to take place, I began to have my doubts... Why was a new library required at all? Didn't Groningen already have a perfectly good library? And one that isn't even that old. I had been at its opening when I studied and lived in Groningen in the 1990s, and I was immediately enthusiastic at the time. With its small windows and large doors, the brick building, designed by the Italian architect Giorgio Grassi, was a sort of warehouse for books. That, in all its simplicity, is exactly what a library should be. Or is that idea now old-fashioned? Libraries today are no longer just about books. They are multifunctional buildings that therefore attract different kinds of visitors and can thus become truly public.

I entered the square in front of the Academy building, facing the sober, but in my view very beautiful back of the old library: an enormous brick wall with even smaller windows. Groningen sobriety fused with Italian elegance. At the time it was built, alderman Ypke Gietema called it the "most beautiful wall in Groningen," and rightly so. Such a wall is the ideal backdrop against which urban life can be played out. Architecture almost as wallpaper rather than something that announces itself in *pontifical* fashion. I was relieved to learn later that the old library has found a new use: the law faculty is moving in. Hopefully, the Forum will also become such a 'shared backdrop'.

When the yearbook *Architecture in the Netherlands 2019-2020* was published in the autumn of 2020, with a delay due to the Covid-19 crisis, its cover bore a photograph of the Forum. To be featured in this way is, apparently, very prestigious: perhaps the highest honour that can be bestowed on a Dutch building in its own country. That cover, with that photograph, annoyed me. The image gives the wrong impression. It makes the Forum out to be the (post)modernist monstrosity that someone like Thierry Baudet will probably see in it. But it is not. Neither is it the pompous temple of culture that he would probably have preferred.

Fortunately, the building was also addressed *inside* the yearbook, which praised the building for its accessibility: it is open 365 days a year, from 9 a.m. to 12:30 p.m. (including for the homeless, provided they cause no nuisance). That praise seems very justified to me: for a building of this kind, nothing is perhaps as important as accessibility. Less justified was its delight that the Forum would function as a 'living room for the city'. That strikes me as precisely the wrong approach: a living room is – thankfully – not so accessible.

The notion of 'domesticity' has an almost intoxicating rosy scent. And not without good reason, but the concept also has thorns, exclusivity being perhaps the sharpest. You cannot aspire to be both a public building and a living room. You can – must! – make a building of this kind accessible and comfortable, but that does not turn it into a living room. A living room exists by virtue of its exclusivity.

Domesticity and comfort have much in common, but not everything. It's difficult enough to create a place where everyone feels at ease, but the idea of a place that everyone considers their home is absurd. Home has too much to do with privacy, the opposite of being in public. At home, you can exclude people you do not consider to be part of your circle. At home, you are allowed to be picky.

Paradoxically, this may provide a useful definition of a good public building: one in which no one feels completely at home but in which most people are at ease. My first impression was that the Forum can indeed become such a public building: a true forum, and not a living room.

It is of course no coincidence that Forum Groningen is also, and perhaps in the first place, a library. The library has made a miraculous comeback all over the world in recent years. While reports of the decline of reading, growing digitisation and the 'death of paper' grow ever louder and more alarmist, the libraries are flourishing again, as true cultural centres. As 'social infrastructure', as the American sociologist Eric Klinenberg calls it in his book *Palaces for the People: How Social Infrastructure Can Help Fight Inequality, Polarization, and the Decline of Civic Life.*

Klinenberg's book is an excellent and accessible study of the role that public buildings, institutions and organisations play in building communities, of "the physical places and organisations that shape the way people interact." It is not about 'social capital' per se, but about the physical conditions that determine whether or not that can develop. For Klinenberg, public buildings and places such as schools, parks, playgrounds, gardens, markets and especially libraries are the building blocks of civic life. His is no abstract account, but one that is backed up with accounts of the many visits he has made to those public buildings and places, and of the conversations he has had with the people who create and, above all, maintain them. But what is lacking, for me, is an explication of the tension that exists between the book's main title and its subtitle.

Klinenberg convincingly demonstrates how the aforementioned social infrastructure, with libraries as a striking example, combats inequality and promotes social life. Polarisation is, as it were, transformed into pluralism: the social infrastructure does not divide, but very subtly streamlines the polymorphous crowd, so that as many people as possible can still live together despite their mutual – sometimes fundamental – differences. That's why, to my mind, it is better not to speak of people's palaces. Palaces neither combat inequality nor promote pluralism.

I used the term 'pontifical' above with good reason, because this is precisely what a public building should not be. It should be ready for informal and casual use. The word 'palace' comes from Palatine, the hill in Rome on which the first emperor, Augustus (the exalted one), had his imperial residence: his *palace*. In my view, a library, or any social infrastructure for that matter, should have nothing regal about it. It should have an informal rather than a solemn atmosphere, convivial but not chummy – that is more for the living room. In short, the atmosphere in a public building such as the Forum should be casual and informal, without being overly familiar.

In order to be accessible to as many people as possible, public institutions, especially libraries, must, of course, be housed in large buildings. But large need not equal grandiose. A library need not look impressive, let alone awe-inspiring. A library building need not attract special attention or be obtrusive. It can be modest and obliging, without being servile: it awaits our arrival slightly aloof and with just the right amount of dignity. Not as a people's palace but as a Big Friendly Butler. And just to be clear, I should add that those capital letters are, of course, ironic.

One of the Forum's urban planning principles was that "a substantial part of the ground floor should function as an extension of the public space of the Nieuwe Markt." Based on this vision, the square was regarded as one of the 'domains' of the Forum. NL Architects made the connection between the building and the square the quintessence of the design. The practice seized an opportunity to surpass spatially the functionally already layered brief.

They intertwined the various functions around a public, vertical landscape of stacked squares: a 'Hoge Markt' that stretches to the roof, as a self-evident continuation of the urban space. This created a continuous line between the city, the square, the building and the roof, with which the architects convincingly drew street life into the Forum.

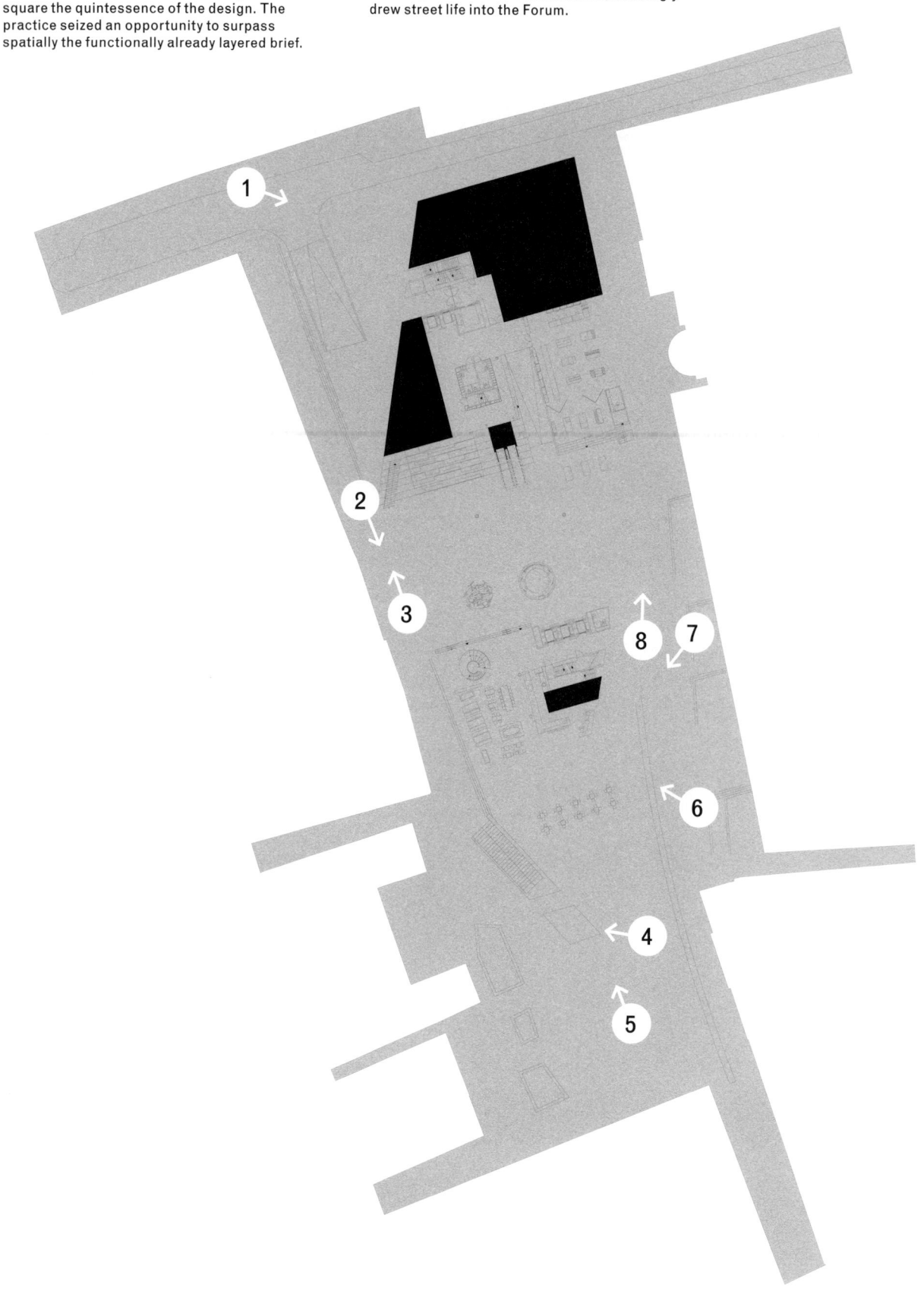

1

2

3

4

5

6

7

8

275

Use

Nooduitgang

vrijhouden

Kirsten Hannema

Forum Groningen Through the Eyes of Herman Hertzberger

What do Herman Hertzberger and Forum Groningen have in common? At first glance, not much. But closer inspection reveals several indirect connections. For example, in 1971-72, as a member of Groningen's city centre team, Hertzberger contributed to the policy document known as the *Maatstavennota* (Standards Memorandum), part of the broader policy document *Doelstelling binnenstad Groningen* (Objectives for Groningen's City Centre) to which an entire issue of *Tijdschrift voor Architectuur en Beeldende Kunsten* (*TA/ BK*) was devoted.[1] Ben Eerhart, one of the magazine's editors, wrote at the time that Hertzberger "makes recommendations that many welfare committees can – and hopefully will – take to heart."

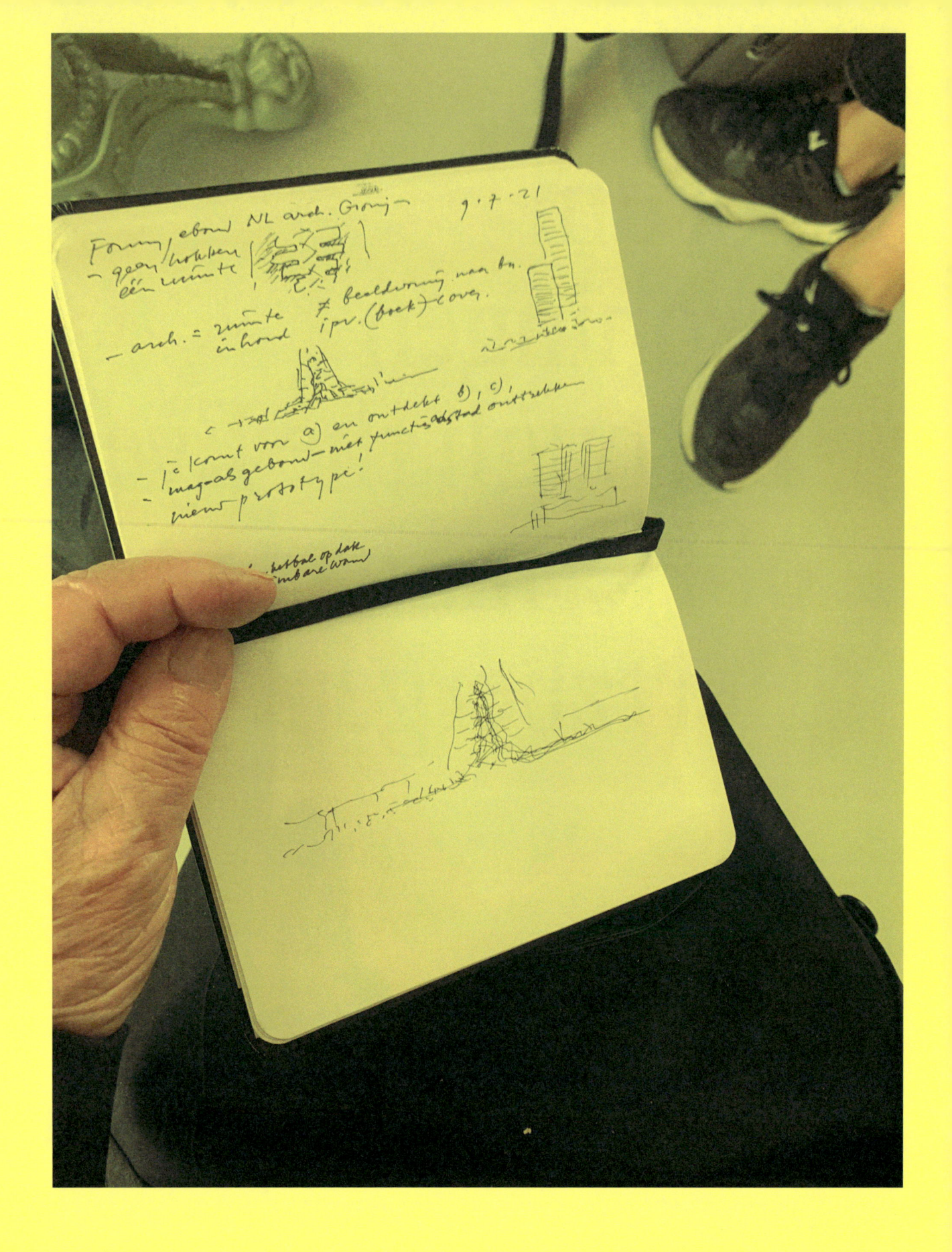

"The city centre is made up of a variety of activities, associations and meanings," Hertzberger wrote in his contribution to *TA/BK*. He spoke of the "exceptional hospitability" that the city should offer, stating that "every new intervention [...] should result in greater hospitability for residents and visitors." Hertzberger thus gave voice to the revolution in municipal planning policy initiated by Max van den Berg, who had been appointed Councillor for Urban Development at the age of twenty-four and who helped to form the first left-wing council, which would take the decision in 1977 to rid Groningen's city centre of cars.[2] The Objectives policy document was an attempt to clarify the starting point for planning within the city centre.

A second connection is that between Hertzberger and Forum's architects. Among the students that Hertzberger taught as professor at Delft University of Technology between 1970 and 1999 were Pieter Bannenberg, Kamiel Klaasse, Walter van Dijk and Mark Linnemann, who cofounded NL Architects after their studies. In 2005, Hertzberger invited the office to design a concert hall for the new Tivoli-Vredenburg music centre in Utrecht. In retrospect, this complex with its stacked venues, organised around a series of internal squares interconnected by escalators, can be seen as a preliminary study for Forum Groningen.

How does Hertzberger view Forum a year and a half after it welcomed its first users? He visited the complex with Bannenberg and Klaasse.

Content Without Image

"When I first saw it in pictures, I thought the building would be much more dominant," says Hertzberger, "but walking through the city centre, I couldn't find it. 'Where is it?' I asked. It doesn't tower above the historical buildings." It proves what Hertzberger taught his students: that you shouldn't rely on images. During the symposium *The Future of Architecture*, organised by Delft University of Technology in 2012 in honour of his eightieth birthday, he started his lecture with two images: the pyramids in Egypt and the Greek amphitheatre in Epidaurus. "The pyramid is an image without content; the amphitheatre is content without image," he explains. His message was: build theatres, not pyramids. "Architecture is about the space it creates, not the form itself." But he sees that the profession is strongly focused on creating images, on making buildings that stand out.

With Forum, this is reversed. "This building is so strongly focused on the activities it fosters within – reading books, watching movies, studying, eating together – that the exterior almost fades from view. I think that's a great quality: the exterior is of little or no importance."

1 The so-called *Maatstavennota* (Standards Memorandum) of January 1972 and the *Doeleindennota* (Aims Memorandum) of October 1971 were eventually merged within the now famous *Doelstellingennota* (Objectives Memorandum), in full *Doelstelling binnenstad Groningen* (Objectives for Groningen's City Centre) of May 1972. To compile the policy documents, the municipality set up the 'city centre team', which, in addition to municipal officials and Hertzberger, comprised Prof. Niek de Boer, Prof. Hendrik Goudappel and Prof. Dr. Jan Lambooy.

2 Van den Berg's full title was Councillor for Culture, Preservation of Monuments, Traffic, Public Works, Public Transport, Social Housing and Urban Development.

"At first I was critical of the idea of housing so many functions together under a single roof. I feared that, in this way, the Forum would drain energy from the city. Once inside, I discovered another aspect: people who had no intention of visiting the library enter it nonetheless from other parts of the building. I think it's very powerful that you encounter all those different functions – possibilities – together, and are seduced into finding something you weren't looking for. Serendipity."

For architecture historian Michelle Provoost "the essence of urbanity is that you get things you didn't ask for." Seen in this way, Forum is a small town. "For me, every building should be a city," says Hertzberger. "It must offer shelter, but also be open to the outside. It's a much-discussed paradox but one for which few solutions are conceived. Here it has succeeded: the city continues inside the building." To clarify what he means, the architect takes his sketchbook and starts making dots, which depict life around the Grote Markt. Around the dots, he draws the contours of the Forum, in which the dots rise upwards, like the bubbles in a fizzy drink, all the way to the roof terrace.

"What we see here," says Hertzberger, pointing to the sketch, "is a vertical shopping street. I don't know where this has been achieved before. A mix of functions in high-rise buildings has certainly been attempted more than once, but in the end those high-rises are subdivided into 'slabs'. The fire department insists on it, they say. Apart from the collaboration between the organisations that share the building, there is little contact." Turning to Bannenberg and Klaasse, he asks: "How in God's name did you get this past the fire department?" The answer: by using sprinklers. That sounds simpler than it is, Hertzberger knows from experience, just as he knows that it is not self-evident that users will leave an open space like this alone. "In architecture, the focus is usually on the private space: the stylish residence, the private garden. You cannot prohibit people from sealing off their environment, but as an architect I think we have to do our best to keep spaces open, and that has succeeded wonderfully here."

"As an architect, my idea has always been to design structures that allow for change. The age of the total design, when the architect drew everything down to the last detail, is over. We live in a 'fluid' society in which everything can change from day to day. Buildings must permit these changes in possibilities and insights. As such, I'm not in favour of designing buildings from start to finish. You have to create spaces *and* leave room. There should always be the freedom to 'fiddle' with a building." He wanders through the Wonderland children's library designed by the architecture collective deMunnik-deJong-Steinhauser and inspects the interior of the cinemas designed by architects and designers &Prast&Hooft. "I think it's good that different architects were allowed to design various parts of this building. That's the right attitude."

In the children's library, Hertzberger stops by the vast suspended net where children are reading, chilling and taking selfies with their smartphones. "It's amazing in your old age to realise how much you were shaped by your youth," he muses. "I remember clearly when I was eight and I lived in Amsterdam, there was a building with an external staircase decorated with huge stone eggs that we used to play on. I can still feel those eggs. Feel what it was like to grasp those stone shapes."

"Buildings are often aloof, when they should be the opposite. Touchable buildings represent architecture at its best. I see possibilities, ways of achieving that. Notice how the residents of Italian cities pass the time sitting on the plinths of the buildings. What I like about your first work, the Heat Transfer Station 8 that you built near Leidsche Rijn in 1998," he says to Klaasse and Bannenberg, "is how you installed a climbing wall on one façade and a window with a basketball net on another. It's a building that doesn't keep its distance but which has a tactile quality expressed in that climbing wall."

"The city is an instrument that can be played over and over again by others, constantly changing but always remaining itself," Hertzberger wrote in 1972 in *TA/ BK*. That is Hertzberger's sole criticism of Forum: the exterior could be even more playable, more accessible. "You could build a 'garland' around it with bars or kiosks so that the transition between the square and the interior space is no longer perceptible, so that it dissolves, as it were." Adding impishly: "I wouldn't mind taking up that challenge."

Striking a fine balance between the route through the building, the stacked squares and the various functions, the Forum's keyhole-shaped atrium operates as an urban interior. The 'traffic structure' at the heart of the building works smoothly because the circulation zone of escalators is not separated from the other spaces but is carefully interwoven with them thanks to layered transitions between routes, places and entrances, just as in an open-air public space.

As an urban structure, the Forum creates a multitude of promenades, unforeseen moments and surprising spatial experiences. In addition, the escalators have an amazing quality that is easily overlooked: they can move in two directions, up and down! In an everyday constellation such as a department store, this yields little, but the way in which the escalators are placed in the Forum means that this hidden capacity can be put to good use here. To act as a catalyst for browsing through the building, the direction of each escalator can be reversed – as if it were an ever-changing vertical ballet. And although this is currently done only as part of the maintenance protocol, it offers the potential to add new routes to the building as needed.

Making a vertically organised building function properly was no walk in the park. In an average shopping street, it is not easy to entice people to the first floor or to the basement of a building, let alone to the upper floors of a ten-storey structure. The only way to achieve a subtle balance between moving, remaining, searching, meeting and visiting within the Forum's building volume was by compactly stacking the rich programme around the atrium. The cinema and the exhibition areas, including the entrances, are divided over three levels. The auditorium and Wonderland are spread across two levels and the other functions occupy one level. The resulting split-level atrium with staggered escalators has proved to have enormous appeal, allowing visitors and users to find their way through the building with apparent ease.

Distributing functions over several levels invited the designers to differentiate and enliven the internal, vertical connections of these clusters. In order to open up the diverse functions within this densely built, raised urban fabric, a new form of the typical Groningen 'alleyway' was needed in addition to the unique constellation of escalators. NL Architects designed five 'specials': urban staircases that facilitate secondary access to the functions. They are generous, lazy, multifunctional, meant for hanging out, playing, relaxing and wandering. The stairs allow visitors to experience the Forum's full depth and density.

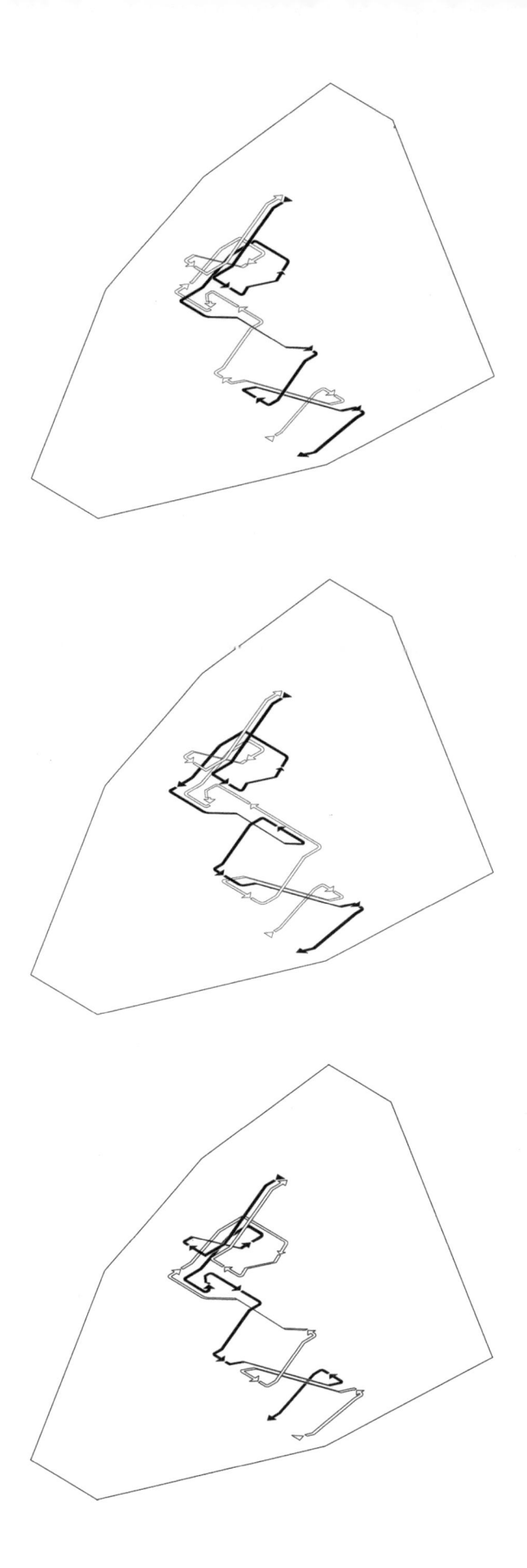

In Groningen, which has been plagued by earthquakes caused by gas extraction, creating a sustainable, 'gas-free' building was an important starting point. In the meantime, the construction of gas-free buildings has become commonplace, but when the Forum was still in the design stage it was quite rare. The question was whether such an immense building could function without gas. Due to ongoing discussions about the earthquakes and gas extraction, which led to a halt to construction, reinforcements of the structure and compensation – the ambition to create a gas-free Forum remained strong. The Forum is heated and cooled with two heat pumps and a heat/cold storage unit, which represents a positive break with Groningen's eventful gas-related history. NL Architects had a suggestion for how to employ the materials that remained unused due to the exclusion of gas in the building. As an ode to the dynamics that the gas extraction problem had brought with it, they used the characteristic yellow gas pipes as a symbol of times gone by, to give visitors a warm welcome in the Forum's central hall.

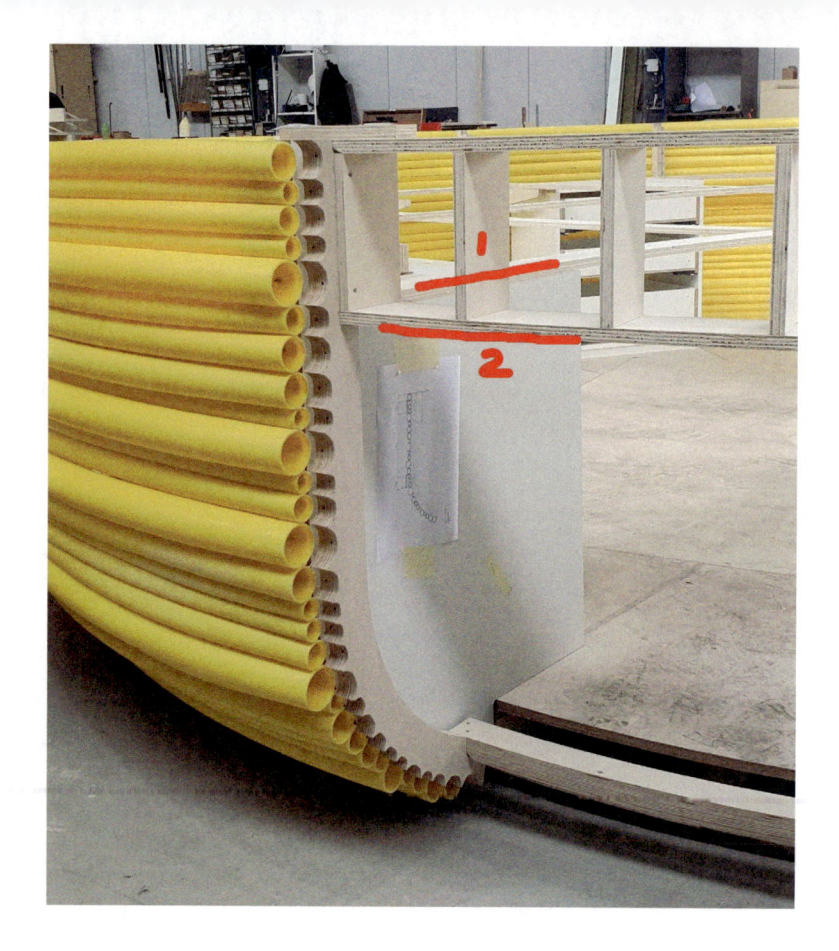

Jeroen Junte

A Public Square

'Known Unknowns'

— and the Design of Serendipity

A Public Square

The interior of the Forum is like an empty shell. Restrained, even austere, with a hard greyish white base colour. It is a blank canvas for colourful worlds full of visual clues and stories. The art cinema full of mirrors and spotlights, the canary-yellow children's furniture in Wonderland, the stately Newsroom: together they form a single generous hangout space thanks to seven clear elements: the welcoming grandstand, lively squares, floating escalators, abundant books, dedicated seating areas, appealing lighting and views everywhere – of the city and of other people.

'Known Unknowns' — and the Design of Serendipity

Three teenage girls are dancing in a secluded lift lobby on the second floor of the Forum. Jackets and a pack of crisps lie on the floor. Faint music emanates from a portable speaker: soft enough not to bother anyone but loud enough for the girls to dance to. The lobby runs from Wonderland to the teaching spaces behind and is rarely used. The girls can fine-tune their TikTok moves undisturbed. The smooth concrete makes the space an optimal dance floor, while the white walls form a neutral background for filming. The girls' most ingenious improvisation is the use of the glass lift doors to study their own choreography: the dark lift shaft turns the glass into mirrors.

A little-used space in the Forum is transformed temporarily into something approaching a professional dance studio. My first thought is that this spontaneous use of the space was probably not a design intervention by the architects. Or perhaps it was?

8.59 a.m.

The Tribune

A queue at the door. Isn't that something for a music venue? Or a Covid testing centre? Not for a public cultural building. At nine in the morning, before the doors have even opened! In barely a year, the Forum has come to occupy an essential place in Groningen's city centre, as if it has always been there. From afar, we see that giant stone from which a sculptural shape has been carved. But it is the interior that has won the hearts of Groningen's residents. Why else would they queue in the cold outside the door to get in?

Inside, the queue evaporates immediately. Students occupy the workplaces, an official with a briefcase strides confidently towards the course room on the second floor. A middle-aged woman is already outside again, on her way to work after returning some novels on the ground floor. A woman, with her coat still on, sits waiting for her friend: for locals this is literally a meeting place. When it rains, it's even busier. After all, there is always something to see or do in this generous building.

The Forum's generosity derives in part from NL Architects' spatial choices. To begin with, that high atrium that opens up the Forum with a single gesture. Thereafter the floor plans have been designed by several different interior architects. But first there is that unambiguous, intimate experience. After passing through the glass sliding doors in the north and south façades – remarkably modest for such an imposing building – we are met by a low ceiling, giving a sheltered feeling after the overwhelming architectural experience entering from the street. The grey floor tiles resemble the paving stones outside, only they are slightly smoother and straighter. This is no coincidence. After all, the Forum aims to be an extension of the city. Finding your way couldn't be easier at the bright yellow information desk (as if you could miss it!), with the help of the numerous screens and interactive whiteboards that hang from an octopus-like artwork, or with the LED screen that measures 4 x 8 metres. The message is clear: there is something for everyone, 365 days a year, from nine in the morning till half past midnight.

The centrepiece of the ground floor – and perhaps of the entire interior – is the robust grandstand. Informal seating areas in this abstract landscape are highlighted with leather cushions. This is where people chat, wait, watch (and are watched), learn and read. Laptops are used in an astonishing variety of ways: lying down with the screen one step lower, sitting in half a circle around a screen one step higher, sitting cross-legged with it on your lap, or squatting over it to quickly look something up. This is Groningen's largest single piece of furniture *and* its most accessible theatre when a fashion show by the Minerva Art Academy or a street dance contest is held on the floor in front of it.

A Physical Browser

The Forum is a building with a characteristic yet elusive form. Just take all that exterior. Even if you walked around the building ten times, it would be difficult to draw it. It yields too much with the city for that. The external walls project and recede from top left to bottom right, obliquely or straight as an arrow. It's the same inside. Because what do we actually see? An intriguing constellation of escalators that tumble over each other, floors that recede or retreat behind seemingly solid walls. The initial spatial experience is diffuse.

This must be a conscious choice on the part of the architect. The interior is defined by what is *not* there. It all begins with spatial demarcation. The public spaces have been, as it were, forced out of a closed and massive building volume using a serrated mould. The closed parts and the high atrium from the ground level to the eighth floor intersect like cogs. This vacant space offers a range of possibilities, but what they are is entirely up to the user.

The Forum is, as architect Pieter Bannenberg of NL Architects puts it, "a building that doesn't want to be a building but rather a physical browser." It is not the architecture itself that is decisive, but the possibilities that present themselves without a fixed sequence or strict set of rules. The first of these is a choice: how do we explore this 'browser'? Actively, by walking through it? Passively, in a lift (which, remarkably enough, you have to make an effort to find)? Or interactively, by asking at the information desk? Or something in between: standing still on a moving escalator, after which the possibilities present themselves naturally? This building has no dead-end corridors: like a Möbius strip, at every turn the interior offers a different perspective with corresponding possibilities. A ceiling becomes a wall; a floor becomes a staircase. And a lift lobby becomes a temporary dance space. By deliberately leaving the interior space undefined, the design gives rise to very specific uses.

The Squares

Toddlers play in the hanging net above the void in Wonderland, imagining themselves unobserved. One has even dragged a beanbag into the thick web of knotted ropes to laze in. Meanwhile, their mothers chat, resting their elbows on the wide balustrade, as if they were sitting on the edge of a sandbox. Because of the yellow walls and comical reading tables, adults play a supporting role in this reading room, without it becoming childish. There are 'real' children's drawings on the bare concrete walls at the spectacular two-way spiral staircase. The colourful book covers are the only decoration. With just a few such effective design choices, even the youngest visitors feel like they can take ownership of the building.

In fact, the interior is an empty shell with an understated and austere palette. The walls and floors are white, grey or greyish white, as if the building might one day have to be surrendered empty again. For architecture collective deMunnik-deJong-Steinhauser, it was a blank canvas to be coloured in with seven lively squares: the busy Information Square full of screens, the News Square with magazine racks and reading tables, the playful Youth Square, the Reading Square with its intimate book niches, the nondescript Expo Square, the inviting Film Square and, finally, the pragmatic Technology Square.

Together, this composition of spaces forms a single large urban plaza, which NL Architects call the 'High Market'. The overwhelming building – almost 20,000 square metres – has thus been brought back to a human scale. Not only is the spaciousness overwhelming, but also the freedom of choice and the quality of time spent here. A library that flows smoothly into a cinema, which is also a café. Just as for the ancient Greeks the 'forum' was also the 'gathering place' for political, social and educational activities.

The Undefined Space

The Forum is designed as a building that although it has physical boundaries, places few restrictions on its use. It offers plenty of options for appropriation by the user. In his book *The Ecological Approach to Visual Perception* (1979), the American psychologist James Gibson called these possibilities 'affordances': to what extent does an object, or in this case the architecture, allow or stimulate personal forms of use? Gibson focused initially on design for animals, but it soon became apparent that his ideas also applied to humans. A common example of affordances is a teacup, whose handle invites it to be picked up using the thumb and forefinger. If the handle is strong enough, an organ grinder can rattle the teacup as an appeal for loose change. The DIY enthusiast can hang the teacup by its handle in the shed as a storage container for screws. Provided the handle is big enough. Same cup, different affordances.

The same principles apply in the Forum. A lift lobby is designed for waiting for the lift, with enough space for a wheelchair and book carts. The glass wall with recessed sliding doors and a wall panel with buttons tell us instantly that this is a lift. That is the formal grammar. But the lobby can also be used as a dance floor. Or as a children's playground, or a place to make a quick private phone call. It was emphatically not designed for such uses, but the design offers the space for them. But that could have been otherwise. A mat in front of the lift door or a bench in the lobby would have limited the affordances here considerably.

The Books

Two middle-aged men walk towards the VR headsets on the Film Square. The first with a purposeful stride, the other following hesitantly. He wouldn't have found his way to the fifth floor of the Forum by himself. His friend puts the VR headset on his head. Barely ten minutes later and they are walking to the exit again, now both with a cheerful smile.

The binding factor in the interior are the six library spaces, although the Forum is emphatically not a library but a cultural complex of cinemas, exhibition spaces, an auditorium, study and meeting rooms, and various eateries. The libraries house almost a hundred thousand books and yet you'd hardly know they are there. Instead of bookcases in the traditional sense, there are multifunctional furniture elements in which the books are kept: a bookcase is also a seat, a vitrine, a meeting place or simply decoration.

The distribution of books over the different squares is indicated by visual hints. The pool table and the padded easy chairs in the Thrillers section allude to detectives and intrigue. Even if the clues are sometimes a little too obvious – a pool table *and* stuffed animal heads are a bit too much – they are usually spot on, such as the metal shelving units with thick bolts and a sliding door on pulleys in the Technology section and a poem on the wall in the Poetry section.

The furniture has a strikingly refined look. The starting point was hospitable rather than 'vandal-proof'. Cupboards are cleverly concealed in the sloping outer walls. The seats are made of soft leather, the carpets are thick and lustrous. Everything is high-quality and meticulously detailed. After all, material refinement promotes refined behaviour. Homelike seating areas have also been created with vintage furniture. This may be a brand-new building, but it seems as though it's always been here.

The utilitarian parking garage houses a pulsating light sculpture by Nicky Assmann, museum art dangling casually amid the exhaust fumes. It turns the Forum into a contemporary People's Palace. Some spaces emphasise the palatial, like the Newsroom, which with its wood panelling and spiral staircase looks like a stately cigar box. Others stress the democratic, like the reading tables on the first floor where everyone is equal, whether you read *De Telegraaf* or *De Groene Amsterdammer*. But even here there are superior finishes: the metal light armatures are one with the tabletop.

In other words, the architecture of affordances is based not on a well-defined function or an aesthetic language of form but on the user's perception and personal interpretation. Whether that user is a visitor or an employee makes little difference. The interior design of the Forum is characterised by this absence of imposed uses. In many areas the space is undefined, or at least multifunctional. That seems like an easy choice – a void here, some abstract forms there – but it requires a deep insight into the workings of the human psyche because the difference between infinite possibilities and an incomprehensible vacuum is as minimal as it is crucial. Rejection or appropriation is therefore an architectural choice. The more possibilities for appropriation an interior offers, the more layered the design is. And the more successful.

A Public Square | 'Known Unknowns'

1.22 p.m.

The Escalators

A family lazily ascends an escalator – only to glide back down again after five minutes. And then up again. The floating escalators not only give the Forum a Piranesi-esque monumentality; they are also the main attraction. Like in a browser, from here you can scroll while the entire building passes you by like a movie. Due to their clever location, the escalators lead smoothly everywhere, with the different worlds distinguished by their colours. The old rose cinema, the moody blue world of the reference books section, the soothing faded brown and moss green of the fiction section, the bright orange Smart Lab, the green screen of the Media Lab with neon letters. Even the stark white of the Expo Square – a nod to the museum white cube – looks sparkling.

In addition to colour, the interior is organised by means of spatial compositions. Take the bookcases in the different reading areas. In the Fiction section they are high with surprising openings that might bring you face to face with a stranger. In sections with less accessible subjects, such as Art and Politics, the closed stacks are close together and connected via labyrinthine corridors, too small to get lost in, big enough to wander through. The high book carousel on the fifth floor, on the other hand, has a truly iconic look.

A girl on the escalator runs her hand gently along the chains that hang as a warning before the narrow stairwell to the ninth floor. The Forum interior's most subtle element is its rhythm of materials. Wooden floors, woollen carpets, soft fabrics, concrete walls, plastic wall panels, a metal fence. Hard and soft alternate, giving the interior a seductive tactility. The materials also influence the acoustics. In the silent reading room, whispers fade through partitions covered with thick felt. The expansive escalators are a literal bridge between all these shapes, colours and materials.

The affordances of the Forum's interior are not about an architectural programme of mezzanines and escalators. And certainly not about the design of functions – a cinema here, an arena for debate there. In fact, it's not even about the physical architecture. That is merely the means. It is about the relationship we, as individuals, have with that architecture, or more precisely: the scope for action that the Forum interior offers. What that action is, or can be, will vary from person to person. For an older user, an escalator is primarily a comfortable way to move around the building, but for a child it is an attraction, especially when part of the sequence of escalators found in the Forum. In NL Architects' interior design, it can be both. And lots more. With its ambition to be a space for encounters within the city, Forum must therefore be accessible to everyone.

At the same time, the building must provide something different for everyone. With its openness and freedom of movement, this is a hyper-individual interior. The stairs from the ground level to the first floor, between the grandstand and escalators, are a shortcut if you're in a hurry or a place to sit if you want to rest. This appropriation can be quite literal. Anyone can lay claim to the space, but it remains public. The interior must be shared with a sense of generosity made possible by an overall design that has been thought through in great detail. The height of a staircase is important, but so too is the depth of the steps, so that you can sit comfortably on them. The placement of a lift control panel must be just as well-considered as the location of the lift lobby.

The design choices are made not to direct users, let alone limit them, but to create new possibilities for action. My Forum is your Forum, but at the same time it isn't. An interior has thus been created in which every inhabitant of Groningen can feel at home. The Forum's interior is exclusively for everyone and therefore truly inclusive. No distinctions are made: everyone must feel welcome. With its options for individual appropriation, it offers a personal experience, regardless of the search term.

3.13 p.m.

The Seating Areas

Two goth girls are sitting on the floor right next to two empty armchairs. They have secluded themselves, with their backs to the rest of the building. The Forum has more than three hundred formal workstations and at least the same number of spontaneous seating areas such as steps, windowsills and tables. So, why sit on the floor? Simply because they can! Rules are there to be broken, especially by rebellious teenagers. And in this interior, everything is possible. Two floors up, five students sit in a circle on the floor because there are no free desks, their coats around them like an imaginary shield. In the middle are two laptops. The students look happy.

The Forum emphatically aims to serve everyone: young and old, rich and poor, with all levels of knowledge. This inevitably results in a dynamic contradiction. Playful toddlers want something different than diligent students or moody teenagers. The furniture smooths out these wrinkles. New perspectives appear organically with every step you climb, space you enter or corner you turn.

There are seats everywhere, each with a specific dynamic. Those who want to be alone for a while are attracted by the high window seats in the stairwell that leads to the cinemas – except when the film starts and the same spot becomes an excellent meeting place. There are round café tables for chatting, picnic tables for families and flirting students, and leather sofas with a chess table between them. The *pièce de résistance* is an 18-metre-long sofa on the eighth floor, with a first-class view of the Martini or St Martin's Tower. The sofa flows into a low bookcase at the back, where people hang out as if it were a sky bar. Many of the furnishing elements function as props, sets that entertain and activate the visitors.

When the Forum functions as a browser, as architect Pieter Bannenberg puts it, the interior is the interface – the intermediary – between the user's query and the experience and knowledge the building has to offer. The most accessible (and therefore the primary) search is for 'known knowns': in this case, a visit the outcome of which is predetermined. The specific target – the amateur techie attending a workshop in the Smart Lab or the film buff watching Wes Anderson's latest movie – will determine the experience. But such self-evident usages are not how the interior design derives its strength. To pick up a book about steam trains on the sixth floor, you must first slowly ascend the escalators along the children's world, a café, countless reading and workspaces, a cinema and an exhibition space. It's like navigating the entire market for a single carton of milk. It's quicker with the lift, but it feels like it takes longer, so why would you? Besides, everyone knows the Forum is all about escalators (a 'known known')!

What the interior is designed for are the 'known unknowns': information or experiences that are useful or convenient, but which are not the user's primary search term. These appear almost automatically in the Forum. The older visitors who come for a lecture by Arnon Grunberg but are also introduced to 3D glasses. Two teenagers who want to chill on the roof after school but casually encounter the temporary exhibition about the history of video games. The interior is designed to allow you to find what you are *not* looking for.

In the Forum, serendipity – the unexpected, chance encounter – is a fully realised aspect of the design. This is a formidable achievement because coincidence simply cannot be directed, let alone designed. If it could, it would no longer be a coincidence. But it is possible to facilitate or even provoke coincidence. For example, by enabling the building's users to unconsciously recognise knowledge they don't have (unknowns): an interior that does not coerce, but rather suggests; a 3D printer prominently displayed in the bright red shopfront of the Smart Lab.

4.44 p.m.

The Lighting

Unrest on the fifth floor. Around four in the afternoon, the screens in front of the windows on the south façade are raised and daylight streams into the building. The students at the workstations in front of the window squint. Some pack their bags and move. Their places are taken by readers who refresh themselves in the direct light. Meanwhile, the lights dim in the atrium and spots are turned on in strategic places. This alternation of light and shadow rearranges the interior.

Accents are created with dimmers, designer lamps or a grid of system lighting. Especially in the evening, when daylight gives way to a sophisticated lighting plan, the seating areas look intimate, while the reading table is bathed in direct and scattered light. Well-aimed spots enhance concentration at the workstations. Wall lamps twinkle like stars in the robust concrete corridors of the cinema. The blood-red walls, floors and ceilings give the toilets a menacing glow. Behind them lie the cinemas like carefully carved-out caves. The cinema itself has become a featured film set thanks to design agency &Prast&Hooft, which also furnishes hip urban restaurants.

Instinctive Architecture

As visitors to the Forum, we are presented with all these knowns and unknowns. They flash by on the LED screen on the ground level. NOW in the Smart Lab: 3D printing consultation. THIS WEEK: a Woody Allen retrospective at the cinema. COMING SOON: a series of lectures on the future of the countryside. Messages such as these activate and stimulate the visitor, but they do not build an intrinsic relationship with the building.

Don't show and don't tell – each individual visitor's appropriation of the Forum interior is based on intuition. The design has taken account of both purely physical and emotional desires. Not through colour or overwhelming forms, or rather not exclusively through the illuminating use of colour or the dramatic revelation from the ground floor of the atrium with all its escalators. It is precisely these places and qualities that each visitor discovers for themselves, by chance, which turn the building into a personal experience. A mother occupies an intimate niche as a place to read to her child, while a teenage couple sees it as a love seat.

In the Forum, there is always a shady *and* a sunny spot, a lively social space *and* one for silent concentration. They simply aren't announced or demarcated anywhere. They are to be found through instinctive searches. The affordances of these 'unknown unknowns' are what sets the Forum apart. The interior takes into account the behaviour or motivations of the individual user, who makes an impulsive choice about how and for what the architecture is used, regardless of the architect's intentions. There are spaces for the reader *and* the talker, for the viewer *and* the flâneur, for a private phone call *and* for a dance routine! But the Forum also transcends these archetypes and generalisations. It not only provides what you know or are looking for, but challenges us to give meaning to what this architecture can be.

6.45 p.m.

The View

The details are inaudible, but he must be having an awkward conversation. The man paces back and forth along the glass wall on the roof, his furrowed brow reinforcing his words. When he hangs up, he stares into the distance, over the city to the meadows beyond. Why does he choose to have that conversation here? Is it the peace and seclusion? Or the mighty thrill of a city at your feet? He feels at home on this roof, that's for sure.

Yet it is no more than a bare surface, without the narrative elements of the squares inside. Except for that large set of steps, which resembles an ancient Greek theatre. In the summer, films are shown here, in the spring and autumn it is a sheltered seating area. Apart from that, there's just the view. Even grander than on the lower floors where you mainly see houses, which enhances the feeling of an urban living room. You are in the middle of the city and simultaneously somewhere else. Exactly where, you can decide for yourself.

The view brings everyone together. You don't have to buy or do anything. You can just be there. Alone or with others. This quality of time spent here is more relevant than ever. We increasingly withdraw behind screens, often even in safe bubbles. Social distancing has disrupted spontaneous encounters. Meanwhile, society is becoming increasingly diverse and inclusivity is no longer an issue, but a given. Where are we meeting again? Here. And it's free too. In an inclusive interior that offers an alternative space alongside work and home. As a hospitable meeting place, the Forum interior focuses not only on the city, but – through books and films – also on other worlds. This building owes its self-evident presence not to its striking exterior that adapts to the city but to its generous interior that adapts to the people who visit it.

A Public Square | 'Known Unknowns'

ACTUALITEITENPLEIN

LEESKAMER
ACTUALITEITENPLEIN

DE STUDIO

index

index

index

index

chillen -
ontmoeten -
lezen

JEUGD

speciale ruimte
6-8 jaar

6-8 jaar

doeplein /
installaties
7 - 15 jaar

vaste tribune

hang- en
chillplekken
multimedia

0 - 5 jaar

'zitkuil' voor
kleinkinderen

VOORPLEIN JEUGD

slimplek   chill plek

chill plek

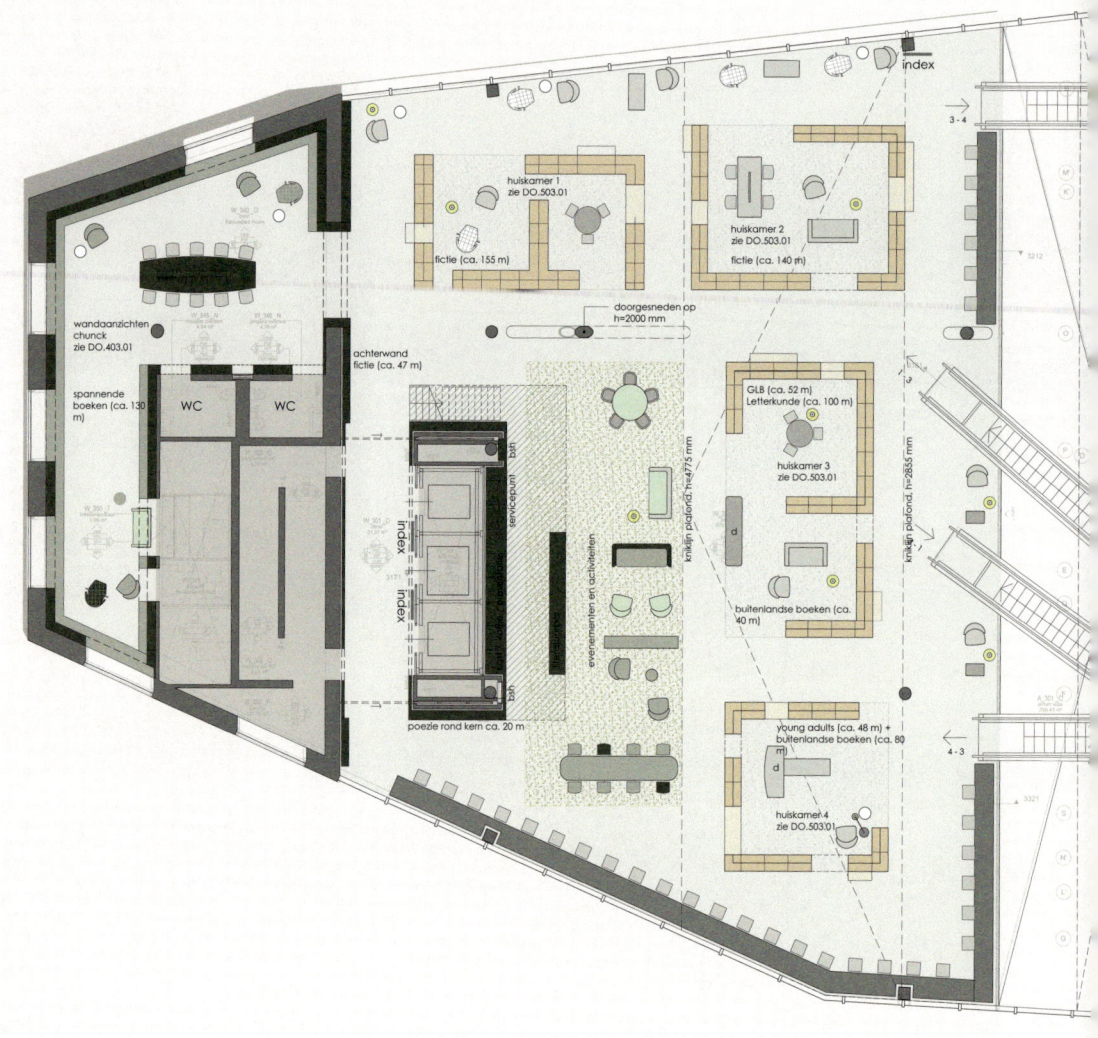

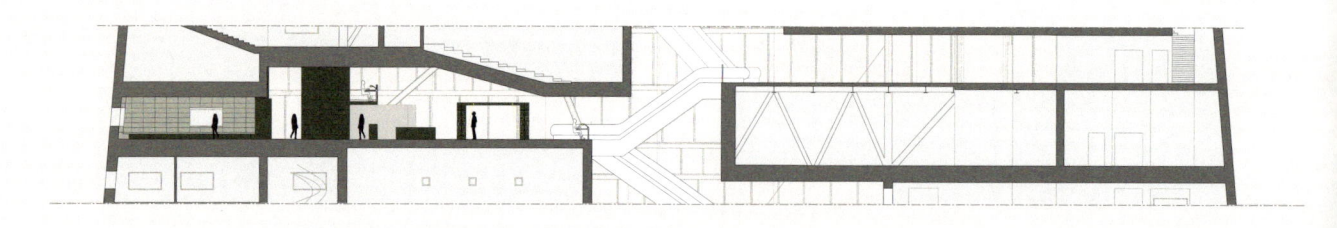

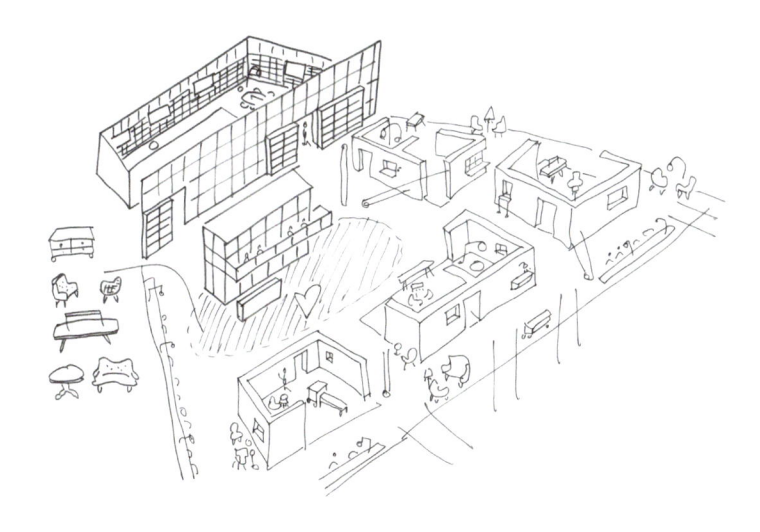

Book square

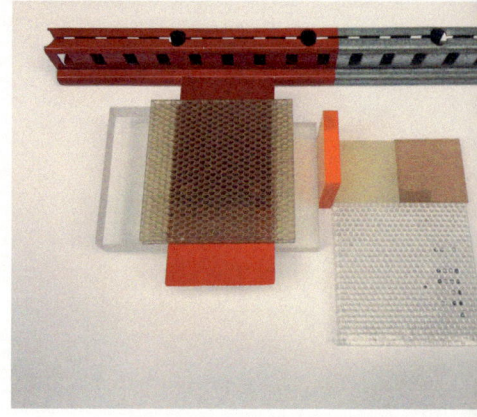

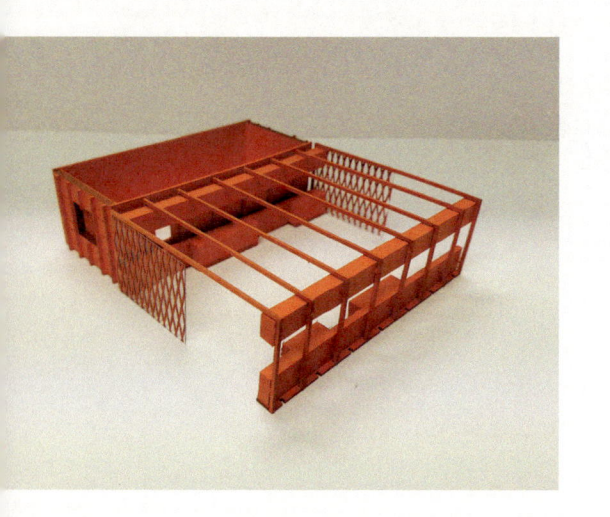

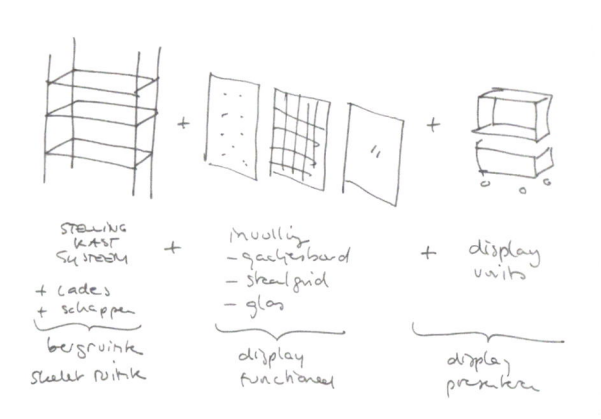

deMunnik-deJong-Steinhauser

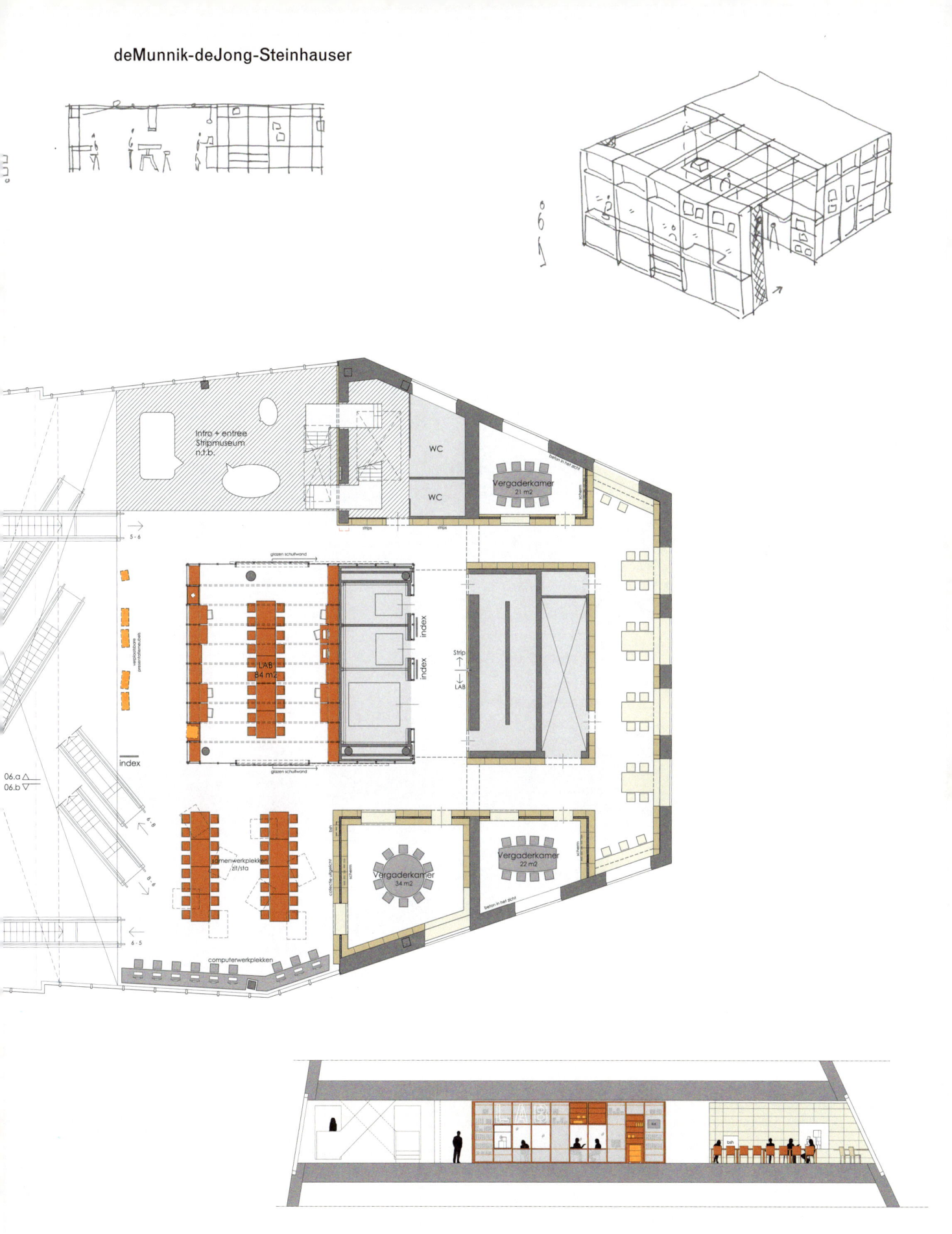

Smart Lab

Use

Use

329

Use

334   Use

Nicoline Wijnja

Turbulence in the

Forum Garage

Groningen is one of the few cities in the Netherlands with a tradition of media art in parking garages. As the most centrally located and eye-catching parking facility, the Forum garage continues this tradition. The idea of installing works of art in parking garages arose from the idea that these spaces are important transfer points and therefore function as gateways to the city. The visitor enters the building as a motorist, at the tempo of the car, and instantly transforms into a pedestrian with a different experience of time and space. Kunstpunt Groningen has commissioned various artworks for parking garages in recent years, in many cases to add interest to these anonymous 'transitional spaces', to give them greater meaning, or to make a connection with the city above. For example, Peter Struycken has designed a light artwork for the parking garage under the Ossenmarkt, and Giny Vos has installed the work *Second Thought* in the bicycle storage facility under the Stadsbalkon, the concourse of Groningen's main railway station.

As the plans for Forum and the garage beneath it took shape, it was obvious to Kunstpunt that the Forum garage would be the ideal place to mark Groningen's newest 'entrance' with an artwork and thus contribute in an imaginative way to the new city-centre development. The starting point for all public artworks in Groningen is the site's specific characteristics, its *genius loci* or 'spirit of place'. With this idea in mind, an art commission was formulated for the Forum garage, which, like the other garages, focuses on media art, in other words, artworks that incorporate light, projections, or other digital media: 'art with a plug'. This art form is characterised by immateriality and mobility, aspects that fit well with the character of parking garages: spaces where people typically stay for a short time and where there is constant movement. From a practical point of view, these interior spaces with minimal daylight provide an ideal setting for media art, and as public spaces with round-the-clock surveillance, they are safe environments for this vulnerable art form.

A specially appointed art committee formulated the principles and parameters for the commission, after which several artists with an affinity for science and technology were asked to produce a sketch design that responded to NL Architects' design, Forum's programming, and Groningen's profile as a youthful city and knowledge centre in which university students account for a quarter of the population. The artists had to consider the possible vantage points from which the visitor could experience the artwork in a location that is five floors beneath ground level. The artwork had to present an exciting image from multiple perspectives and be capable of surprising the viewer on repeated visits.

The artwork selected was *Turmoil* by Nicky Assmann, who came up with a proposal that appealed to the imagination but also posed a major technical challenge: to realise a double-sided screen in the shape of a tornado with moving images that refer to natural phenomena. The strength of the design was that it could be spatially integrated into the central interior space and that it fitted neatly with Forum's programming and with Groningen as a university city: the images on the screens refer to natural phenomena such as turbulence and fluid dynamics and the science behind them. The design's innovative techniques and cinematic character make a direct link to Forum's programming: the artwork refers to the place where films can be seen and where technological innovations are made accessible to a large audience.

The strength and persuasiveness of Assmann's first designs for *Turmoil* were matched by the complexity of its development and execution. A thorough investigation of form and material was required: a spatial investigation to allow the form to swirl logically and to integrate it seamlessly into the architecture, and a technical-digital investigation into the hardware and software needed to create exciting images. Assmann explored the shape and scale of *Turmoil* with paper and plastic in the garage while it was still under construction and then engaged a team to translate the design into a physical construction.

As her first permanent artwork in a public space, this commission represented a new step in Assmann's artistic practice, providing an opportunity to further develop and deepen her work in a new context. This fits well with the Municipality of Groningen's tradition of affording artists opportunities for development. Like Forum itself, *Turmoil* was embraced by the public from day one. It is much more than a marker of the entrance to Forum and the city for the motorist. It is an artwork that attracts people to the garage expressly to see it, an artwork so astonishing and jarring that you wonder what you are actually looking at. And so you keep looking.

With a background in film and ArtScience, Nicky Assmann combines art, science, and cinematographic elements to create sensory experiences. She develops her own screens from diverse materials, following in the tradition of expanded cinema. *Turmoil* originated from years of research into the natural movement patterns of turbulence and fluid dynamics. Assmann became fascinated by how those kinds of patterns repeat themselves at the smallest and the largest scales: from a small frozen soap bubble to a storm on Jupiter. She has distorted photographs and videos of these natural phenomena beyond recognition using two specially designed video synthesisers in accordance with the physical principles of turbulence, fluid dynamics, and reaction-diffusion. The images, combined with the intense colours that are so characteristic of Assmann's work, seem to splash off the 20-metre-long LED sculpture. *Turmoil* is Assmann's first permanent artwork in a public space.

Turbulence in the Forum Garage

Arnon Grunberg

Mortal Souls and their Parking Garages

On 5 November 2011, the daily newspaper *NRC* published an article by two doctoral students at the law faculty of Leiden University, Thierry Baudet and Bastiaan Rijpkema. It was about architecture. Its closing sentence was incorporated in the headline: 'Fuck the context? Fuck the Koolhaas!' A reference to Rem Koolhaas' famous statement: "Fuck context." I believe I read on an architecture website that Koolhaas's 'motto' comes from one of his books. I like that idea: the architect as author.

What fucking the context means was neatly summarised in 1994 by Ole Bouman in *De Groene Amsterdammer*. The idea of urban community – 'civitas' – was disappearing, and nobody had understood that better than Koolhaas. He had, Bouman wrote, abandoned "any illusion of social engineering, governance, and urban planning coherence" and rejected "historical sentimentality." What remained was chaos and 'bigness'.

Baudet and Rijpkema were thus rather late to the party with their criticism, accusing Koolhaas and his followers of destroying Rotterdam. "Modern architects" were wrapping their contrivances in a theoretical framework of "intellectual claptrap" to make everyone forget how "ugly" they are. For Baudet and Rijpkema, it is not an architect's job to change things but simply to provide a pleasant place to live and a small dose of beauty. The instinct of common sense, the kind of reasoning the *NRC*, the Netherlands' biggest newspaper, has long relied on.

The piece is worth rereading, and not so much because Rijpkema would later break with Baudet and suggest in *De Groene Amsterdammer* in 2021 that it might be time to ban the Forum for Democracy, the political party founded by Baudet in 2016, and that other extreme-right Party for Freedom as well. Incidentally, we shouldn't draw the facile conclusion that what starts with an aversion to modern architecture and suchlike (for example, atonal music) ends with hatred of society itself and reflexes that appear to lean towards fascism. As Rijpkema has demonstrated, other outcomes are possible – although I suspect that combating the ugliness of modern architecture is no longer his top priority. No, the piece is worth reading because it neatly summarises many assumptions about contemporary architecture that were popular thirty years ago and, I'm afraid, still are today. The greater the uncertainty, it seems, the more attractive historical sentimentalism becomes.

As an example of how things should be done, Baudet and Rijpkema give, among others, the centre of Warsaw, where those in charge have done their level best to pretend that the Second World War never took place, at least in the field of architecture. Done well, but this is historical sentimentalism *avant la lettre* nonetheless.

Just how slow the pace of development is, became clear to me in the summer of 2021 when, after a lecture in Mönchengladbach, I got into a discussion about the city with the local librarian. To her mind, the city required a rethink because it was no longer needed for shopping. So, what is it for then? Living? Working? The city as a parking garage for mortal souls.

Parking garages have long fascinated me, not because I use them often – I have neither a car nor a driver's licence – but because I know of no other places that are so completely stripped of sentimentality and frivolity. No matter which parking garage you enter, you will find nothing but functionality. Some people may be sentimental about their cars, but not about where they park them: the parking garage is permitted to be as utilitarian as an abattoir shed.

Baudet and Rijpkema quote the website of the Netherlands Architecture Institute (now Het Nieuwe Instituut), designed by "Koolhaas clone" Jo Coenen, which, they claim, states that the use of concrete in the building was intended to "avoid associations with a parking garage." This statement puzzled me – why would one want to avoid associations with parking garages per se? – even though Baudet and Rijpkema somewhat disparagingly call that statement "incomprehensible."

Mortal Souls and their Parking Garages

We certainly need parking garages, but we'd rather not live or work in them. In many films, they are the setting for ominous scenes, the place where murders are committed or initiated. If that context has truly disappeared anywhere, it is in the parking garage, where citizens temporarily store their instrument for mobility, the symbol of their freedom (now perhaps also *the* symbol of pollution and one of middle-class values, in both the good and bad senses). The parking garage is the place where Western people's mobility resides and so has become the home of freedom.

When I visited the designers of the Forum, Pieter Bannenberg and Kamiel Klaasse of NL Architects, in December 2021, they told me that they have been fascinated by parking garages since their student days. They praised the Van der Valk Hotel in Amsterdam Zuid designed by Wiel Arets (and voted the best building of the year 2021) because of the creative way he dealt with the parking garage.

If the city is, first and foremost, the possibility or impossibility of parking, then the Western urban dweller is indeed one who has parked his soul. Or perhaps we should go further: just as managers and some social workers today like to talk about 'parking our problems', so we can say that the city is the place where life itself gets parked. Perhaps this is why Koolhaas became interested in the countryside: to find life that is not in the parking position.

The architects of the Forum, a place I have visited only once, take the position that the city can still have a real urban culture without falling into historical sentimentalism. As this building proves, the urban designer is certainly not doomed to the role of set designer in an open-air museum, something that Ole Bouman feared in his 1994 article in *De Groene Amsterdammer*. The threat or the blessing of the open-air museum lurks in every city worthy of that status, and where that threat does not lurk, decay has taken on museological qualities.

The good thing about the Forum is that the building takes the city seriously as a city without falling into sentimentalism or lazy irony. Sadly, I haven't been in the Forum's car park. But reviewing the building in the *NRC*, Bernard Hulsman wrote that the Forum has the most beautiful one in the Netherlands.

The car enthusiast with zero interest in books has a solid reason for visiting the Forum, where he will find that even using the parking garage in a library and cinema complex is an aesthetic experience, well worth the detour. And sooner or later someone, perhaps Bannenberg and Klaasse, will build a parking garage that doubles as a home. I would like to live in it, perhaps not forever but at least for one winter.

Mortal Souls and their Parking Garages343

Biographies

Anneke Bokern studied the history of art and architecture at the Freie Universität in Berlin. She has lived in Amsterdam since 2000 and writes about architecture and design in the Netherlands as a freelance journalist. Her articles have appeared in *Baumeister*, *DAMN°*, *DETAIL*, *Mark*, *Topos*, *Werk* and *Uncube*, among others. She has contributed to various books and is the author of *Architectural Guide: Rotterdam* (2021). In 2004, together with Dutch architect Paul Vlok, she founded Architour, which organises architecture tours in the Netherlands. She is a cofounder and member of the board of the international network Guiding Architects.

Erik Dorsman studied the history of art and architecture at the University of Groningen and wrote his thesis on the influence of the Cold War on the reconstruction of East and West Berlin. As an independent architecture and urban-planning historian, he worked together with chief city architect Niek Verdonk on Groningen's architecture policy, and from 2009 was secretary of Groningen's preservation committee. He is the author of *Grote Markt Oostzijde – 20 jaar stadsontwikkeling in 40 verhalen* (2022) about the transformation of the east side of Grote Markt, of which the Forum is part.

Joseph Gardella studied architecture at the Hanze University of Applied Sciences in Groningen and is studying for an MA in the history and theory of architecture and urbanism at the University of Groningen. He intends to complete his training as an architect, integrating theory and practice. With an interdisciplinary and holistic view that stems from his interest in anthroposophy, he aims to fuse poetry and philosophy with architecture and design. Part of that quest is the development of an organic theory of architecture, based on the writings of Johann Wolfgang von Goethe.

Arnon Grunberg made his debut as a writer at the age of twenty-three with the novel *Blue Mondays* (1994). Since then, he has written sixteen novels, including *The Asylum Seeker* (2003), *Tooth and Nail* (2010) and *Death in Taormina* (2021). His columns, essays and short stories have appeared in numerous Dutch newspapers and magazines, and he has contributed to international debate on issues such as migration policy, discrimination, racism and human trafficking in *The New York Times*, *Le Monde*, *The Times*, the *Neue Zürcher Zeitung* and the *Süddeutsche Zeitung*. He was the recipient of the P.C. Hooft Award in 2022.

Kirsten Hannema studied and practiced architecture before becoming an architecture critic and journalist. She writes for *de Volkskrant* and various architecture magazines, and from 2016 to 2021 was editor of the annual publication *Architecture in the Netherlands*. In addition to her work as a writer, she is a guest lecturer at the Delft University of Technology, the Academy of Architecture in Amsterdam and the Rotterdam Academy of Architecture and Urban Design, and regularly sits on architecture juries.

Simon Henley studied architecture at the University of Liverpool and the University of Oregon. He is a principal of London-based architects Henley Halebrown, whose Chadwick Hall student housing for the University of Roehampton was shortlisted for the Stirling Prize in 2018, was nominated for the EU Mies Award in 2019, and won the Fritz Höger Silver Award for Brick Architecture in 2020. A monograph on the practice was published by Quart Verlag in 2018. Henley is a postgraduate unit master at the Kingston School of Art and is the author of *The Architecture of Parking* (2007) and *Redefining Brutalism* (2017).

Pieter Hoexum studied monumental design at the ArtEZ University of the Arts in Arnhem and philosophy at the University of Groningen. He sold books on art and philosophy at the Athenaeum book shop in Amsterdam and since 2000 has written philosophical articles about architecture and housing for various newspapers, magazines and websites. He is the author of *Kleine filosofie van het rijtjeshuis* (2014) and *Thuis – Filosofische verkenningen van het alledaagse* (2019), an exploration of the various spaces in the home. He is currently working on a book about the spaces between houses.

Ronald Hooft studied visual art at the Rietveld Academy in Amsterdam and began designing shop and restaurant interiors around 1990. In 2013, he founded &Prast&Hooft with architect Herman Prast, with whom he first worked around 2000. The practice has designed several housing projects in Groningen's historic centre, interiors for private clients and numerous successful restaurant interiors. Until recently, Hooft wrote a weekly column on architecture and urban planning in Amsterdam for *Het Parool*.

Jeroen Junte studied history at Leiden University, the Freie Universität in Berlin and the University of Amsterdam. He writes on architecture and design for *de Volkskrant*, *de Architect* and *Museum* magazine, among others, and is founder and editor-in-chief of the online and offline platform DesignDigger. He has taught at the Rietveld Academy, the Sandberg Institute and the Design Academy Eindhoven. He is the author of *Think Dutch: Conceptual Design & Architecture from the Netherlands* (2014) and *Do It Ourselves: A New Mentality in Dutch Design* (2019).

Jacqueline Knudsen studied mass communication and film studies and the history of art and architecture at Utrecht University and architecture restoration at the Delft University of Technology. She worked for several architecture practices before shifting to publishing. She is an editor for magazines and websites such as *ArchitectuurNL*, *Bouwwereld* and *Het Houtblad* and writes on contemporary construction techniques. She has been active for many years in the Bouwnetwerk, which strives for a better position for women and promotion to higher positions in architecture, construction and related professions.

Koehorst in 't Veld is the Rotterdam-based design practice of Jannetje in 't Veld and Toon Koehorst. The office has designed books and exhibitions for clients that include Het Nieuwe Instituut, the Zeeuws Museum, Museum Boijmans Van Beuningen, the Mauritshuis and the Rijksmuseum Twenthe.

Marijke Martin studied the history of art and architecture at the University of Groningen and conducted research at the Institut Français d'Architecture in Paris. She gained her PhD in 1997 with her thesis on the development of Maastricht. In 1991, she joined the department of architecture and urban history at the University of Groningen, which she headed from 2012 to 2016. She has been a guest lecturer at the Delft University of Technology and a visiting professor at the Architectural Institute in Prague. She is a member of the management committee of European Cooperation in Science and Technology.

Jola Meijer studied at the Minerva Art Academy in Groningen and taught in schools for ten years while completing her master's degree in the history of art and architecture at the University of Groningen. In the late 1980s, she joined the Spatial Planning and Economic Affairs department of the Municipality of Groningen, working as a project leader on events such as *What a Wonderful World!* (1990), *A Star is Born* (1996) and *Blue Moon* (2001). She has also worked on complex urban renewal projects, such as the renovation of Groningen's large urban parks and the Kop van Oost.

NL Architects was founded in 1997 in Amsterdam, but its three partners, Pieter Bannenberg, Walter van Dijk and Kamiel Klaasse, have been working together since the early 1990s. Because they lived in Amsterdam and studied in Delft, they started out as a carpool office in a metallic-blue Ford Escort Estate. Their recurring fascination with mobility and tarmac can be traced back to their 'education' on the motorway, which explains their bumper sticker logo, while the dot before the 'NL' indicates their love of the digital highway. Their projects often focus on the everyday aspects of life, including the negative or unappreciated, which they sublimate or manipulate to bring to the surface the unexpected potential of the things that surround us. In addition to the partners, the office has a staff of around twenty employees, consisting of a core of veterans supplemented with interns from various backgrounds.

Niek Verdonk studied architecture at Eindhoven University of Technology before joining the department of Spatial Planning and Economic Affairs at the Municipality of Groningen, where he was director of urban development, construction and housing from 1988 to 2001. He was appointed Groningen's Chief City Architect in 2004 and initiated a new series of design manifestations, including *De Intense Stad* (2004), *Intense Laagbouw* (2009) and *Bouwjong!* (2011). He has been an external advisor to the office of the Chief Government Architect of the Netherlands, he supervised the Grote Markt Oostzijde project and is a member of the Groningen Spoorzone Quality Team.

Gerard Vos studied at the Fontys Academy of Journalism in Tilburg. As a journalist, publisher and industry consultant, he promotes sustainability and circularity in construction. Together with OVG Real Estate and Andy van den Dobbelsteen, professor of climate design and sustainability at Delft University of Technology, he is cofounder of the platform Duurzaam Gebouwd. He has been a project leader at the Living Daylights Foundation and until recently managed communications for Active House Netherlands. He is the author of *Circulaire gebouwen – Strategieën en praktijkvoorbeelden* (2020), commissioned by the Netherlands Enterprise Agency.

Cor Wagenaar studied history at the University of Groningen, gaining his PhD in 1993 with a thesis on the reconstruction of Rotterdam. He taught at Delft University of Technology from 2000, and in 2016 was appointed professor in the history and theory of architecture and urbanism at the University of Groningen. He is chair of the scientific council of the European Network Architecture for Health and co-founder of the journal *Cities & Health*. He has written extensively on the history of urbanism and on the health aspects of architecture and urban design.

Dirk van Weelden studied philosophy at the University of Groningen. He co-authored the novel *Arbeidsvitaminen – Het ABC van Bril & Van Weelden* (1987) with Martin Bril and made his solo debut in 1989 with *Tegenwoordigheid van geest*. Around this time, he worked regularly with artists, photographers and architects. His 1991 novel *Mobilhome* was awarded the Multatuli Prize in 1992. Since then, he has published more than a dozen subsequent novels or collections of essays. He has been editor of the cultural and literary journal *De Gids* since 1999, the year he received the Frans Kellendonk Prize.

Micha Wertheim studied cultural studies at Maastricht University and wrote his thesis on Franz Kafka. He joined the stand-up comedy group Comedytrain in 1998, and in 1994 presented his first one man show at the Leiden Cabaret Festival, which won both the public and jury prizes. He has performed in English in comedy clubs in London, New York and Tel Aviv since 2001 and appeared at the Edinburgh Fringe Festival in 2008. In addition to his work in the theatre, he writes columns, children's books, essays about art and the occasional poem about his birthplace, Groningen.

Nicoline Wijnja studied the history of art at the VU University in Amsterdam. She is a project leader for art in public spaces at Kunstpunt Groningen (formerly Centrum Beeldende Kunst) and has recently taken charge of the programming for the pavilion on Hereplein designed by Bernard Tschumi. She works from the conviction that art is a significant factor in the design of public spaces. She previously worked for Museum De Paviljoens in Almere and Stichting Kunst & Openbare Ruimte (SKOR) in Amsterdam.

Chris Zwart studied the history of art and architecture at Groningen University. He has worked as a freelance writer and editor since 2016. As editor of the online architecture and urbanism magazine *GRAS*, he writes reports, stories, interviews and podcasts, nearly always with a human dimension. He recently worked as a writer on the art project *Ik blijf hier* (I'm Staying Here), which produced four honest portraits of residents of neighbourhoods in Groningen that are undergoing renewal.

Colophon

Concept
Erik Dorsman, Toon Koehorst, NL Architects, Jannetje in 't Veld, Niek Verdonk

Text and picture editor
Erik Dorsman

Copy editor
Chris Zwart

Authors
Anneke Bokern, Erik Dorsman, Joseph G. Gardella, Arnon Grunberg, Kirsten Hannema, Simon Henley, Pieter Hoexum, Ronald Hooft, Jeroen Junte, Jacqueline Knudsen, Marijke Martin, Jola Meijer, Niek Verdonk, Gerard Vos, Cor Wagenaar, Dirk van Weelden, Micha Wertheim, Nicoline Wijnja, Chris Zwart

Translations
Dutch – English
Gerard Forde (except p. 100 by Micha Wertheim)
English – Dutch
Leo Reijnen

Photography
Marcel van der Burg, Peter de Kan

Graphic design
Koehorst in 't Veld

Printing and lithography
NPN Drukkers, Breda

Edition
400

Publisher
Marcel Witvoet, nai010 publishers

Image credits and sources

AAS Architecten, *Beeldkwaliteitsplan Poelestraat achterzijde*, commissioned by the Municipality of Groningen, February 2009: p. 58 top | ABT: p. 169 | Auk Archive / Alamy Stock Photo: p. 8 (915-3827) | Eric Ausema (photography): p. 137 bottom left | Aviodrome Lelystad: p. 41 bottom (Groningen Archives: NL-GnGRA_1785_7102, maker: KLM Aerocarto, aerial photo of the destroyed Grote Markt, 26 July 1946) | Groninger Museum collection (1937.1048): p. 40 top (Cornelis Pronk, 1754, photography: Marten de Leeuw) | deMunnik–deJong–Steinhauser architectencollectief: pp. 316 left, 317 top, centre, 318, 319 left, bottom, 320-321 except top left | 'De stad, een plein,' thematic issue *Forum*, Quarterly Magazine for Architecture, no. 34, July 1990: p. 47 | Robert Dijkstra (photography): p. 137 row 3 right | Erick van Egeraat Associated Architects: p. 110 | Foreign Office Architects: p. 112 | Forum Groningen: photography p. 21 row 2 right, p. 27 row 3 left, p. 31 row 2 right, row 3 left: Bob de Vries; p. 21 top right, row 2 left, row 3 right, p. 23 top left, p. 25 row 2 left, row 3 left, bottom right, p. 29 bottom left, p. 312 bottom: Knelis; p. 21 row 3 left, p. 23 row 3 left, p. 25 top left, p. 27 bottom right, bottom left, p. 29 row 3 left, p. 31 top right: Siese Veenstra; p. 23 row 2 left, bottom left: Susan Pathuis; row 3 right, p. 31 top left: Douwe de Boer; p. 29 bottom right: Marleen Annema; p. 23 row 2 right, p. 25 top right, row 2 right, row 3 right, p. 27 top right, row 2 left, p. 29 top left, row 2 right, p. 31 bottom left | Joseph G. Gardella: pp. 153-154 (atrium diagrams, 2021).

Municipality of Groningen: pp. 3, 172 bottom, 175 top, 188-189, 200-202, 203 left, right, 204-206 centre, 208 left, 209 left, 210 right, 211 left, 213, 224 (photography: Marieke Kijk in de Vegte); pp. 5, 11, 17-18, 21 top left, bottom left, 23 top right, bottom right, 27 top right, row 2 right, row 3 right, 29 top right, 31 row 3 right, row 2 left, bottom right, 58 bottom, 61 bottom, 63-68, 82-83, 86-87, 137 top right, row 2 right, row 3 left, 145 left, 162, 166, 178-184, 190, 191 centre, bottom, 192-193, 196-199, 214, 226-234, 258-260, 264-273, 275 top right, row 2, row 3 left, 276, 280, 284-286, 289-293, 295, 306 top, 310 top, 312 top, 313 top, centre, 324-325, 330-331, 334, 341, 343 (photography: Peter de Kan); p. 14 (BVG, municipal information system); p. 61 top (photography: Stefan Müller, commissioned by Thomas Müller Ivan Reimann Architekten); p. 83 (original design drawing for Groningen Public Library, Giorgio Grassi, 1989, photography: Peter de Kan); p. 55 bottom right (*Naar een ontwikkelingsvisie voor de Grote Markt*, December 1996); pp. 71-73 (*Doelstelling binnenstad Groningen*, 1972); p. 76 bottom (*Ruimte voor Ruimte*, masterplan for the redesign of public spaces, in partnership with Mecanoo, 1990); p. 108 (*Grote Markt Oostzijde – Concept-Programma van Eisen Stedenbouw, Openbare Ruimte en Verkeer*, appendix 2. 'Illustrations to explain the urban planning principles for the Groninger Forum,' in partnership with Johannes Kappler, June 2006); pp. 109, 125 (photography: Erik & Petra Hesmerg); pp. 275 top left, row 3, bottom left, 277-279 (photography: Marcel van der Burg); p. 338 (photography: Cor van der Veen).

Groningen Archives: p. 4 (NL-GnGRA_1785_11723, photography: K.A. Gaasendam, 1965); p. 6 (NL-GnGRA_2290_4549, photography: Gerard Til, May 1988); p. 40 bottom (NL-GnGRA_1785_9527, ILVO photo-topography department, 1918-1922); p. 41 top (NL-GnGRA_2138_3816, Folkers press photo agency, 1945-4); pp. 10, 45 top (NL-GnGRA_1785_19750, photography: P.B. Kramer, 1947); pp. 45 bottom, 55 top left, bottom (NL-GnGRA_2138_3280 [2731_07415], Municipality of Groningen Mediateque collection [2731_07423], NL-GnGRA_2138_3279 [2731_07426], made by Bert Koenderink after a design by A. Natalini, designed as part of the Nieuwe Noordzijde (New North Side) urban plan, 1997-2000); p. 49 (NL-GnGRA_2138_3275 [2731_07404], NL-GnGRA_2138_3276 [2731_07405], made by John Stoel after a design by R. Krier, designed as part of the Nieuwe Noordzijde (New North Side) urban plan, 1997-2000); p. 51 (Municipality of Groningen Mediateque collection [2731_02185, 2731_02188], Maarten Schmitt, Anco Schut, 1989); p. 53 (Municipality of Groningen Mediateque collection [2731_02178], 1988); p. 55 top right (NL-GnGRA_2138_3282 [2731_07432], Jo Coenen Architecten, 1997-2000); Collection RHC: p. 56; p. 75 bottom (NL-GnGRA_2290_5470, D. van der Veen press photo agency, 1965-1976); p. 75 top (1536-8025/2, design: Abe Kuipers, 'Loop Map' of the Traffic Circulation Plan, Municipality of Groningen, 1977, c/o Pictoright Amsterdam 2022); p. 76 top (Municipality of Groningen Mediateque collection [2731_08775], Verbindingskanaalzone model, 1987); p. 186 top (NL-GnGRA_817_4034, G. Acker Stratingh, 1837).

Cor Harteloh (photography): p. 346-347 | Simon Henley (photography): p. 191 top | Het Geheugen/Royal Library: p. 2 (photography: unknown, 1911) | Jacqueline Knudsen (photography): pp. 174, 175 bottom | Koehorst in 't Veld (photography): p. 9 | Kunsthalle Basel: pp. 88, 97 centre (Hans Arp, *Plakat Basel*, exhibition poster, 1961) | Kunstpunt en Nicky Assmann: p. 335 (photography: Paula Lambeck); p. 337 (photography: Jenne Hoekstra) | Manntech (Alimak Group Benelux): p. 235 | Cristina Garcia Martin: p. 100 | A. Natalini, Monumento Continuo, Primary Structure (Superstudio, 1969): p. 52 | Neutelings Riedijk Architecten: pp. 79, 92-96, 97 top (*Studie Grote Markt Groningen*, commissioned by the Municipality of Groningen, May 2003); p. 114 (Forum competition design) | NL Architects: pp. 11, 62 (after the maps by AAS Architecten, *Beeldkwaliteitsplan Poelestraat achterzijde*), 81 right, 84, 97, 99 bottom, 130-133, 140 bottom, 141, 143, 145-148, 152, 156-161, 170-171, 172 top, 177, 184 bottom, 194, 203 centre, 208 right, 209 right, 210 left, 211 right, 212, 215-223, 236-237, 274, 288, 298 (documentation of realised situation); pp. 91, 98, 123, 126-128, 140 top, 150 (Forum competition design); 134, 138 bottom, 139, 144 (design research Forum competition); 287, 296-297 | NL Architects and ABT: pp. 21 bottom right, 25 bottom left, 29 row 2 left, row 3 right, 84 right, 101-102, 137 top left, bottom right, 165, 176, 195, 238, 251-256, 263, 275 bottom right, 294, 300-301, 302-305, 306 centre, bottom, 307-309, 310 bottom, 311, 313 bottom, 314-315, 316 right, bottom, 317 right, 319 top right, centre, 320 top left, 322-323,

326-329, 332-333, 348 (photography: Marcel van der Burg); p. 137 row 2 left (photography: Deon Prins); pp. 168, 225, 240-249 (BIM) | Giambattista Nolli, *Pianta Grande di Roma* (1748): p. 81 | Noordinbeeld.nl: pp. 77, 78 bottom, 187 (photography: Koos Boertjens, 2021) | rovimage (photography, 2020): p. 7 | Camillo Sitte, *Der Städtebau nach seinen künstlerischen Grundsätzen*, as included in Hegemann and Peets, *The American Vitruvius: An Architect's Handbook of Civic Art* (1922): p. 80 | Shutterstock: p. 78 top | Corné Sparidaens (photography): p. 207 centre | Stichting Clubhuis voor Doven: p. 138 top (https://www.facebook.com/dovenclubhuis/videos/539206946807087/?t=5) | Thomas Müller Ivan Reimann Architekten, *Beeldkwaliteitsplan Grote Markt — Oostwand*, commissioned by the Municipality of Groningen and Volker Wessels Vastgoed, June 2008 (revised June 2014): p. 59 | UN Studio: p. 116 | Niek Verdonk (photography): p. 282 | C. Wagenaar, *Tussen Grandezza en Schavot. De ontwerpen van Granpré Molière voor de wederopbouw van Groningen*, Wolters-Noordhof / Egbert Forsten, Groningen, 1991 (Municipality of Groningen): p. 43 | Siebrand H. Wiegman (photography): p. 206 right | Wiel Arets Architects: p. 118 | Peter Wiersema (photography): pp. 351-352 | Zaha Hadid Architects: p. 120.

Projectcredits

Client: Municipality of Groningen: Bert Popken, Klaas van der Wal, Bert Karsens, Elzo Dijkhuis, Erwin Kloen, Marcel Slijkhuis, Sietze Bodewits, Hilvert Doornkamp, Wessel Rothstegge, Esseline Schieven, Alfred Kazemier, Tjerk Ruimschotel, Fokke van der Veer, Jaap Dallinga, Anneke Miedema, Rein Mebius, Leo Bijl, Ilona Rooks, Michel Boer, Henk Zuidhof, Jasper Schweigman, Mark Floor | Delegated client: Twynstra Gudde: Iljan van Hardevelt, Peter Groeneveld, Frank Velthuis, Henk Weulink | Delegated client for the interior: abcnova: Sjoerd Groen, Ylze Lindeboom | Gross floor area: 20.300 m² (building), 14.500 m² (parking garage) | Start of the competition: 2006, first price | Completion: November 2019 | Architect: NL Architects with ABT | Forum Groningen: Bas van Kampen, Dirk Nijdam, Koen van Krimpen, Peter Bon, Pernille Claessen.

Design team NL Architects: Pieter Bannenberg, Kamiel Klaasse, Walter van Dijk, Thijs van Bijsterveldt, Florent Le Corre, Sören Grünert, Iwan Hameleers, Sybren Hoek, Kirsten Hüsig, Mathieu Landelle, Zhongnan Lao, Barbara Luns, Gert Jan Machiels, Sarah Möller, Gerbrand van Oostveen, Giulia Pastore, Guus Peters, Jose Ramon Vives, Laura Riaño Lopez, Arne van Wees, Zofia Wojdyga en Gen Yamamoto met stagiaires Christian Asbo, Nicolo Bertino, Jonathan Cottereau, Marten Dashorst, Rebecca Eng, Antoine van Erp, Tan Gaofei, Sylvie Hagens, Britta Harnacke, Jana Heidacker, Sergio Hernandez Benta, Johannes Hübner, Yuseke Iwata, Cho Junghwa, Linda

Kronmüller, Jakub Kupikowski, Katarina Labathova, Ana Lagoa Pereira Gomes, Qian Lan, Justine Lemesre, Amadeo Linke, Fabian Lutter, Rune Madsen, Phil Mallysh, José Maria Matteo Torres, Victoria Meniakina, Shuichiro Mitomo, Solène Muscato, Lea Olsson, Pauline Rabjeau, Thomas Scherzer, Michael Schoner, Martijn Stoffels, Jasper Schuttert, Bartek Tromczynski, Carmen Valtierra, Elisa Ventura, Benedict Völkel, Vittoria Volpi, Murk Wymenga, Qili Yang, Yena Young, Alessandro Zanini.

Design team ABT: Ruud Arkesteijn, Caspar van Belle, Jos Berentsen, Martin Bijsterbosch, Harm Boel, Gerbert Boezewinkel, Ivonne Bönisch, Ben van den Bosch, Mark Bosveld, Theo te Braak, Erwin ten Brincke, Han Brinkman, Wil Bronkhorst, Harmen Bunk, Krijn Dieleman, Leendert Dijkhuis, Eppo Dokter, Bert Everts, Richard Fielt, Björn Francissen, Constantijn Fuchs, Robert Gips, Lonneke van Haalen, Kars Haarhuis, Michel Haverkamp, Ewoud Heijink, Jan Heijne, Roy Heugten, Widy Heuver, Sandra Hombergen, Daan Hornman, Matthijs van der Hulst, Kim Jager, Jorg Janssen, Ostar Joostenz, Marco Kimenai, Paul Klunder, Han Krijgsman, Jeroen van Kuijk, Edgars Laposka, Dion de Leeuw, Harm Lesmeister, Mart van de Leur, Stamatina Lialiou, Niki Loonen, Shen Ma, Erik Massar, Casper Meijer, Michaël Menting, Hans van Mierlo, Miriam Molenwijk, Shayer Nijman, Jan Nillezen, Rogier Penning, Cock Peterse, Marco van der Ploeg, Roel van der Putten, Maurice Radstake, Jeroen Rindertsma, Ton Roelofs, Jelle Roks, Jens Roozendaal, Rudi Roijakkers, Siebe Sjoerdsma, Ed Smienk, Corinne Smits, Robert Smits, Frank Spaen, Walter Spangenberg, Ton van Straaten, Marcel Tabak, Zana Uthman, Martijn van der Velden, Wendy van Veldhuizen-Schriever, Mark Verbaten, Hans van Vliet, Gert Voorhoeve, Onno Wennekes, Bas Wijnbeld, Lies Wijnveld, Henk Willemsen.

Elaboration of the architectural plan: ABT with NL Architects (and Bureau Bouwkunde during the competition phase) | Consultant for structure, geotechnics, construction costs, construction logistics (design phase) and specifications: ABT | Installation advice: Huisman & Van Muijen: Will van der Weijden, Imre Janse | Building physics and fire safety: DGMR: Frank Jakobs, Bert Vrijhof, Erik-Jan van Pelt | Acoustics consultant: Peutz | Seismic consultant: abtWassenaar, ABT, BAM Advies & Engineering | Natuursteen: Van Stokkum: Twan Smedts | Interior design: NL Architects together with deMunnik-deJong-Steinhauser (public tribune, library, Media Lab and Smart Lab), &Prast&Hooft (cinemas with foyer and film café), NorthernLight (Storyworld) and Tank (restaurant NOK) | Design of public space: Municipality of Groningen: Chris Emaar, Dariusz Kwiatek | Parking garage artwork: Nicky Assmann | Client artwork: Kunstpunt: Jan Samsom | Building contractor: BAM: Marc de Vreede, Erik te Duits, Jan Kempkens, Tiede Swart, Johan, Wegman, Jos Rona, Date Jan de Haan, Ivar Beukers, Martin Wiersma, Mark de Vries, Jasper Pluijmert, Mark Scheepstra, Roy Haaijer, Lianne Heidekamp, Willem de Bruin, Janet Oosterkamp, Wesley Billekes, Ronald Kleijer, Klaas Lautenbach, Erwin Nijenkamp, Andries Miedema, Arnold de Jong, Alex Sinnige, Menno Glas, Richard Enninga, Harold Buisman, Wiljan Eerland, Paul Jansen, Henk Broekmans, Ewout Stel, Freddy Wierenga, Joris Hesselink, Joop Hermans, Freek Hesterman, René Sterken,

Mischa Falger, Marc Spanenburg, Jelte Hoving, Henk Bloemert, Eddie Schildmeijer, Henk Post, Alie Stevens, Harald van der Bij, Guido van Dijk, Wim van Willigen, Harry Venema, Hans Verkoelen, Peter van Leeuwen.

This publication was commissioned and financed by the Municipality of Groningen, with the support of ABT, BAM, DGMR, Huisman & Van Muijen, Twynstra Gudde, Van Stokkum.

Making both the city and province of Groningen stronger economically!

The Groninger Forum project has been made possible with funding from the Regiospecifiek Pakket Zuiderzeelijn (RSP)

www.provinciegroningen.nl

Distribution and sales
nai010 publishers is an internationally orientated publisher specialized in developing, producing and distributing books in the fields of architecture, urbanism, art and design.
www.nai010.com

nai010 books are available internationally at selected bookstores and from the following distribution partners: North, Central and South America - Artbook | D.A.P., New York, USA, dap@dapinc.com. Rest of the world - Idea Books, Amsterdam, the Netherlands, idea@ideabooks.nl.

For general questions, please contact nai010 publishers directly at sales@nai010.com or visit our website www.nai010.com for further information.

Printed and bound in the Netherlands

ISBN 978-94-6208-676-0

NUR 648
BISAC ARC000000
THEMA AM

Thanks to Leo Reijnen and Chris Zwart for their close reading of the texts in this volume.

351

The realisation of the Forum has resulted in a new type of public space that blurs the traditional boundaries between cultural functions: the Forum is not a library, nor a museum, nor a cinema, nor a conference centre. In the same way, *Forum Groningen* is not an architecture book, magazine, newspaper, periodical or review. It is a collection of diverse texts, images and illustrations that transcends a traditional architecture publication. The series of visual rhymes with which the book begins is the prelude to a search for the design of the Forum: for its shape, structure, materials, construction, experience, and its place in the city. Although exuberant in composition, the stories are carefully intertwined and arranged in three parts: *city*, *design* and *use*.

If the Forum is a three-dimensional Wikipedia, through which we browse endlessly and where, by definition, we find more than we seek, *Forum Groningen* is the two-dimensional register, in words and images, that helps us explore the building and its origins. In analytical essays, reflections, columns, interviews and a poem, authors from diverse backgrounds employ different perspectives to shed light on the comprehensive spectrum that the Forum has become. This publication portrays the building's many faces. Just as the Forum itself has augmented Groningen's characteristic series of squares with a public space that is traversed vertically, *Forum Groningen* offers ever-changing panoramas of the building in the city, in order to stimulate the exchange of knowledge and ideas about it.

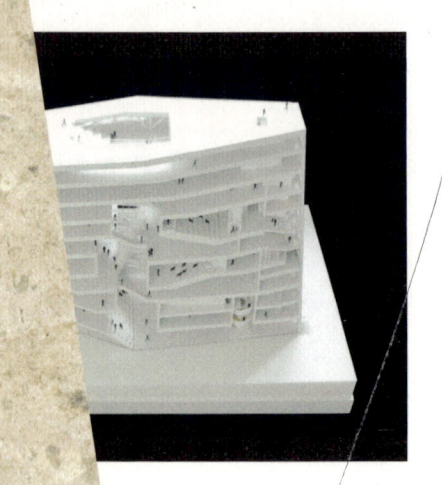

nai010 publishers
www.nai010.com

ISBN 978-94-6208-676-0